The GLORY *of* BEADS

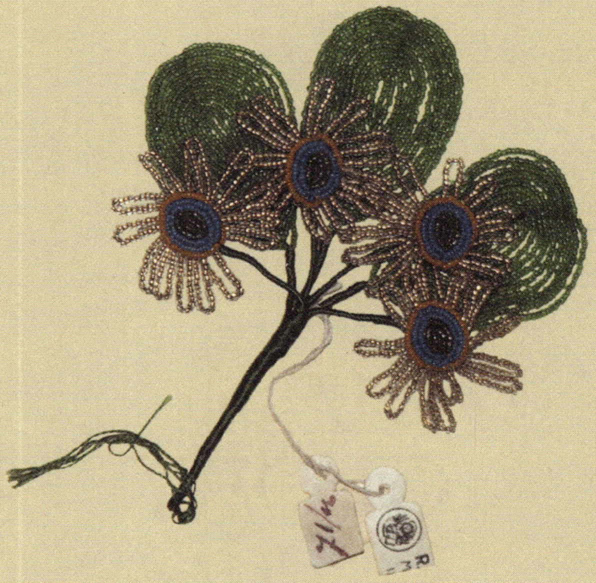

About the cover:
Purchased by the author in an antique market in Venice, this sample cloth was made by the Rova Company in 1896 on the island of Giudecca. The glass seed beads were strung on a loom, creating many colorful and intricate patterns. Rova Company salesmen used the sample cloth to solicit sales (note the original tags). Typically, customers would order patterns by the meter, which were used to create tobacco pouches, handbags, and trimmings for dresses, necklaces, cushions, belts, small coin bags, and lampshades.

ISBN 978-0-692-88200-9

The GLORY *— of —* BEADS

The Rise and Fall of the Società Veneziana per l'Industria delle Conterie

NICOLE ANDERSON

For my family

The scribe's profession increases his wisdom; whoever is free from toil can become a wise man.

How can he become learned who guides the plow, who thrills in wielding the goad like a lance, Who guides the ox and urges on the bullock, and whose every concern is for cattle?

His care is for plowing furrows, and he keeps a watch on the beasts in the stalls.

So with every engraver and designer who, laboring night and day, Fashions carved seals and whose concern is to vary the pattern. His care is to produce a vivid impression, and he keeps watch till he finishes his design.

So with the smith standing near his anvil, forging crude iron. The heat from the fire sears his flesh, yet he toils away in the furnace heat. The clang of the hammer deafens his ears, His eyes are fixed on the tool he is shaping. His care is to finish his work, and he keeps watch till he perfects it in detail.

So with the potter sitting at his labor, revolving the wheel with his feet. He is always concerned for his products, and turns them out in quantity.

With his hands he molds the clay, and with his feet softens it. His care is for proper coloring, and he keeps watch on the fire of his kiln.

All these men are skilled with their hands, each one an expert at his own task;

Without them no city could be lived in, and wherever they stay, they need not hunger.

They do not occupy the judge's bench, nor are they prominent in the assembly; They set forth no decisions or judgments, nor are they found among the rulers;

Yet they maintain God's ancient handiwork, and their concern is for exercise of their skill.

SIRACH 38:24–34

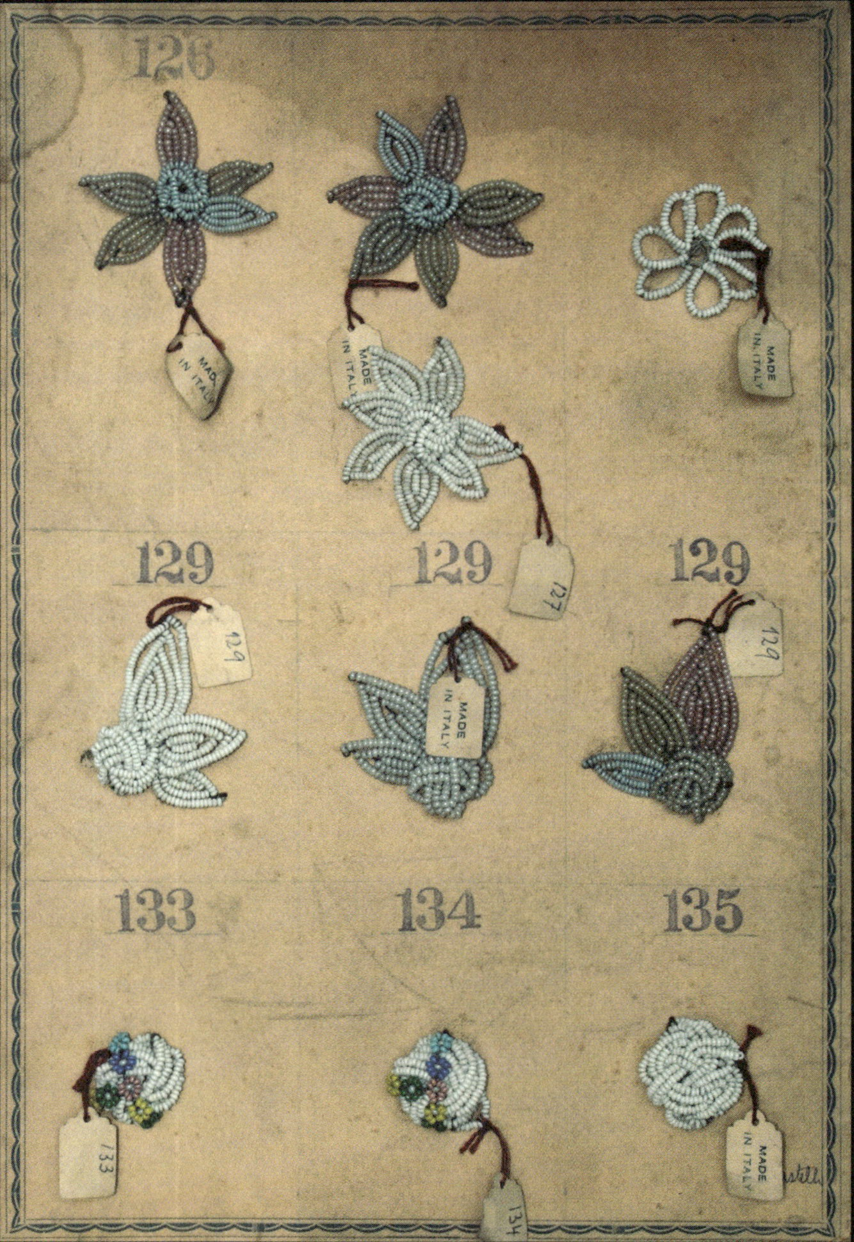

< SEED BEADED FLOWERS strung on metal wire were sent from Venice to France. The French women assembled the flowers onto a large metal frame, creating a funeral wreath for the fallen military soldiers of WWI.

—*Table of*— CONTENTS

BEAD CARDS PHOTOGRAPHED BY STEFANO PANDIANI

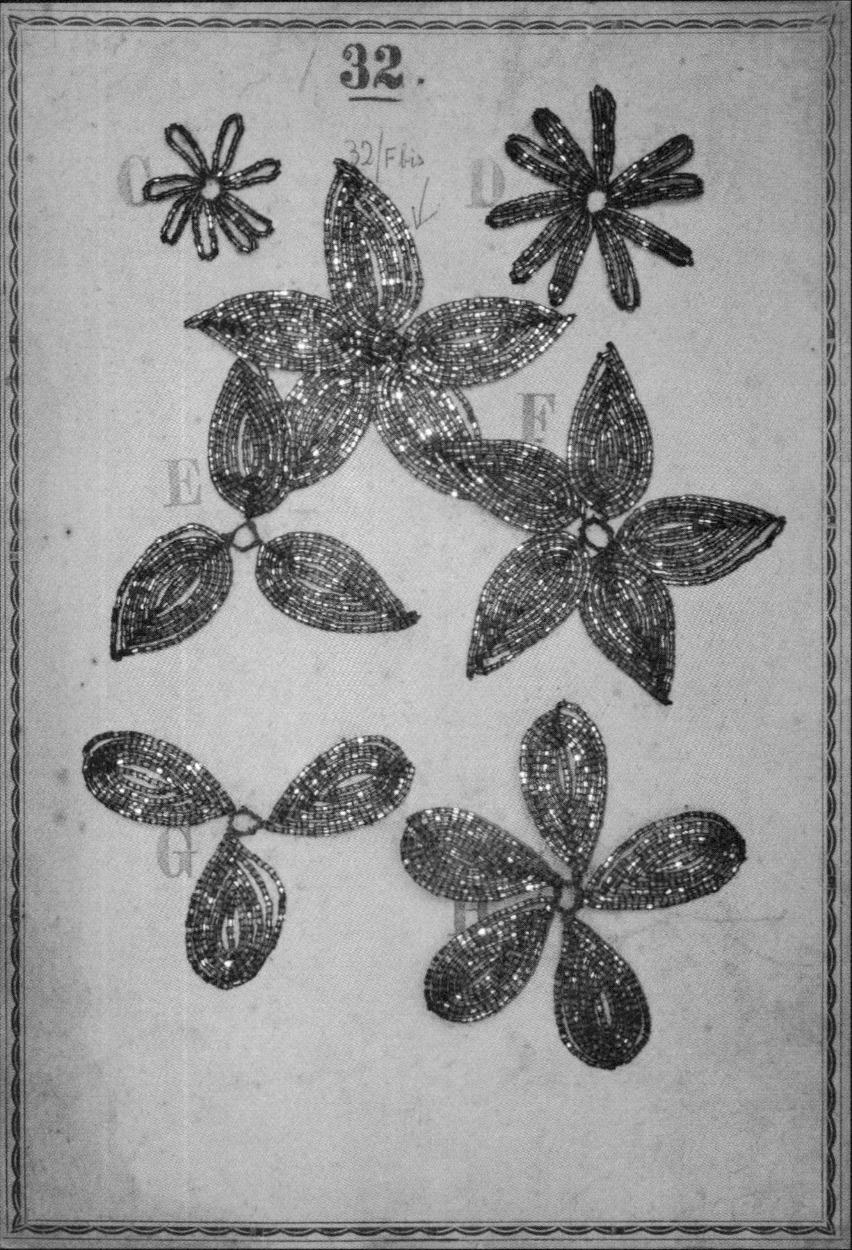

< SILVER-LINED seed beaded flowers.

— *Foreward* —

In an age where everything seems to be mechanized, seed beads and handmade glass beads from Murano will preserve their unique and irreproducible characteristics for eternity . . . works of the human spirit. The journey that the author, Nicole Anderson, has undertaken, a long and winding road rich in art and history of the production of glass beads, is encompassed in this book and is a double victory.

The first victory is entirely personal in view of the effort of a foreign researcher in a world of hidden truths, unrevealed secrets, complex historical and bibliographical research, which represents the merit of achievement and a life dedicated to love which fascinates and surprises us every day.

The second victory is devoted exclusively to the reader who, thanks to the tenacity and perseverance in the research conducted by the author, will admire and be captivated by the rare images of real lives with accurate descriptions of a different perspective.

This wonderful journey takes the reader beyond the borders of Murano and Venice to France where, in particular, the reader will discover how Murano production was appreciated and used to enrich and honor the graves of the deceased with embroidered wreaths of colorful flowers made with seed beads.

I'm certain that this book will fascinate and cultivate the knowledge of readers who love this amazing art form.

Giacomo De Carlo
Bead Historian
Venice, Italy

Wherefore I saw that there is nothing better, that a man should rejoice in his works, for that is his portion; for who shall bring him back to see what shall be after him?

ECCLESIASTES 3:22

—Preface—

My interest for glass beads began in 1985. After graduating with a Bachelor of Arts Degree in Communication Arts from Saint Mary's College of Orchard Lake, Michigan, I found a job as a special events coordinator for a concert venue (Center Stage, in Canton, Michigan) which had a seating capacity of nearly two thousand people. Friday nights were dedicated to alternative new wave and punk music, and I was thrilled to be the disc jockey spinning vinyl albums. One night the teens insisted that I play pop music, but I refused because this type of music was scheduled to be played on Saturday nights, not Friday nights. Soon the deejay booth was crowded with angry teens each fighting for the right to hear their favorite genre of music. Losing my cool, I grabbed the microphone, shouted a few curse words and then played "Let's Have a War" by the band Fear. The punks went wild and screamed with victory as they slam danced, overturned tables, broke glasses, and threw chairs in the air. I was fired on the spot.

Two weeks later, I bought a one-way ticket for one hundred fifty dollars to Brussels, Belgium on People's Express, a no-frills airline company. When my money ran out, I planned to return to the United States to launch a promising career . . . or so I thought. Little did I know that this travel adventure would change my life forever.

I hitchhiked alone throughout England, Scotland, Ireland, and Wales. Six weeks later, I traveled throughout Europe using a train pass and sleeping in youth hostels. I soon found myself in Venice, Italy—a destination I knew I couldn't possibly overlook. From the get-go, I was mesmerized and spellbound with Venice. Everything in front of my eyes was beautiful, artistic, romantic and enchanting, including the Venetian man I met. Our subsequent marriage was short-lived; it was all Venice's fault.

My first job in Venice was painting masks for Carnivale. Much as I enjoyed my job, I knew that if I wanted to earn more money, I had to learn more about the glass industry. I was hired as a salesperson in a very elegant glass store near Saint Mark's Square. My boss, Signore Bepe, taught me a lot about the artistic glass of Murano, as well as how to skillfully convince tourists to buy our glass. The atmosphere in this store was tense. We were pressured to finalize as many sales as possible, and if a customer left our store without buying something, we'd get the evil-eye or criticized.

Signore Bepe's store had a vast collection of lovely glass beaded necklaces, earrings, bracelets, and pendants. Playfully, I would wear this jewelry for the day, never anticipating that I'd sell it right off my neck. It wasn't long before my boss recognized I had an innate ability to sell glass beaded jewelry. Whenever a customer showed even the slightest interest in our jewelry, Signore Bepe immediately summoned me to handle the sale. I never felt it was necessary to forcibly persuade someone to buy; I simply shared my awe over these miniature pieces of art and, effortlessly, convinced hundreds of tourists from all over the world to buy our jewelry. It was a natural transition for me to collect and study Venetian glass beads, and soon I began to design my own pieces. Eventually, after several years of working in glass showrooms in Venice and Murano, I decided to participate in a few bead shows in the United States. Finally, it dawned on me: selling opulent glass chandeliers was not nearly as fun as selling small glass beads. There is a passage in the Bible that reminds me to never underestimate the power of just one bead: *"and upon finding one pearl of great value, he went and sold all that he had and bought it."* (Matthew 13:46) Beads (*perle*, in Italian) can change your life, your career, your direction, and your priorities. And that's exactly what happened to me.

In 2002, I was honored to give the Keynote Address during the Recursos Bead Expo in Santa Fe, New Mexico. I gave a slide presentation consisting of fifty black and white photographs taken in the early 1920s. The photographs illustrated the operations of the factory—the *Società Veneziana per l'Industria delle Conterie*. I'll never forget that evening. I think there were over one hundred people in the audience. I was very nervous as I briefly explained each photograph. After the presentation, many people approached me and complimented on the delivery, the photographs and the content of the address. "You really need to take that presentation and turn it into a book," commented one woman. "It was a beautiful presentation, Nicole. Did you ever think about writing a book on it?" added another. "There are grants from bead societies that could help finance a book. You should look into it." After hearing many encouraging remarks and suggestions, I began to think seriously about writing a book on the history of the Società Veneziana per l'Industria delle Conterie.

A few months later, I submitted a grant proposal to the Northwest Bead Society and the Bead Society of Greater Chicago. It was a bittersweet moment when those grants were approved. Part of me was very happy that these bead societies supported my project, but another part of me was thinking, "Be careful what you wish for, you just may get it." In my grant proposal, I stated that I could complete the book in one or two years. If I could re-write that proposal, I would have never put a time limit on this project. I never imagined how much of my life would be consumed in serious archival research, translating, reading, writing, interviewing, and editing. Many aspects of my life were put on hold as I closed myself in my tiny Venetian apartment for months at a time, focusing on the book and nothing else.

All the Italian-English translations were done by myself. The Italian dialogue is similar to one of their meals . . . it goes on forever. One sentence, in Italian, can take up half a page. The Italian language is poetic and the cadence is phonetically beautiful. Hopefully, nothing got lost in translation and the content is accurate. In regards to the terminology when describing the production of glass, I decided to use the word "cane" (instead of the word "rod") because "cane" sounds most similar to the same word in Italian, which is *canna*.

After I received the grants, I announced to my family and close friends that I was embarking on a very serious project and that I needed their constant support and motivation. Everyone stepped up to the plate, especially my dad, who wouldn't hesitate to scold and curse, "When are you going to finish that book? What the heck is the matter with you? What are you waiting for?" Even as an adult, I was still frightened by the wrath of my father. Despite his constant and harsh reminders, I wouldn't allow him to control the journey of this book, even if it meant he'd never live to see it published.

All too often, friends and acquaintances would ask me why it was taking so long to finish the book. It seemed no one understood that I had bills to pay, bead shows to organize and attend, and elderly parents to care for. Any free time I found was dedicated to the book; it was just hard finding that free time.

Meanwhile, many friends (and even strangers) recommended their own effective formulas on how to complete a major project. Everyone had the perfect solution, the perfect balance, a guaranteed result, and the suggestions kept rolling in. What they didn't understand was that once I put the book on hold for a period of time, re-opening it was like starting all over again. I would take two steps forward and one step back. In order to make progress, it was necessary to create a substantial amount of uninterrupted free time, allowing me to accelerate and gain some sort of momentum. However, starting and stopping this project was like driving a stick-shift. By the time I reached the sixth gear, it was time to terminate the research, fly to the United States, and embark on an annual ten-thousand-mile bead-show tour.

The first year of my research was the most difficult and challenging. I had to learn how to use the national libraries and archives. It took me one year to figure out how the Italian system worked and how to successfully retrieve information. I was on my own, with no friend to guide me or show me the ropes, and I was scared and nervous. To my benefit, I speak fluent Italian and possess Italian citizenship, so when it came time to submit my legal documents to obtain a library card, or to get permission to look at an ancient book, I was no foreigner and no one raised an eyebrow.

Retrieving information from the libraries wasn't an easy task. It seemed every time I visited, I broke some sort of code of conduct. I was scolded for reading a book on my lap, reprimanded for sitting in the wrong seating section, criticized for wanting too much information too soon, and taunted when I mistook the book's location number for an @ sign when, instead, it was a fancy "C" written in old-school calligraphy. Many times I left the library frustrated, humiliated, and crushed in spirit. There had to be another way to be taken seriously and slowly, slowly, I learned a few tricks. I noticed the more often I frequented the library, the more receptive and helpful was the staff. Sometimes I would buy a staffer a coffee in the bar next door, and this gave me a little edge in my progress — instead of receiving the allocated two-book requests at one given time, I was sometimes able to receive three or four. I'll never forget the time I submitted a request to see a book, written in 1866. After thirty minutes, the clerk returned to the distribution desk and said that the book was indeed in their inventory, but that it was simply "unreachable." In all my years of studying in libraries, I had never heard of such a thing. She suggested I return one week later, allowing the staff ample time to retrieve it. I left the library that day, scratching my head, wondering how the book got there in the first place. After one year of mastering how to use the Venetian libraries and archives, I can now enter with confidence, without feeling anxious or intimidated. Over the years of this research, I have learned to just roll with the punches, expect some delays, perplexities, frustrations; and if you're a woman, it always helps to wear a smile and a little lip gloss.

Obstacles, obstacles, obstacles. Although some things went smoothly, there were also many periods of frustration. I found discrepancies in several books, which kept me searching for the truth, but ultimately resigning myself to the fact that everything can be disputed. The translations weren't easy either, especially if the material was written in the Venetian dialect. Then, there were the deaths of a few Venetians and Muraneses whom I had interviewed. If I wanted additional information from them, I was out of luck. There were also periods of doubt and fear where I thought this project was too big, too complicated, and a greater undertaking than I could possibly endure. I would pray to God and ask Him to bless my work. I would say the rosary, go to church and light a candle, sprinkle holy water around my work space, light incense, and telephone my dad. The old man, stubborn and ornery, was always good for instilling determination, albeit in a most authoritarian approach. Raised during the Depression, he was strong as steel and expected his children to prevail over life's challenges. By the grace of God, I was able to move forward, however slowly, and overcame any self-defeating thoughts.

Oftentimes during my research, I felt like a baseball batter in a slump. I'd spend one full day in the library and come out with nothing. The following day, the same result. Even though I convinced myself that the process of elimination could be considered progress in itself, I was still striking out, day after day, and walking home with my head held down. Then, one day I'd get my first hit. Then, I'd hit a double, then a triple, and sometimes I'd even hit a home run.

One of those "home runs" occurred when I was searching for information regarding the man who made the needles for the *impiraresse* (the women who strung the *conterie* beads onto threads). The only information I had on this gentleman was his name, Aldo Bullo, given to me by a signora in the neighborhood who had a career in the bead business. She told me that Bullo belonged to a church in lower Castello (a district of Venice). She suggested that I go to this church, talk to the priest, and get Bullo's date of birth and death. Having Bullo's personal information, I could possibly estimate the approximate period of his artisan production of needles. One afternoon I went to the church only to find a sign on the door that read, "Out for Spiritual Reflection." A few days later there was another sign posted, "Out for Sacred Meditation." And again another day, "Repose for Holy Hours and Prayer." No luck. Either the priest was highly devoted or someone was taking a nap. A few days later, I was at the bank waiting in line with the caretaker of the same church, who just so happened to be the brother of the signora who gave me the initial information on Bullo. We chatted about the weather and then I casually related my disappointment in not finding the priest or any information on Bullo. That was the extent of our conversation. A few days later, the signora arrived at my door. She just returned from a funeral where she suspected the daughter of Aldo Bullo was in attendance. On my behalf, she approached Bullo's daughter, recounted that there was an "Americana" living in the neighborhood who was working on a book, and who was interested in learning more about Signore Bullo. Before I knew it, I had not only Bullo's date of birth and death but his fascinating life story as well. Grand slam.

More obstacles and delays occurred while writing this book when my brother Lorne, a Vietnam veteran, died suddenly. His death was a devastating and shocking blow to my family. Then, two years later, late in the summer of 2009, both of my parents died just fifteen days apart. It seemed the entire year of 2009 was occupied with caregiving for my sick parents, nursing them until death, organizing back-to-back funerals, and then dealing with their estates. How could I find enthusiasm and energy to work on the book while I was in a perpetual state of mourning? It seemed my life had taken a nose dive and, consequently, the book was put on the back burner. Caring for my parents was an honor, not an obligation, and in the wake of their absence, I was soon suffering the "empty nest" syndrome. My greatest cheerleader and critic was now gone, but I could still hear him yelling at me, "Finish the book, gosh darn it!"

In retrospect, the book saved my life. Had I finished it years ago, I wouldn't have had a project to focus on during a period where I felt orphaned, abandoned, lost, and depressed. "The Glory of Beads" occupied my time, kept me productive and hopeful, and gave me a sense of purpose when I needed it most. The completion of this book was a monumental challenge and in many cases a sacrifice, but it was also therapy, a victory over defeat, life over death, and a labor of love.

Nicole Anderson
Author

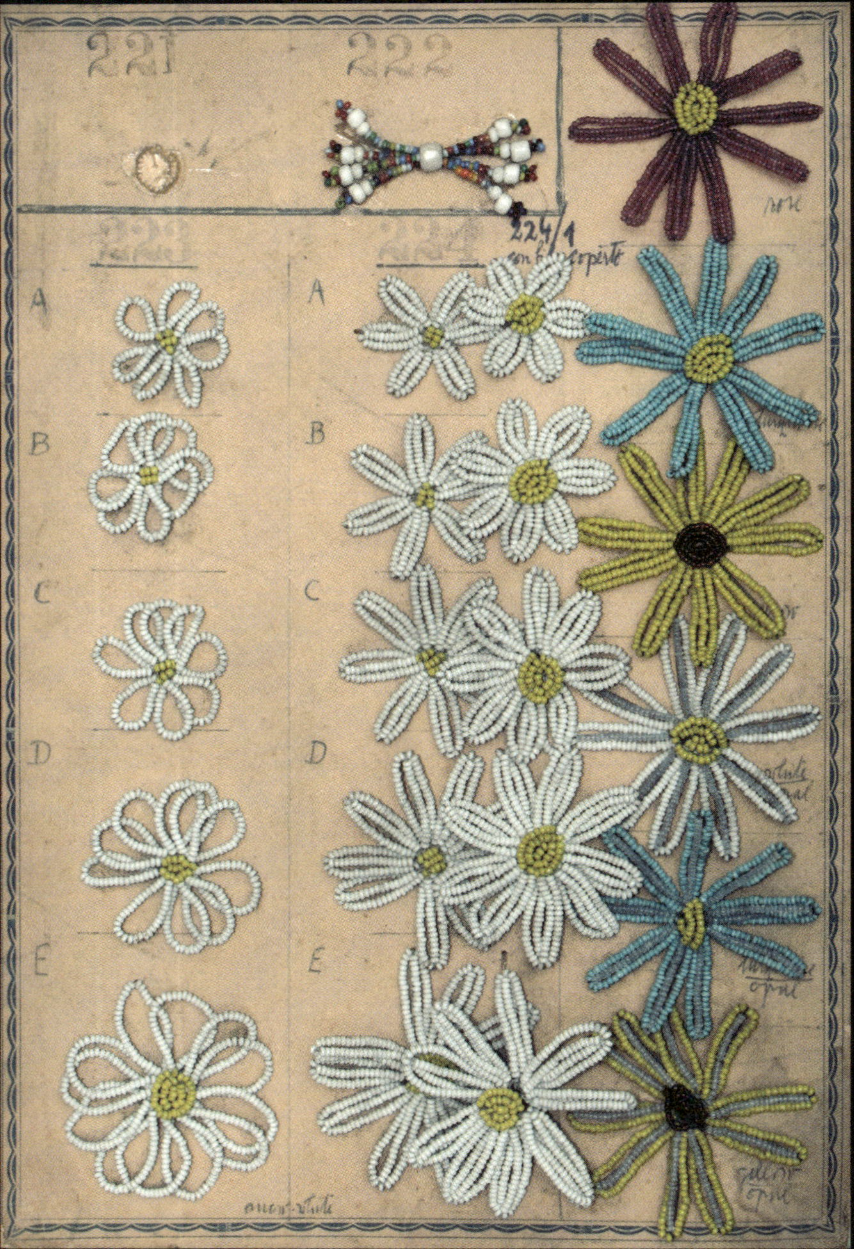

< DAISY FLOWERS str
a metal wire.

—*Acknowledgements*—

This book was made possible with the financial support of the Northwest Bead Society and the Bead Society of Greater Chicago. As a grant recipient, I realized that I had a responsibility and obligation to prove these bead societies made the right decision when they chose my proposal. Although I felt compelled to complete the book in a timely manner, these societies never questioned my progress. They were always kind and supportive. Thanks to their grants, I was encouraged to finish the book and realize a goal that was once just a dream.

I'd like to express my gratitude to my dear friend, Mary Donovan with whom I've been friends since junior high school. Mary has been a professional technical writer for over thirty years and notwithstanding her busy family life and a full-time job, she dedicated many hours editing and proof reading the chapters. Her expertise and contribution to this book are greatly appreciated. I am forever grateful.

A heartfelt thanks go to Muranese, Iginio Costantini, a kind and intelligent man who has a wealth of information, whose memory is as sharp as a nail, and who never lost his patience as I struggled to understand the mechanisms of the conterie bead production. Iginio provided me with more information than most books. I appreciate and enjoyed all the time he spent with me.

My layout designer, Kathy Dorian, gets the credit for making this a beautiful, tasteful, artistic book, one that I could have never imagined. Thank you so much for your ideas, understanding, guidance, and thank you for allowing me to also play a part in this design process.

Considering I am an American, female, and have no lineage in the Murano glass industry, I was worried that the doors of Murano would be closed and that I would have a difficult time retrieving information and scheduling interviews, but this was not the case. Everyone in Murano was kind and hospitable, all the doors were wide open, one thing would lead to another, one person would introduce me to another, and before I knew it, my research found its way into this book. I would like to thank all the Muraneses and glass historians especially Vettore Zaniol, Paolo Zecchin, Giacomo DeCarlo, the Murano Glass Museum, Dottoressa Chiara Squarcina, Vladimiro Rusca, Franco Moretti, Mario Cavagnis, Sereno Serene, Luigi Ferrigno, Vittorio Visman, Franco Lunetta, Francesco Ferro, Arnoldo Toso, Giampaolo Nason, Livio Seguso, the Stazione Sperimentale del Vetro, and the many friends and acquaintances on the island who continue to encourage me and open their doors.

I thank my father who, on his deathbed, commanded that I finish the book and with tears in my eyes, I promised to do so. I thank my mom for her gift of writing and for giving me life.

Although my family and friends couldn't help me with the research or translations, they were my greatest cheerleaders especially my sister Michelle and her family, my brothers Carl, Lorne, and Keith and their families, Uncle Donald, Aunt Peggy, Aunt June, Uncle Bobby, my godmother Eulene McGuinness, and Dawn and Fred Bause.

Little did I realize, way back in high school, when I went to Florida on spring break with my girlfriends that we would share a friendship that would last for decades. After our college educations, we all went in different directions. I moved to Venice, Italy, leaving behind my closest friends and the city life as I once knew it. However, each time I returned to Detroit, it was an excuse for us to get together, and so our little clique of chatty girlfriends has remained intact despite the miles between us. We've shared everything from laughter at weddings to tears at funerals. These women have been a wonderful, loving, humorous, and strong support group, not only during the writing of this book, but during my entire adult life as well—they are Susan Swims, Mary Donovan, Colleen Zemmin, Lorraine McDermott, Regina Townsley, and Nancy DeVergilio.

I'd like to acknowledge my Christian spiritual advisors Mary Beth and David Burke who continually encouraged me to pray for guidance and healing graces during some of the most painful and shocking moments of my life. Whenever I fell into despair, they responded with sacred words, prayers, and the reminder to never surrender, to use my God-given talents, and that it was okay to have a bad day just as long as I counted my blessings and put God first. Without their support, I may have never finished this book.

A special *mille grazie* goes to my Venetian friends who have shared all my joys and trials during the period of writing this book—they are Ruggero Moronato, Antonella Sfriso, Flavio Farenea, Nevia Rampini, and Luigina Zennaro. These friends have always been right by side, encouraging me to focus on the book and giving me a "family" when I was so far from home.

My neighbors—the Mazzoleni family, the Venuti family, and the Rosada family are perfect examples of what it means to "Love Thy Neighbor." During a period when I was grief stricken, they fed me and comforted me. They continue to help me with minor repairs on the house or pull in my laundry on rainy days. And whenever I needed the definition of a long-lost Venetian word, they never hesitated to help me. They are the best neighbors anyone could ask for.

Many bead stores continue to give me moral support. As a Venetian bead dealer, I have organized trunk shows in these stores and have established both a business relationship and a friendship that has grown over the years. They are as follows: Alethea Gaston of A Better Bead & Craft in Brevard, NC, Gail DeLuca of White Fox Beads in Knoxville, TN, Jennifer Lowe of Beaded Venus, in Mt. Pleasant, SC, Glenda Paunonen of Crystal Creations Bead Institute of West Palm Beach, FL, Jean Blaire of the New Orleans Glassworks & Printing Studio in New Orleans, LA, Robert Steinberg of Stone Mountain Bead Gallery in Albuquerque, NM, Dannelle Gundlach of the Beaded Iris Store in Albuquerque, NM, Carole Tripp of Creative Castle in Newbury Park, CA, Sandy Murphy of the Bead Jungle in Henderson, NV, Deena Seloff of Spring Beads in Spring, TX, Lauren McChrie of Oskadusa Beads in Solana Beach, CA, and Kim West of Stony Creek Beads in Ypsilanti, MI. It has been a joy and honor to work with these people and their staff.

I'd also like to thank the members of the Bead Society of New Mexico and the Great Lakes Beadworkers Guild, Alan Kay, David Kay, Arthur V. Liu, Pat and Gerry Colman, Kristen and Paul Young, Linda and Steve Petilli, Catherine Hetherington, Susan Barrett, Marjorie Bernbaum, Pam Collins, Lisa and Paul Kahler, Karen and Gianni Zanatta, Jamey Allen, Kathleen Meyers McKay, Joan Gibson, Claire Reid, Shannon Bastianello, Jeff Haller, Eddy Bettiol, Alessandra and Laura Bullo, Laviana Ventura, Lia Favero, GianLuigi Moretti Facchin, Stefania Moronato, Patrizia Semenzato, Stefano Da Villa, Daniele Resini, Stefano Rossi of the Museo Storico Navale da Venezia, Dottoressa Silvia Lunardon of the IRE and Tomaso Fillipi Archivio, the Curia Patriarcale di Venezia, the staff at the Marciana Biblioteca Nazionale, the Biblioteca del Museo Correr, the Archivio Fotografico Fondazione Musei Civici di Venezia, the Archivio di Stato di Venezia, and my friends at beadcollector.net.

Many thanks to award-winning photographer Stefano Pandiani for photographing the bead sample cards and glass objects. Thank you for always being available for me.

Some of the people I interviewed have since died. These people gave me their time and welcomed me into their homes and I thank them very much. They are Franco Mian, Alfredo Barbini, Lucia Gavagnin, and Ilde Torcellan. May their souls rest in peace.

My husband, Francesco Bungaro, came into my life when I wasn't looking. He has been a pillar of strength, love, courage, joy, and optimism since the first day I set eyes on him. Thank you for always protecting me, motivating me, and sharing my dreams.

I thank God for putting His signature on every one of these pages and for showing me His presence during this entire journey!

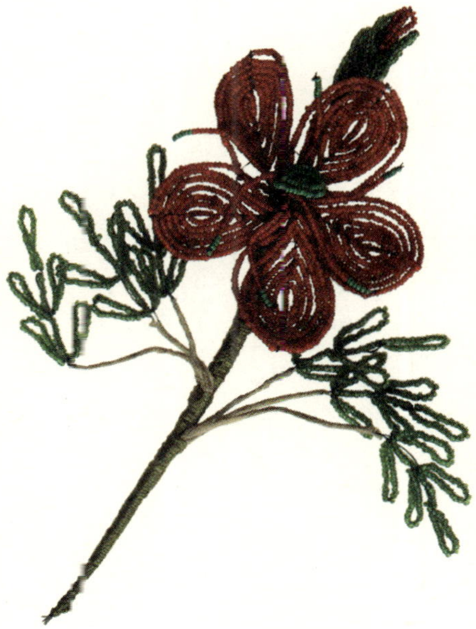

The
GLORY
— *of* —
BEADS

We are not makers of history, we are made by history.

MARTIN LUTHER KING, JR.

Baptist Minister and American Civil Rights Leader

(1929–1968)

Murano in Retrospect

The island of Murano, once known by the ancient name of *Amurianum*, is located in the Venetian lagoon, just one kilometer from Venice. Murano is comprised of seven small islands, two of which are united with a long bridge extending over the wide Grand Canal of Murano. The circumference of Murano is only about four kilometers, but despite its size, Murano has a wealth of history that dates back to the 5th and 6th centuries.

Like many islands in the lagoon, Murano was a sanctuary for refugees from the Veneto mainland of Altino and Opitergio who sought freedom from barbaric invasions such as those from Attila the Hun in the mid-400s.[i] One hundred years later, in 568, the Lombard invasion sent another wave of refugees to the islands of the Venetian lagoon. Aware and fearful that the mainland was still populated by brutal invaders, the Lombards settled permanently in Venice. As a result, the population of Venice increased as did its number of glass workshops.[1]

Many of these glass workshops, constructed of wood, were destroyed by fire. Hence, on November 8, 1291, the Chief Advisor *(Maggior Consiglio)* of Venice ordered their demoli-

1 | The Lombards/Longobards/Langobardi were a Germanic tribe originally from northern Europe who invaded Byzantine Italy in 568 under the leadership of King Alboin. They established a Kingdom of Italy which lasted until 774 when it was conquered by the Franks. *(Extracted from http://en.wikipedia.org/wiki/lombards last modified on September 14, 2008.)*

> RIO DEI VETRAI: A narrow canal of approximately 500 meters that flows between the Grand Canal of Murano and the Marani Canal. It gets its name due to the many glass factories that were once situated here.

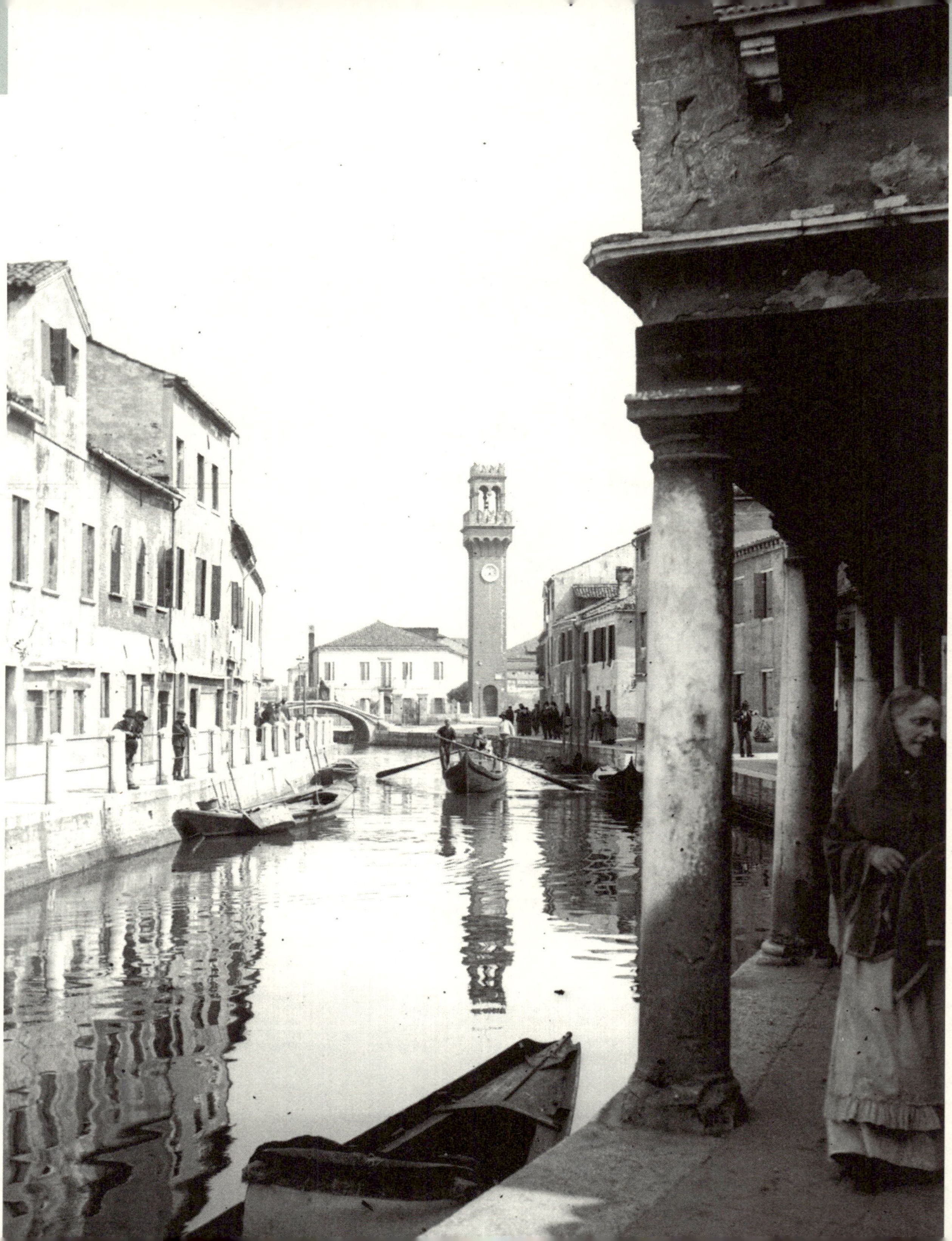

tion and relocation. During this period, glass workshops had already existed in Murano and, recognizing the island was isolated from Venice, yet still nearby, it was chosen as the ideal place to continue the art of making glass. Moreover, any fires would be confined to the island of Murano, sparing Venice. The decree also gave the Venetians, who were very much aware of the economical importance of the glass industry, greater surveillance and restrictions over this trade. Murano and its glass factories then became more guarded and protective of its glassmaking techniques, contributing to its aura of intrigue and mystery.[ii]

A second decree, dated January 8, 1295, was issued to severely discipline any Murano glassworker who fled to a foreign land and failed to return within an established time limit. The Chamberlain of Art (*Gastaldo*) lamented of this painful fact:

"Many artists leave Venice without realizing the fragility of the punishment as they go to enrich another city and make their home there. Therefore, it has been added in the Capitolare delle'Arte that all those who leave Venice to practice glass elsewhere are considered an outcast and if they return to their homeland, they can no longer work with glass in Venice and in the Veneto regions, such as in those cities that already have glass furnaces—Treviso, Padova, Vicenza, Mantova, Ferrara, Ravenna, Ancona, and Bologna. Also, those few that are recalled to Venice will no longer be given an export license for raw materials used for making glass."[iii]

Shortly after this decree, the artisan workmanship of producing glass beads arrived in Murano, thanks to the adventurous travels of merchant Marco Polo. The event, narrated by Carlo Nejmann Rizzi in 1811, recounts how two men founded a new trade, the *Arte dei Margariteri,* which is the production of glass beads to imitate gemstones or *perle false*.[2]

According to legend, in the late 1200s, when Marco Polo returned to Venice from his journey

2 | A Margartieri is one who works in the production of the so-called *'verixell'* or conterie beads. For example, a Margartieri can be the worker who separates the cane, or who cuts the cane, or who polishes the beads, and so on.

in Asia and the coast of the Indian Ocean, he described to two Murano glassworkers, Christopher Briani and Domenico Miotti, the beautiful gemstones he observed in these faraway lands, how they were used, and the fondness the people had for them. Polo convinced the two men that if they could produce perle false out of glass, they could make a lot of money. Miotti and Briani dedicated themselves to this new idea and performed many experiments. Eventually, they were able to produce the first Murano glass beads to imitate gemstones such as agate, amethyst, garnet, sapphire, and chalcedony. The first shipment of these beads went to the port of Basra, Iraq, earning the two glassworkers a very large profit. Although this account of the origin of the perle false is based more on hearsay than evidence, Briani and Miotti, nonetheless, are considered to be the founders of the Art of the Margariteri glass trade in Murano.[iv]

Despite being closely connected to Venice, the Muraneses always safeguarded their independence and had their own local administrative government. Unlike Venice, in 1602, Murano had a "Book of Gold" (*Libro d'Oro*) where descendants of pure Muranese lineage were registered and given priority citizenship, especially those who worked in the glass industry. They were allowed to carry two knives instead of one. Also, non-Muraneses were excluded from participation in the activities of the glass factories and only children of glass masters, or children from an owner of a glass factory, were permitted to build a factory.[v] In addition, neither the police nor the chief of police of Venice was allowed to set foot on the island of Murano. In the event a crime was committed, the magistrate of Murano would ensure that the guilty party was handed over to the superior magistrate of Venice.[vi]

The Venetian government, which prospered from the glassworks of Murano, granted Murano the distinct privilege to create a specified amount of its own currency represented as medallions *(oselle)* made of silver or gold and having the Latin inscription, *Munus communitatis*

Muriani,[vii] or "gift from the community of Murano." The dated coins also had the epigraphs of the current reigning Doge[3], the Podestà[4], the Treasurer of Murano, and the island's insignia, which is a rooster bearing a fox on its back and a snake in its beak, symbolizing vigilance/surveillance, acuteness/cleverness, and wisdom/knowledge.[viii]

"But the most honorable of all privileges was the one which allowed the marriage of a patriarch aristocrat from the Veneto region to the daughter of a Murano glass master, without losing any of his rights or privileges and preserving the legitimacy of all levels of nobility. This privilege was truly extraordinary, especially coming from a government eminently aristocratic and which took great lengths to uphold the nobility of the region."[ix]

By the early 16th century Murano reached its greatest splendor when nearly thirty thousand inhabitants, seventeen churches, several majestic Gothic palaces, beautiful villas, libraries, monasteries, convents, art schools, shops, lush gardens and orchards grew alongside glass factories, confirming the prosperity of this community.[x] Although the residents of Murano lived in poverty, the island was a retreat for noble Venetians where famous poets and writers would linger in the fragrant gardens in conversation. For many years, these gardens were the pride of the Venetian aristocrats. The gardens of Murano were abundant with trees of cypress, bay, evergreen, cedar, fruits, as well as many exotic species of plants and flowers. Poets and writers praised the beauty of the gardens of Murano, comparing it to the famous 16th-century gardens of Florence, the Orti Oricellari.[xi]

On May 12, 1797, the last Doge of Venice, Lodovico Manin, surrendered without a battle to Napoleon Bonaparte's French army. After more than one thousand years of independence, the Serenissima Republic of Venice fell to foreign invaders. Nine months after the invasion,

3 | The Doge (or Duke) of Venice reigned rather than governed; his powers were limited and his actions were severely controlled. He was elected for life and usually chosen from among the most shrewdest and aristocratic Venetian families. *(Extracted from Knopf Guides,* Venice, *Alfred A. Knopf, Inc., New York, page 231.)*

4 | The Podestà was a magistrate sent from the Doge to a territory to oversee the laws and administer justice. He was the director of the administration of the municipality. *(Extracted from Il Novissimo Melzi, Dizionario Linguistica, Antonio Vallardi Editore, Milano, 1970.)*

Napoleon gave Venice to Austria in the Treaty of Campo Formio, but not before taking an unprecedented booty to France.[5] Napoleon's wrath succeeded in stripping Venice and Murano of most of its wealth, artifacts, and historical properties. Almost all of Murano's churches, bell towers, schools, and monasteries were demolished and plundered. Of the seventeen churches in Murano, only three survived. Destroyed or looted were grandiose libraries rich with antique manuscripts, marble statues and columns, antique mosaic pavements, opulent ceiling panels, reliquaries, hand-carved wooden altarpieces, sterling silver relics, ecclesiastical paintings, and even tombs. Numerous Gothic palaces were destroyed, in addition to schools, oratories, convents, and gardens. Moreover, the oldest church on the island, Saint Salvador, founded in the 5th century by the Altino fugitives, was demolished. Napoleon's army succeeded in erasing most of Murano's history. Glass factories, along with tools, ovens, and equipment did not escape Napoleon's fury. Describing the state of the glass industry in Murano of 1799, author Silvano Tagliapetra wrote:

"It is a trade that almost no longer exists. The furnaces in operation could be counted on one hand. Everything had been disbanded."[xii]

After the devastating loss of architectural monuments, sacred treasures, and being savagely stripped of its historical identity, it took years before Murano could regain its strength and power. But with perseverance and the innate mastery for glass, the Muraneses—known for their vigilance and resourcefulness—were determined to rebuild their factories and revive its glass industry.[xiii] In effect, by the mid-1800s, the glass industry was back in full force, winning many honors and recognitions in artistic exhibits throughout the world.

Murano maintained its autonomy until December 31, 1923 when it was forced to join the

5 | The Treaty of Campo Formio gave France control of most of northern Italy but a secret clause promised Venice to the Austrians. Venice was under French and Austrian occupation from 1797-1866. *(Extracted from http:/www.historyworld.net, http://en.wikipedia.org, and http://it.geocities.com.)*

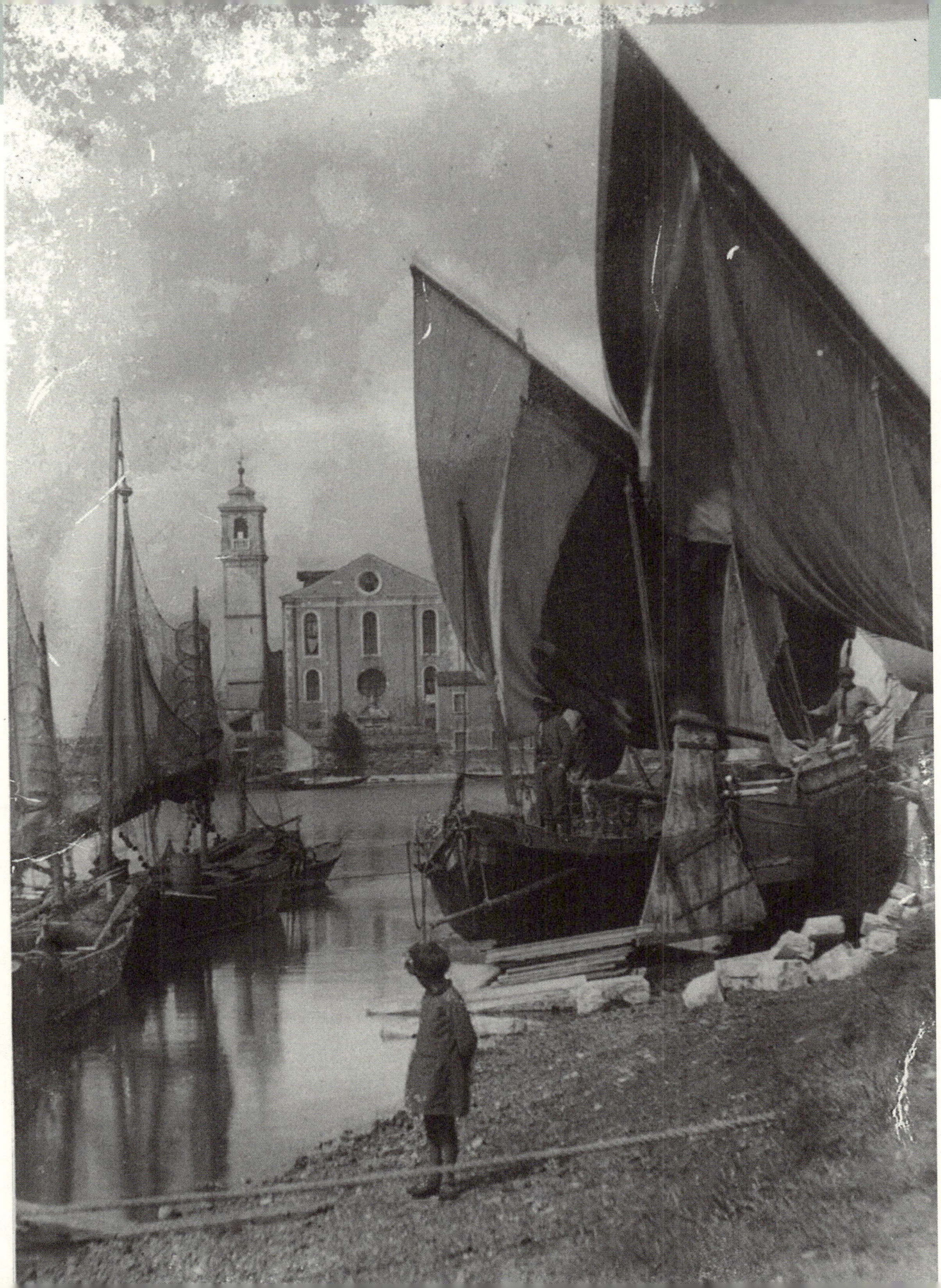

< CHURCH OF SANTA MARIA DEGLI ANGELI. One of the three remaining churches left standing in Murano after Napoleon, in 1797, overthrew the Most Serene Republic of Venice (*Serenissima Repubblica di Venezia*). The origins of the church date back to 1188 and was rebuilt in 1498–1529. Note the fishing nets on the boats (left) and the people standing in the boats (right). The Venetians were champion fishermen long before they became glass masters.

municipality of Venice despite many loud protests and disorder from the Muraneses. The annexation of Murano was the result of a law during the fascist dictatorship of Benito Mussolini in which all small municipalities were united to larger ones.[6] The Muraneses protested with tumultuous demonstrations. Many angry factory workers were armed with blowpipes ready to assault a police officer if he dared to penetrate their protests. The church bell towers were continuously overtaken by rebellious teenagers who were able to climb up and strongly hammer the bells, creating noise and disturbance. Dozens of arrests were made. A curfew was established but that didn't stop the destruction of the street lights, leaving the narrow streets and residents in the dark. For weeks, the protests continued. As a form of protest, graffiti-painted roosters (the symbol of Murano) were drawn hastily on many walls and columns around the island, never to be cleaned or repainted as the Muraneses chose to be reminded of their proud past and independence.[xiv] Per contra, the most beautiful, creative, and non-violent form of protest came from the celebrated glass masters Ulderico Moretti and Giuseppe Barovier[xv], who in 1923–1924, made several *murrine* with the image of the rooster.[7] The murrine were cut, polished, framed in gold, and then made into tie clips and lapel pins worn by the men of Murano. The same murrine were fashioned into rings, pendants, earrings and brooches for the women, all worn to affirm their allegiance with their beloved Murano.

WWII had a forcible impact on the island. Infrastructures in Europe were damaged and electricity was often reduced or completely disabled. Consequently, the operations of the glass factories shut down. It was a difficult period for the Muraneses. Suffering from hunger, poverty, illnesses, despair, fear, joblessness, and sometimes the loss of a loved one from the war, they struggled daily to survive.

6 | Benito Mussolini was appointed Prime Minister of Italy by King Victor Emmanuel III in 1922 and soon became Italy's dictator until 1943. Fascism opposed class war and instead supported strong unity, class collaboration, collectivism, and extreme nationalism. Fascists promote the unification and expansion of a power and/or territory of their nation in order to realize its greatness. (*Extracted from <http://en.wikipedia.org/wiki/fascism> last modified on October 17, 2008.*)

7 | A murrina (or plural murrine) is a slice of glass cane that has been cut, assembled with other slices of glass cane, and then re-heated in order to create a specific design or image. The glass cane is then stretched (or drawn out) to create a long rod while maintaining the design throughout the length of the cane. There are three different techniques to produce murrine: lampwork, furnace, or bundling thin rods together while the glass is cold.
For detailed information see Giovanni Sarpellon's book, *Venetian Beads, Mosaic Glass and Murrine.*

Il Gazzettino Illustrato

Settimanale delle Tre Venezie

	Nel Regno	Estero
Anno	L. 10.–	Fr. 12.50
Semestre	» 5.50	» 6.75

Per le inserzioni rivolgersi all'Amministrazione del "Gazzettino„ in Venezia, e negli uffici succursali di provincia, nonchè presso l'Unione Pubblicità Italiana.

CONTO CORRENTE COLLA POSTA

UFFICI DELLA RIVISTA
Palazzo Gritti Giustinian Faccanon (prop. del "Gazzettino„)
VENEZIA
Merceria, Calle delle Acque
I manoscritti non si restituiscono

Anno III - N. 23 — VENEZIA - 10 Giugno 1923 — Centesimi 20 la copia

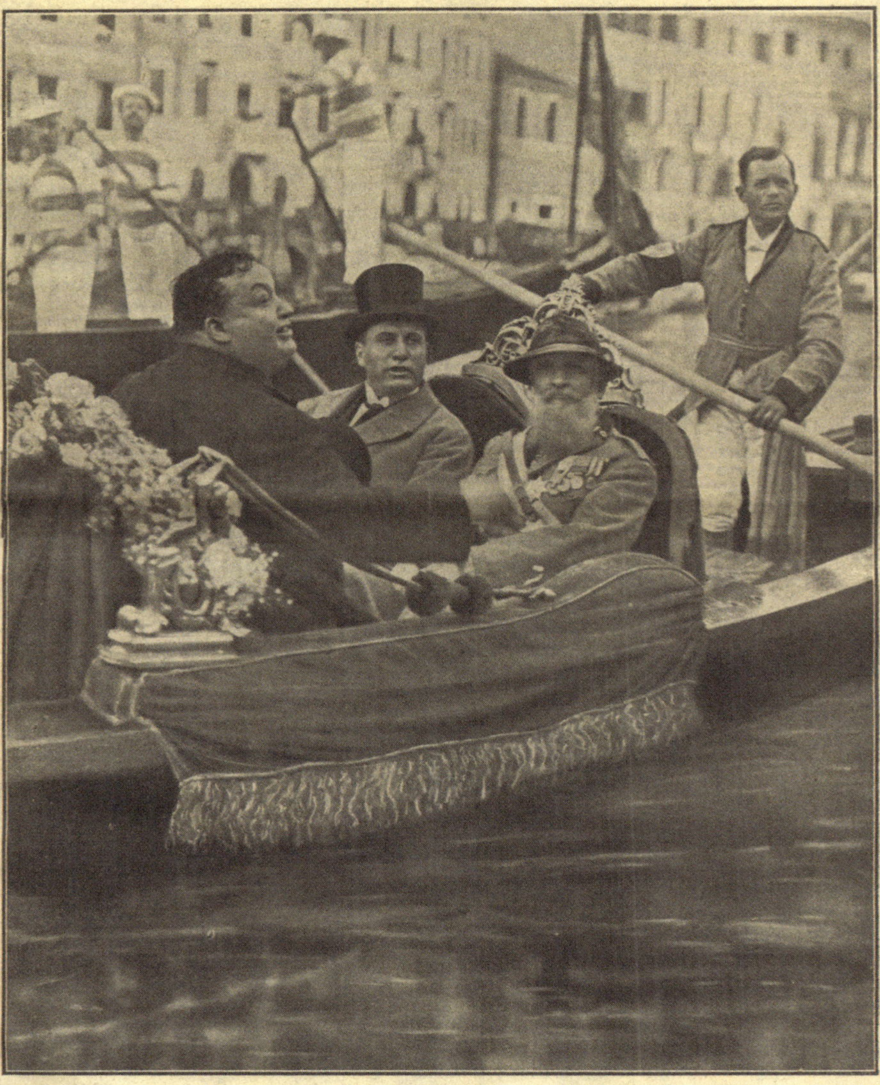

MUSSOLINI A VENEZIA

Sabato e domenica scorsa il Presidente del Consiglio è stato ospite della nostra città che gli ha tributato calorose accoglienze. La nostra istantanea coglie l'on. Mussolini appena sceso nella gondola di gala, avendo a sinistra il Commissario straordinario prof. Giordano in divisa di Console medico della Milizia nazionale e di fronte il prefetto gr. Uff. D'Adamo. (fot. Ferruzzi - Venezia)

< MUSSOLINI IN VENICE: The President of Council, Mussolini (wearing a top hat) was given a warm welcome in Venice in June 1923. The snapshot captures Mussolini, sitting in a regal gondola used for special occasions. On his left is Commissioner Professor Giordano in his uniform of the National Militia, and in front of Mussolini is Prefect Officer D'Adam.

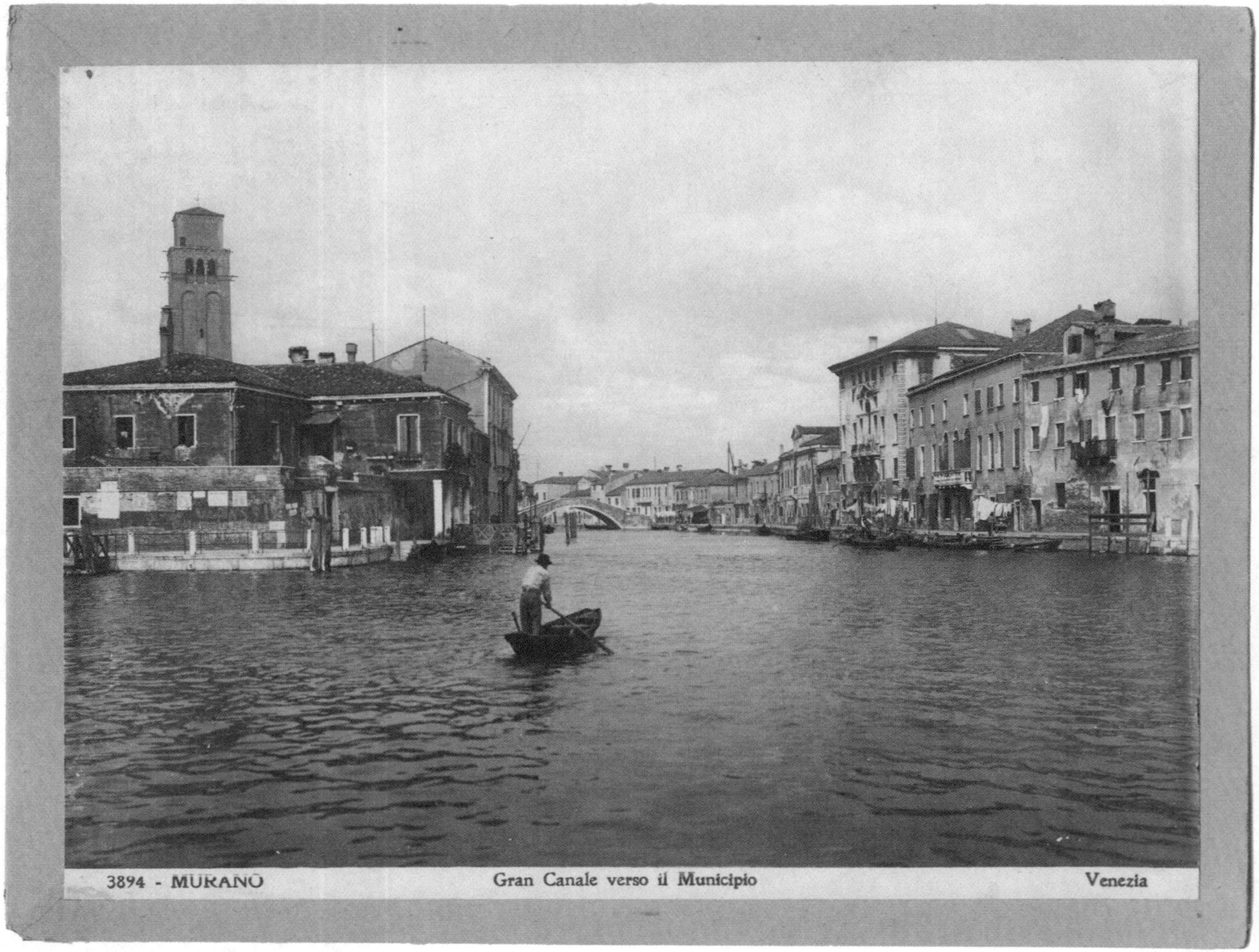

∧ SITUATED NEAR THE GRAND CANAL OF MURANO, the administration offices of the SVC occupied the 16th century Palazzo Trevisan, the tall white building on the right. The four-story tower on the left side of the canal (now demolished), was constructed to string beads in a free-fall operation.

"In the streets of Venice, no more cats could be found; during the night they were killed by delinquents and later sold as rabbits. We were lacking, literally, in everything: no milk, no flour to make bread; we lacked the raw materials to make glass, and there were no combustible materials to fuel the ovens."[vxi]

In 1951, the total population of Venice was 157,205—nine thousand of whom lived in Murano. Soon methane gas arrived in Venice, then the television. Although the Muraneses were still a poor community, their economic condition started to improve. However, in 1965 many glass factories began to transfer their activities to the mainland.

Situated on an island, Murano's glass factories were isolated from the mainland's commerce and trade. Moreover, all of the raw materials, which were necessary to make glass, had to be delivered by boat from the mainland, increasing each factory's expenses. Specialty glass shops in Murano saw increases in profits due to heavy tourism, but this was not the case for the factories and those who labored there. Many Murano glassworkers began to leave their jobs to work in other fields such as in construction, the public sector, hospitals, restaurants, retail, and so on. Witnessing an exodus of glass factories and its workers to the mainland, a group of Muraneses (composed of glassworkers, factory owners, artisans, professors, and other professionals) proposed constructing a bridge from the island to the mainland. This project (and its supporting newsletter) was called the *Muran Nova* or the New Murano.[xvii] The project proposed a bridge as a means to access raw materials, transportation, shipping companies, and workers. In addition, the bridge would encourage more tourists to arrive directly to the island (instead of Venice). The proposed bridge was refused by the municipal of Venice, leaving Murano isolated, struggling with its antiquated system of commerce, and suffering nostalgia over the loss of its autonomy back in 1923. Venice's indifference toward

Murano exacerbated the poor economic situation over the years.

Acknowledging the decline of Murano's identity, a group of Muraneses wrote the following in the *Muran Nova* newsletter in 1965:

"The Muraneses have inherited a great wealth: the name of Murano![xviii]
How is it today? How will it be tomorrow?
Muraneses, study the possibility to renew your island!
Muraneses, no one knows your needs better than you!
Muraneses, no one better than you can defend your interests!
Muraneses, wake up, think, ask, question, insist, and demand to be defended,
otherwise in twenty or thirty years we will have two Torcellos."[8]

By 1967, fifteen glass factories made an exodus to the mainland, taking with them one thousand five hundred workers and artisans.[xix] The factories that elected to stay on the island, perhaps out of respect for tradition, could not defend themselves properly, noting the emergence of many glass stores yet fewer glass factories and workers. Fake "Murano glass" products could now be found all over the world, making it necessary for Murano to regulate the market of its own glass. A law which would require the trademark of origin was opposed by the Italian Senate, handing the Muraneses yet another blow that could have otherwise protected and secured their interests. The aftereffect of the Senate's decision enabled the influx of so-called Murano glass (from nearby cities on the mainland, as well as from the Czech Republic and China) to easily find its way onto the shelves of glass stores in Murano and Venice.[xx]

Many glass factories were now resisting an economic crisis. Some glass factories closed

8 | Today's population of the island of Torcello, founded in the 5th and 6th century, is about ten people. (*http:/ www.corrieredelveneto.corriere.it*)

for a brief period and many glassworkers went on strike for higher salaries. The future of Murano appeared bleak.

The 1970s to the 1990s marked a gradual exodus of both Venetians and Muraneses who abandoned their historical roots in favor of the faster-paced cities and suburbs on the mainland such as Mestre and Marghera. These cities offered greater job opportunities, newer housing, shopping conveniences, and entertainment.[xxi]

By 2003, the number of glassworkers employed in Murano fell to 1,577, compared to 3,142 in 1971 and these numbers continue to fall.[xxii] Once boasting a population of thirty thousand inhabitants five hundred years ago, Murano's population is now approximately five thousand.[xxiii]

Although the economic prosperity of the 1980s and 1990s saw a boom in tourism, the high cost of upgrading factories (in order to comply with the pollution emission regulations and health standards), along with the higher costs for raw materials and mandatory salary increases, attributed to the rising prices of artistic glass. Meanwhile, tourists were demanding inexpensive, affordable glass. To appease the tourists, some shops resorted to importing cheaply made glass from foreign countries and marketing it as "Murano" glass. Not recognizing any difference between authentic Murano glass and the cheaper imported counterfeits, tourists continued to buy foreign glass, unaware they were doing so. Consequently, fewer orders for authentic Murano glass attributed to the ongoing closures of factories. This practice continues to threaten the true Murano glass industry.

Sadly, only a few glass masters and glassworkers want to pass their trade on to their sons. As has been the case for centuries, many who work in the trade began their careers as children working seven days a week and under unlawful conditions. Furthermore, working in a glass factory requires considerable physical strength, long work hours, the ability to endure the blistering heat, and health risks. For this reason, today's glassworkers are more likely to encourage their sons to seek a higher education in business, law, medicine, engineering, and computer technology rather than carry on the tradition of working with glass.

While the world, including Murano, continues to develop and modernize, the Murano tradition of producing unique, artisan glass continues today, albeit on a very small scale with very few workers and factories. The glass factories and artisans that have remained are trying to keep the traditions alive by participating in exhibitions, fairs and events to promote their art while drawing attention to their cultural patrimony. Today's glass masters include those who are recognized for their furnace work, such as Lino Tagliapetra, Livio Seguso, the late Pino Signoretto, and Davide Salvadore and those who are well-known for their lampwork such as Lucio Bubacco, Cesare Toffolo, and Vittorio Costantini. These artists are continually promoting their Venetian heritage by participating in exhibitions all over the world and offering classes and workshops.

While Murano glass production has declined, Murano glass continues to represent centuries of specialized skill and artisan workmanship, using ancient color recipes and techniques to produce unique creations of high design, quality and beauty. Authentic Murano glass can be found all over the world, gracing the most opulent palaces, castles, casinos, and hotels with crystal chandeliers and light fixtures to the most modest homes in rural areas with its charming decorative items and vases.

With trade, pride, education, and allegiance, the Murano glass industry hopes to maintain a prosperous and healthy future.

CHAPTER ONE *Endnotes*

i Domenico Bussolin, *Guida alle Fabbriche Vetrarie,* 1842.

ii Ibid.

iii Riccardo Vianello, *Murano—La Sua Grande Storia ed i Suoi Grandi Uomini,* Tipografica Minoese, 1964.

iv Elena Bertagnolli, Maria Teresa Sega, Rossana Urbani DeGheltof, *Perle Veneziane,* Consorzio Venezia Perle, Venezia, 1989, p. 27; Luigi Zecchin, "Un Ricettario Muranese dell'Ottocento," in *Vetro e Silicati,* 1964; Domenico Bussolin, *Guida alle Fabbriche Vetrarie,* 1842.

v Domenico Bussolin, *Guida alle Fabbriche Vetrarie,* 1842.

vi Vincenzo Zanetti, *Guido di Murano e delle Celebri Sue Fornace Vetrarie,* Tipografica Antonelli, 1866.

vii Vincenzo Zanetti, *Delle medaglie di Murano denominate oselle—Monografia,* Venezia 1881.

viii Marco Toso Borella, *Lo stemma della Magnifica Comunità di Murano ovvero il Giallo del Gallo,* Venezia/Mestre, Associazione per lo Studio e lo Sviluppo della Cultura Muranese, 2003.

ix Ibid.

x Ugo Stefunutti, in *Guido di Murano e delle Celebri Sue Fornace Vetrarie,* Vicenzo Zanetti, Tip. Antonelli, 1866.

xi Riccardo, Vianello, *Murano—La Sua Grande Storia ed i Suoi Grandi Uomini,* Venezia, Tip. Minoese, 1964.

xii Silvano Tagliapietra, *I Muranese nel Settecento,* Edizioni Helvetia, 2002, page 337.

xiii Borella, p. 25.

xiv Ibid, p. 52-59.

xv Giovanni Sarpellon, *Venetian Beads, Mosaic Glass and Murrine,* Palazzo Rota, Venezia, 2003, pp. 119-122.

xvi Silvano Tagliapietra, *Cronache Muranesi—2 Murano Veste La Divisa 1926-1950,* Edizioni Helvetia, 1982, pp. 105 and 138.

xvii Silvano Tagliapietra, *Cronache Muranesi—Il Tempo della Muran Nova (1951-1975),* Edizioni Helvetia, Venezia 1990, pp. 88-90.

xviii Ibid. pp. 91-92.

xix Ibid. page 98.

xx Ibid. page 136.

xxi Http:/www.comune.venezia.it, La Populazione del Comune di Venezia, page 36, December 31, 2006.

xxii Scuola del Vetro Abate Zanetti, *La memoria del vetro—Murano e l'arte vetraria nelle storie dei suoi maestri (a cura di Andrea Tosi),* Marsilio, Venezia, 2006, pp. 19-20.

xxiii Http:/www.comune.venezia.it (census report of 2015)

Chemists are, on the whole, like physicists, only 'less so'. They don't make quite the same wonderful mistakes, and much of what they do is an art, related to cooking, instead of a true science. They have their moments and their sources of legitimate pride. They don't split atoms, as the physicists do. They join them together, and a very praiseworthy activity that is.

ANTHONY STANDEN

British chemist and author

(1906–1993)

The Chemistry Department

In every glass factory there is a technician who follows a specific recipe for a determined color by adding and mixing various substances such as sand, soda, ash, limestone, chemicals, and minerals. In the early 1600s, this technician was called the *conciatore;* in 1866, the name *acconciatore* was used.[i] Although these two terminologies have long lost their cultural significance, the term get its name from the word *concito,* meaning to agitate, stir up, bring together, assemble.[ii] In the Murano glass factories today, this technician is simply known as the glass *composizionatore.*

For hundreds of years, the Muraneses documented their experimental achievements and failures in small booklets. The creation of different types of glass and colors (transparent and opaque) were cultivated from true specialists. The jealously-guarded recipe books, containing secret ingredients and tricks of the trade, was an authentic and valuable instrument for the chemist of the factory. The book was the mirror of his knowledge and was passed down from generation to generation. The Murano glass factories depended on the chemist to invent new colors and tonalities, especially those that no other factory possessed.

> A LAB BENCH IN THE CHEMISTRY DEPARTMENT shows the various test apparatuses for measuring and mixing fluids and minerals, for conducting experiments, and for inventing new colors and tonalities to be used in glass. A wide variety of colors and hues can be created by adding specific minerals, metals, and elements. For example, magnesium oxides produce a violet shade, cerium molybdate produces a light blue tonality, and copper oxides produce an aquamarine color. (*Il Vetro Trattato Generale di Technologia Vetraria*, Felice Franceschini, Hoepli, Milano, 1955).

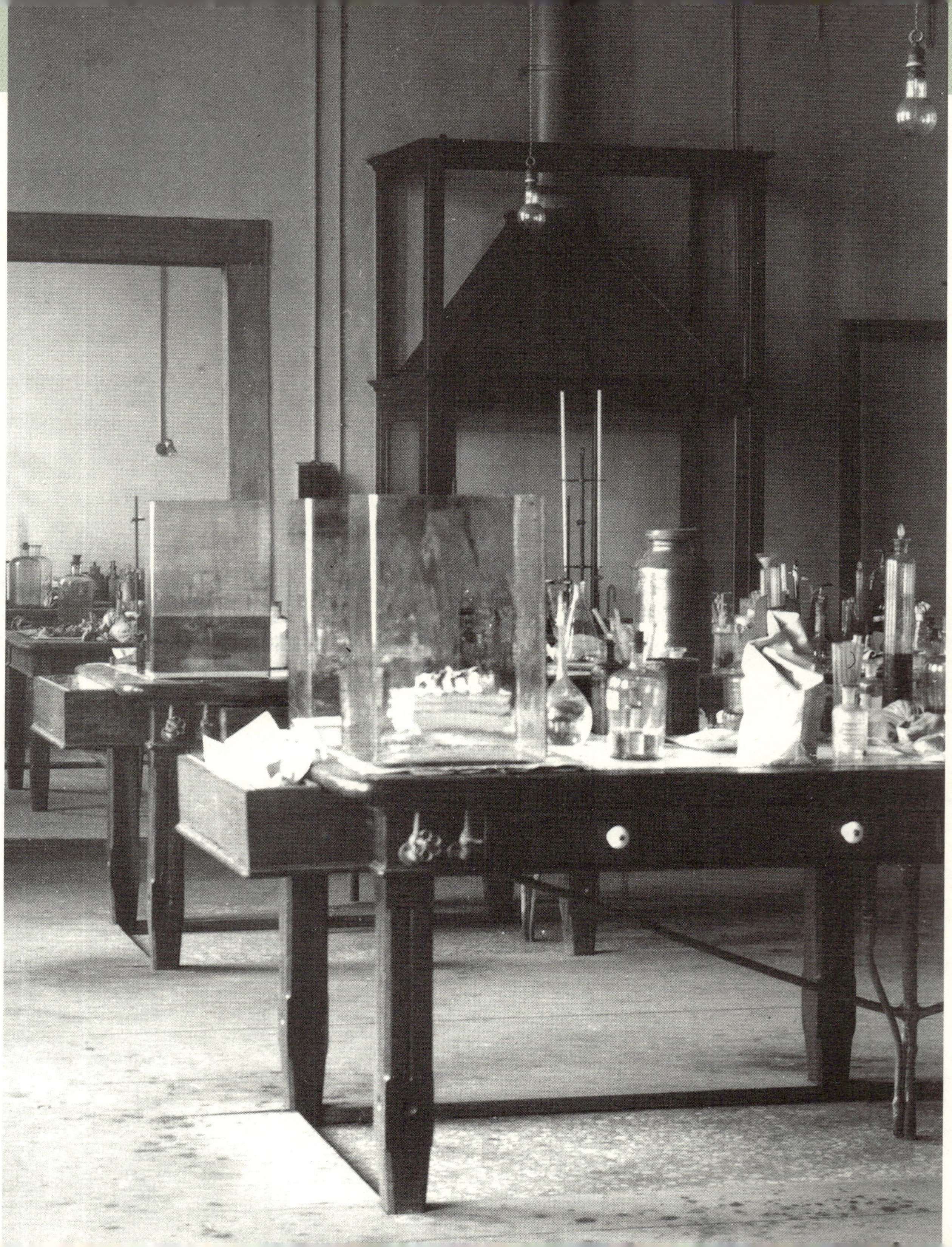

However, many of these so-called "chemists" were the offspring of true specialists and in possession of a very coveted and relevant recipe book, but with no scientific intellect or experience in the field of chemistry.[iii]

"There is no stopping the contempt for chemistry. The technicians in the conterie who empirically work in this field do not feel bad for wasting raw materials or ruining combustible materials just to make unknown colors and retry new experiments without even having a scientific clue to lead them. They throw firewood or glass in the furnace and wait to see what happens. In secret, they consult their dusty recipes and reproduce the mixtures either for the love of novelty or because they are suspicious of the poor results that came from similar recipes. They would add something of their own [to the batch] and take notes of everything while keeping a watchful eye on the oven hoping and fearing of some result. It wasn't too long ago when there was also the practice of throwing an old slipper into the fire."[iv]

Glassmaking techniques were fundamentally unaltered until the end of the 18th century when advances were made in the field of chemistry. The traditional mixtures and customary working procedures, which required the greatest prudence, were modified only if compelled by the negative results of the glass. For the Murano glass dynasties, the allegiance to the family's secrets and traditions constituted an indisputable high, artistic honor.[v]

In 1902, in a monthly newsletter dedicated to the Murano glass industry, journalist Alessandro Zecchin reported how the field chemistry was not very advanced considering the intense and ongoing scientific studies. However, the article credited the SVC for its progress in bead chemistry, citing its consolidation as the reason.

Embarking on a new period of the conterie industry, the SVC now had *"the most competent and current technicians available, forcing the conterie industry to come out of its state of stagnation (that has lasted for hundreds of years) and take advantage of all the mechanical and chemical resources, such as the advancement of chemical knowledge, allowing this industry to progress and develop more efficiently."*[vi]

There are two types of compositions for making glass cane used for bead making. One is a transparent glass (*canna di vetro*) made for producing ordinary conterie beads called *conterie ordinarie*. The other type of glass is called *smalti* (enamel glass), which is an opaque glass used for producing *conterie fine*, simply a "finer" quality of glass used for the production of conterie beads. The method for making these two types of glass is similar, except for a meager difference in its composition. Gold and silver are added to the composition of the *conterie fine*, making the enameled glass more expensive than the ordinary transparent glass.[vii]

The compositions for making glass in Murano has changed over the past seven hundred years. Due to fluctuations in the availability of raw materials, increasing health regulations, and the advancement of chemistry by numerous experiments executed by factory technicians, the colors and tonalities of glass once achieved hundreds of years ago are now a thing of the past. As such, the color can often determine the approximate age of a glass bead. Furthermore, the chemists of the factory jealously guarded their recipes, never allowing anyone to see their secret formulas. Many of these unique recipes were lost, damaged, and even buried in the tombs with its keeper.

In the mid-1800s, the raw materials used for making ordinary glass cane and enamels for the production of conterie beads were as follows: sand from Pola (Istria, Italy), sand from

Catania (located in Sicily), natron from Egypt, arsenic, manganese, minium (red lead), antimony, nitrate, and other minerals.[viii]

In 1866, glass historian and founder of the Glass Museum in Murano, Abbott Vincenzo Zanetti, identified the quantity of minerals used to produce glass enamels. The factory (which he did not name but used as an example) produced 954,095 *libbre Veneta sottili* in one year (or approximately 287,000 kilos).[1]

1 | This unit of weight fluctuates according to city or region. A *libbra Veneta sottili* corresponds to 301.23 grams. Most recipes up to the 19th century were expressed in *libbre*. (*Cesare Moretti,* Glossario del Vetro Veneziano: dal Trecento al Novecento. *Venezia, Marsilio, 2001.*)

Zanetti went on to describe that in one year, *"the factory for glass enamels consumed 470 klafters of wood*[2]*, 10,808 of fine gold oxides, 113,942 kilos of potassium nitrate, 113,942 funte (pounds) of minium*[3]*, 7,356 funte of antimony, 40,260 funte of arsenic, etc."*[ix]

Having the capacity to fabricate nearly three hundred thousand kilos of glass cane in one year was a remarkable accomplishment, considering the period of history and the artisan production. The glass factories in Murano today are fueled with methane gas, providing a greater luster and clarity to the glass due to the high temperatures of the furnaces. The raw materials currently used in glass include sand, soda, limestone, calcium, potassium, boric acid, barium, and a variety of other minerals.

To create glass with particular colors and tonalities, selected minerals and precise quantities are added to the composition. For example, to make blue, cobalt minerals are needed. For green tonalities, copper minerals are often added. For yellow tonalities, resin and sulfur minerals are added, and for ruby (*rubino*) tonalities, real gold is necessary, making rubino one of the most expensive enamels to produce. In fact, recipes in the early 1900s that called for rubino tonalities used "Napoleon gold" and "Ongari silver" which are actual gold and silver coins.

2 | *Klafter* is a traditional German unit of volume for stacked firewood, comparable to the English cord. A *klafter* of wood was generally one *klafter* tall and one kiafter long but there was less agreement on its width which is the length of the logs. (*Http://www.unc.edu/~rowlett/units/index.html. Ross Rowlett and the University of North Carolina at Chapel Hill.*)

3 | A traditional Russian unit of weight or mass corresponding to the German pfund (pronounced "funt."). The *funt* corresponds to approximately 0.9028 pound avoirdupois or 409.5 grams. The plural is *funte.*

Beyond the primary colors, there were numerous recipes to encompass a wide spectrum of shades. Using green as an example, the Muraneses had recipes for Parrot green, Agate green, Emerald green, Uranium green (made with uranium oxides), Special green, Antique green, and Green grass. The chemists also looked to their Italian cuisine for such color names as Olive green, Pistachio green, Pea green, Lime green, Green Apple, Leek green, and even Bottled green. The chemists were also influenced by floral and horticulture, giving names to colors such as Rose, Iris, Lily, Sunflower, Lavender, Poppy, Acacia, Hydrangea, and Heliotrope. Many glass beads were purposely created to resemble quartz and gemstones (*perle false*), thereby giving names to compositions such as Lapis Lazuli, Turquoise, Amethyst, Coral, Opal, Emerald, Agate, Chalcedony, Carnelian, Amber, Celestial, Garnet, Jet, Sapphire, Peridot, Aquamarine, Ruby, and Topaz. Some color names could be linked to the destination of the conterie beads such as Paris Lily, German Green, American Green, India Lemon, Zanzibar Pink, and Cairo Pink, or to aristocracies such as Imperial, Bishop, and Empire.[X]

Long before the arrival of methane gas in Murano, the ovens for fusing glass were first fueled by wood, then in the mid-1800s by carbon, followed by petroleum (naphthalene-based oil called naphtha), until finally, in 1954, by methane gas. The procedure for fusing glass using methane gas is much easier and cleaner than it was when the ovens were stoked by wood or naphtha.

Hundreds of years ago, the process of fusing glass was much more complex and time-consuming. In fact, glass was once obtained in two separate phases: one was the preparation of frit (*fritta*), the other was the fusion itself in a crucible. Alchemist and priest, Antonio Neri, explained in his recipe book, L'Arte Vetraria (1612) that in order to create glass, it was necessary to first make crystal frit—the indispensable and fundamental material used for the

> THE FURNACES IN THE EARLY 1900S were stoked by coal, attributing to the dozens of men employed in the coal yards at the SVC.

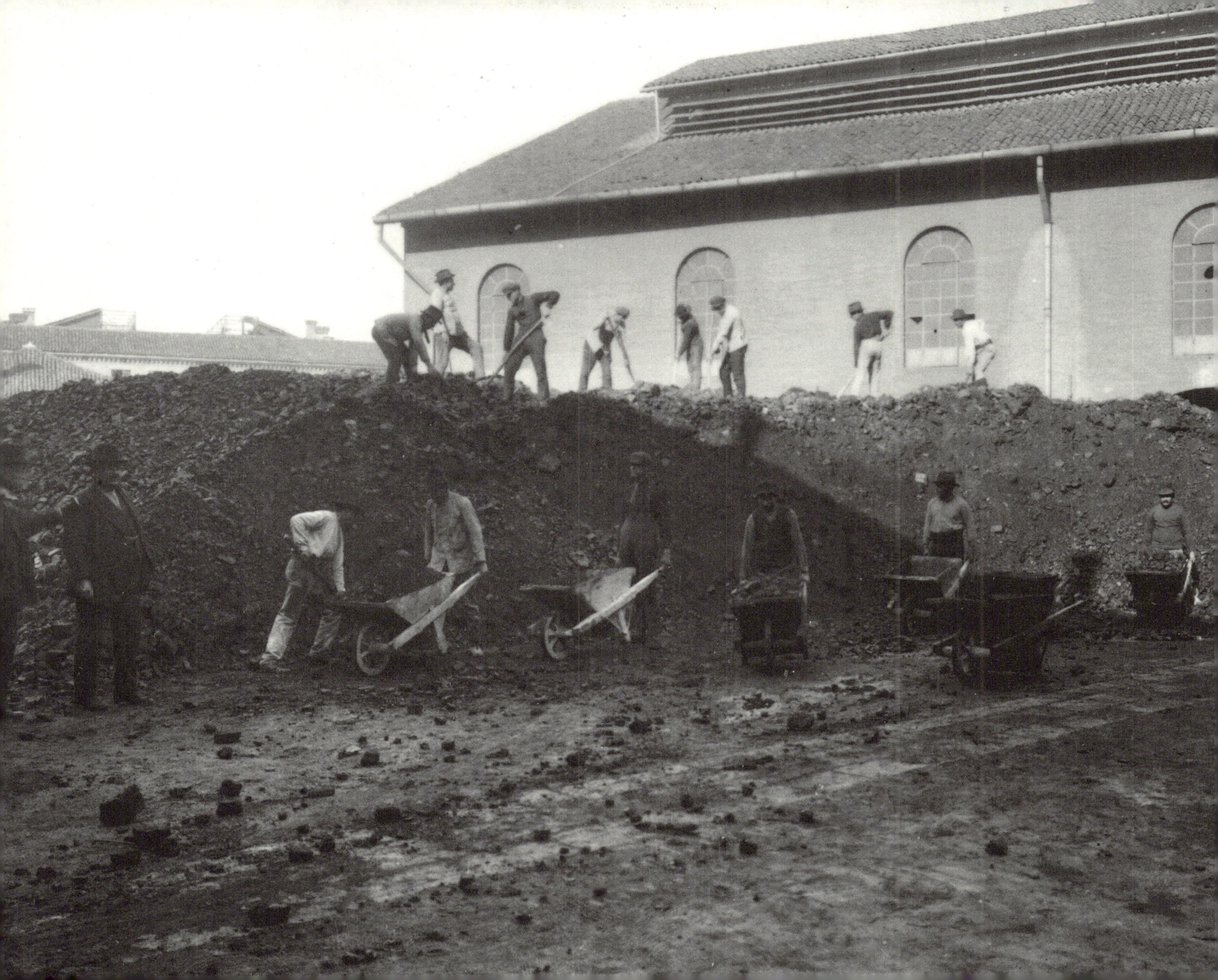

fusion of glass at that time. During that era, the ovens were stoked by beech wood (a type of wood that does not generate much smoke when burned) resulting in slow-rising and moderate temperatures for the fusion of glass. Frit was used to help speed up the time of fusion in the crucible, as well as to discharge the gas bubbles caused by the first chemical reaction in the fusion of glass. The process of eliminating the gases during the first fusion of glass was called *affinaggio*.[xi]

To make frit, Neri described the use of a stone mortar and iron pestle to crush a large quantity of hard white marble (*tarso*) into a fine powder.[xii] The Muraneses found an abundance of this type of quartz in Northern Italy in the river Ticino, calling these rock/quartz fusions *cogoli* or *ciottoli*. These ciottoli were heated in an oven and then thrown into cold water so that the thermal shock would break the pieces into fragments. The fragments were then pulverized into a very fine powder using a *pestrino*, which was a steam-operated grinding machine.[xiii] After the ciottoli were finely grounded and sifted, salt was added and the two materials were blended thoroughly and sifted to create a fine, powdery mixture called frit. The frit mixture was then put into a kiln (*calchera*), which was a reverberating furnace, and left at a moderate temperature of 700-750 degrees Celsius.[4] Here the raw materials experienced their first chemical reaction, but would not reach the point of fusion, and the process of affinaggio occurred. After approximately six to twelve hours, the frit would transform into a solid mass of small rocks, then were removed from the calchera to be slowly cooled in an annealing oven called the *ricottura* (meaning "re-cooked") and then be stored for later fusion.

4 | A reverberatory furnace or kiln is one in which the material under treatment is heated indirectly by means of a flame deflected downward from the roof. (*The American Heritage® Dictionary of the English Language, Fourth Edition copyright ©2000 by Houghton Mifflin Company. Updated in 2009.*)

Neri explained, *"If you want to have fine crystal, then in this you must exercise great diligence; when the frit is made with this careful attention, it will be white and pure like snow from heaven."*[xiv]

To achieve certain colors, specific minerals and glass fragments were added and blended with the frit. This mixture was then fed into a crucible which was positioned in a round oven (*forno fusorio*) used for fusing glass at 1000-1200 degrees Celsius. This is considered the second phase of the production of glass, however, the time of fusion is now accelerated due to the previous process of making the frit. In the 16th century, it took four to five days for the glass to fuse. By the early 18th century, the Muraneses discovered that potassium nitrate could accelerate the fusion of glass, thus eliminating the lengthy and antiquated process of making frit. Today, the raw materials are mixed and blended together by the compositioner of the factory who still follows a scripted recipe.

"When weighing the given amounts, be extremely precise . . . it is the only way to avoid making a mistake." (Girolamo Pavanello, Personal Recipe Book, Murano, 1928.)

The powdery mixture (*miscela*) is then fed into a crucible that is set in an oven fueled by methane gas. The temperature of today's ovens can now reach 1400–1450 degrees Celsius; the time of fusion is approximately eight to twelve hours.

In 1954, the institution of the *Stazione Sperimentale del Vetro* (Experimental Station for Glass) was formed to promote *"technology progress in the Italian glass industry through surveys, studies, research, and analysis. The Stazione Sperimentale del Vetro is Italy's only official body devoted to studying all the scientific and technological issues of the glass industry."*[xv]

On behalf of this institution, the glass technicians of Murano can obtain information, answers, and suggestions regarding the outcome of their glass. Over the years, the institution's highly trained staff has assisted the Murano glass industry immensely, solving many enigmas and difficulties. Prior to this time, the Muraneses did not have a supportive institution to consult for guidance. Some glass enamels took hundreds of years of trial and error to perfect, such as *avventurina* (goldstone). The diligent fabricators of glass enamels had to rely on their own tests, studies, documentation, experience, and above all, perseverance and fortitude. On account of the determination of these technicians, Murano glass, in its splendor of colors and tonalities, has made a great and lasting impact on the world of art.

CHAPTER TWO *Endnotes*

i Antonio Neri, *L'Arte Vetraria: The Art of Glass,* translated and annotated by Paul Engle, Heiden & Engle, USA, 2006; Vincenzo Zanetti, *Guida di Murano e delle Celebri Sue Fornace Vetrarie,* Venezia, Antonelli, 1866.
ii *Oxford Latin Dictionary,* University Press, Oxford Great Britain, 1982-1985.
iii Giuseppe Morazzoni, *Le Conterie Veneziana,* Società Veneziana Conterie e Cristallerie, Venezia, 1953, page 70
iv Alberto Errera, *Le industrie nel Veneto,* Milano, Zanatti, 1868, page 8.
v Morazzoni, page 70.
vi Alessandro Zecchin, *La Voce di Murano,* February, 1902, Murano.
vii Zanetti, 1866
viii Ibid., pages 22-25.
ix Ibid., page 29.
x Extracted compositions from personally written recipe books from Muranese Giudo Utimpergher (1893-1969) and Girolemo Pavanello (1928).
xi Paolo Zecchin, "La Nascita delle Conterie Veneziane", *Journal of Glass Studies,* The Corning Museum of Glass, Corning, NY, Vol. 47, 2005; Cesare Moretti, *Glossario del Vetro Veneziano dal Trecento al Novecento,* Venezia, Marsilio, 2001, page 44.
xii Neri translated by Engle, Vol. 1, pages 15-17.
xiii Ibid., pages 22-24; Zanetti, page 22.
xiv Neri/Engle, pages 16-17
xv Extracted from the promotional brochure of the Stazione Sperimentale del Vetro, Via Briati 10, Murano.

Chance favors only the prepared mind.

LOUIS PASTEUR

French Chemist and Founder of Modern Microbiology

(1822–1895)

The Star of Murano

The enamel that is called *avventurina* (goldstone) is an opaque glass which contains reflective mineral inclusions that lend a shimmering, glistening effect. Avventurina is commonly a copper color but it can also be made in green and blue.

While the SVC did not invent avventurina, the bead artisans employed by the factory frequently used it to decorate lampwork beads. Avventurina can be used as an accent to gild stripes, flowers, feathery designs, or it can be used to coat an entire bead.

The history of avventurina production has spanned hundreds of years. The avventurina formula (commonly known to the Muraneses as its "composition") has been lost, found, modified, lost and found again, and revived. The fabrication of enamels was practiced exclusively by the competent factories of Murano who were granted privileges from the Inquisitors of the State and the Council of Ten[i] to specialize and produce enamels and glass cane for the glass bead production. Considered to be the most beautiful and precious of Murano enamels, Muranese author Vettore Zaniol describes avventurina as the "Gold of Murano."[ii]

Although the word avventurina gets its name from the Italian phrase *"per avventura"* (meaning, "by chance"), it is called avventurina not because it was discovered by accident, but because of the difficulty in achieving the result.[iii] A stunning glass that shines like a galaxy of stars, avventurina was also called *stellaria*, taken from the word *stella* (star), but by 1873, this term was no longer in use.[iv]

An early document describing avventurina comes from a Venetian, Rimondo Rimondi who, in 1626, listed his inventory as *"22 pairs of earrings in Venturina, 180 assorted buttons in Venturina, and [approximately 14 kilos] of pieces of Venturina."*[v]

During this period, avventurina was treated as a semi-precious stone and was shaped using a grinding wheel to produce such items as buttons, earrings, small boxes, tablets, brooches, and inlaid tabletops. It wasn't until many years later that it was used on blown glass pieces.[vi]

Perhaps the oldest documented formula of avventurina comes from the recipe book of Giovanni Darduin in 1644. The Darduins were a family of Murano glassworkers who were repeatedly registered in the *Libro d'Oro* (The Book of Gold) since 1605.

In his notes, Darduin writes, *"It is still unknown and for certain if the so-called enamel or formula of Venturina will come out nice and so it is called Venturina and for a good reason because the results are more of an adventure rather than a science."*[vii] Darduin concluded that avventurina was *"a glass whose composition is very eccentric and misleading and this is clearly seen because sometimes an entire crucible was made—many of them—and one year there were 40 or more made and not one came out good. So there is nothing more to say about it except that it is something very dubious, uncertain, and misleading and this is also the reason why it is sold at such a high price."*[viii]

PHOTOGRAPH BY STEFANO PANDIANI;
ALL PIECES PROPERTY OF AUTHOR.

> THE AVVENTURINA TABLET, *"Ricordo di Venezia"* (Souvenir of Venice) was made in the early 1900s. Note the inlaid winged lions of Venice—the symbol of the Veneto region. The lion is holding open the Gospel of Mark who is the patron saint of Venice. The bouquet of glass flowers is made with glass micro mosaics. The tablet measures 7.5 cm x 11.5 cm and is 1.5 cm thick.

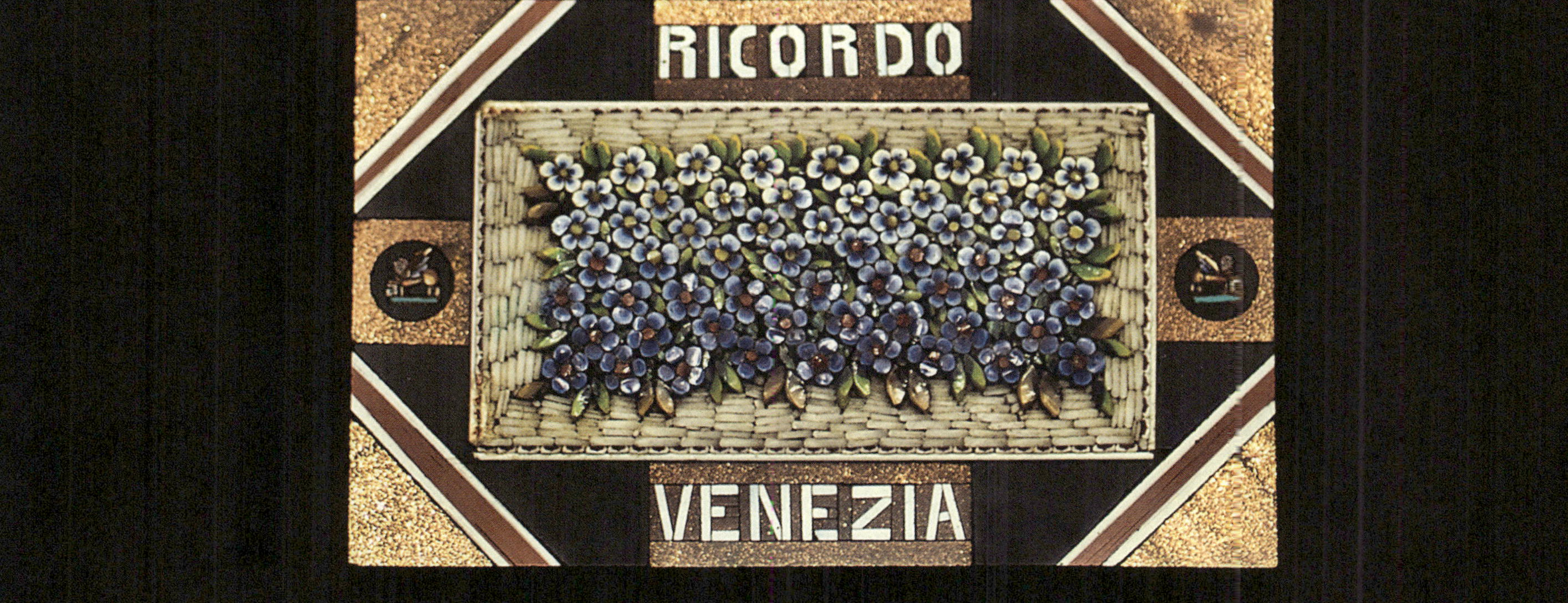
RICORDO
VENEZIA

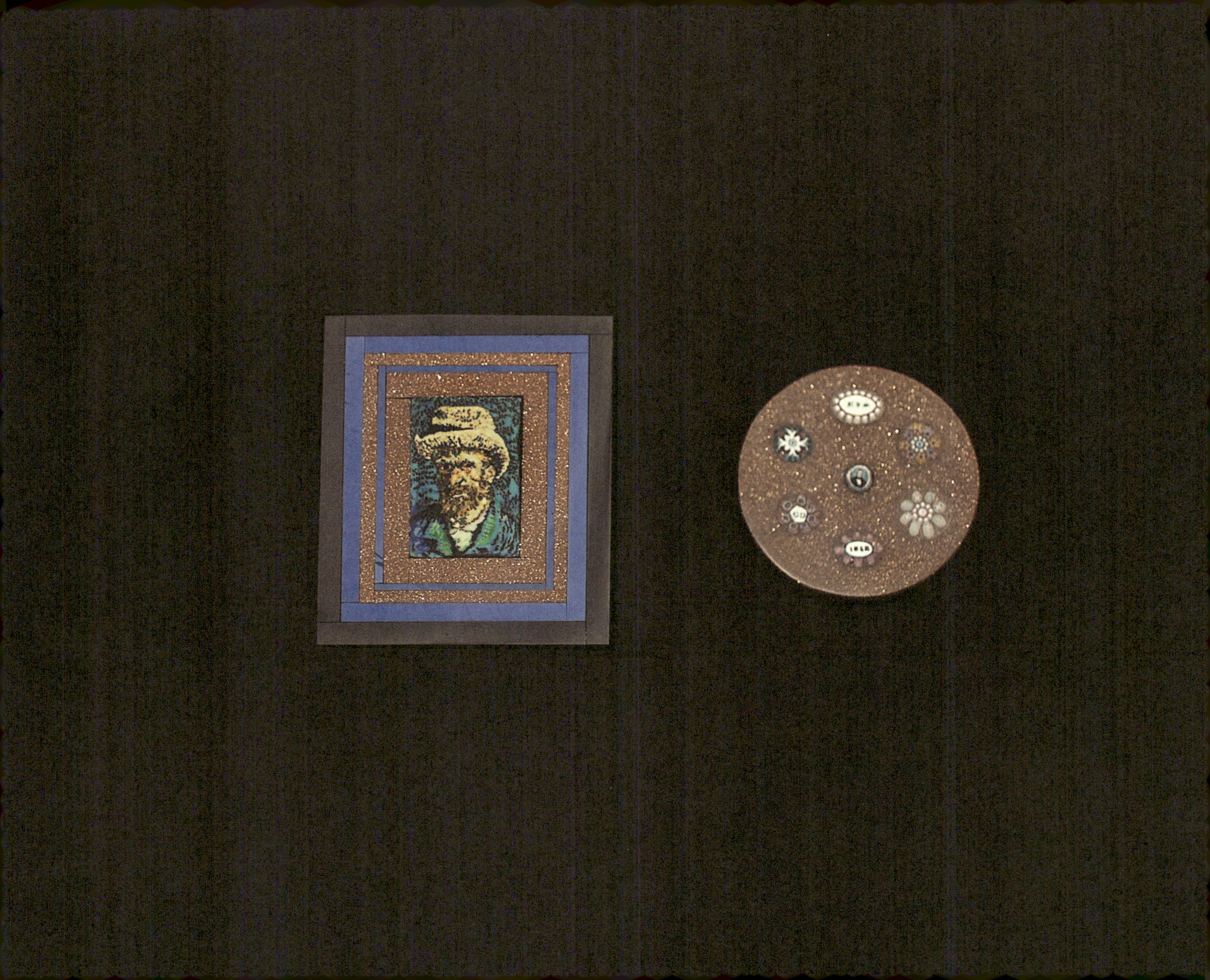

< THE VAN GOGH MURRINA was made by Mario Dei Rossi of Burano (an island in the Venetian Laguna). Using over 50,000 hair-thin "stringers" of glass, the strands are tightly assembled together (while cold) in a copper ring to create the image. After months of bundling/assembling, the finished piece is placed in an oven so that the strands are fused together. Once the murrina is fused, it is removed from the oven and a small gather of molten glass is applied to its center (with a pontil) so that the piece can be stretched/pulled to the desired length of the artist, creating a glass cane. The image appears throughout the entire length of the cane. The cane is then put in a kiln for tempering. Once tempered, it is cut into slices, polished, and can be set into different applications such as earrings, pendants, brooches, tie clips, rings, and used in vases, bowls, sculptures, and in this case, incorporated in a paperweight. Using Dei Rossi's murrina, intarsia artist Gianni DeCarlo of Venice created this beautiful glass paperweight with inlaid avventurina. The paperweight measures 5.2 cm x 6.2 cm and is 2.5 cm thick.

< THE SPARKLING AVVENTURINA DISK is 4.3 cm in diameter and composed of seven inlaid murrine. The floral murrine were made by Giovanni Battista Franchini circa 1840–1843. The initials and numbers were made by his son, Giacomo, circa 1843-1848, as well as the center murrina, made in 1862, which is a portrait image of Camillo Benso, Count of Cavour, who was the first Prime Minister of Italy. All the murrine were crafted on a primitive torch, fueled by animal fat. Using their beadmaking skills and techniques, the Franchinis were pioneers in creating complex millefiori and figurative murrine canes, producing many masterpieces in the art of glass. *(Venetian Beads, Mosaic Glass and Murrine,* Giovanni Sarpellon, Albignasego (PD), 2003.)

PHOTOGRAPH BY STEFANO PANDIANI:
ALL PIECES PROPERTY OF AUTHOR.

Giovanni Darduin died in 1654, and one year later, so did his only son. The avventurina recipe was then passed on to Darduin's daughter, Angela, who happened to be married to Daniele Miotti, a chemist, whose family had a long history of fabricating glass cane and beads.[1] Although this union seems coincidental, it wasn't. At that time, it was common for the sons and daughters of glass masters to marry within their trade for socio-economic reasons, as well as for strengthening the family's trade or profession. Miotti, a very competent and hard worker, was given the coveted recipe. Miotti set out to rediscover avventurina, however, producing the unpredictable enamel proved to be quite challenging.

In 1669, Daniele Miotti re-copied precisely Darduin's recipes and notes into his own personal recipe book. Later, Daniele's son Vincenzo did the same. For this reason, Miotti was given credit as the creator of avventurina by the historian Muranese Abbott Vincenzo Zanetti in 1873. In 1717, the Miottis were reconfirmed by the Inquisitors of the State with the privilege to fabricate "every type of glass and to work with their particular secret," but the written permission made no specific mention of avventurina.[ix] The Miottis studied the chemical reactions that occurred in the furnace during the fusion of avventurina and tried to establish a scientific explanation with formulas.[x]

Although documented by Darduin, and popularized by the Miottis, there is evidence that an enamel, very similar to avventurina, existed well before them. Roman excavations in Ostia uncovered a cruet for holding tears, which was decorated with stripes of blue, green, and an avventurina-like enamel. This artifact, dating to 700 B.C., was placed on display at the Etruscan Gregorian Museum at the Vatican.[xi] In 1994, archeological excavations in San Antonio di Polesine (Ferrara, Italy) uncovered a beautiful goblet that was undoubtedly manufactured in Murano. It was made of an opaque milky-white glass (*lattimo*) with colors of blue, red, black, and included an avventurina-like enamel dating to the second half of the

1 | The Miotti family dates back to the 13th century when Domenico Miotti, together with Cristofo Briani, began the production of glass beads to imitate gemstones on the suggestion of Marco Polo.

16th century.[xii] While artifacts decorated with an avventurina precursor exist, it is the Miotti family who perfected the enamel in the 1700s and who are credited with its high popularity and demand throughout Europe in the 18th century.[xiii]

In 1873, Zanetti narrated the discovery of avventurina as the *"tradition that has stayed alive amongst our glassworkers and artists."* According to his narrative, Miotti was commissioned by a goldsmith to make a red glass, known commercially as *rosso da bisse* or *rosso copo*.[2] After working several hours and doing many tests to achieve the desired tonality, Miotti was unsuccessful. Tired and discouraged, he abandoned the crucible and extinguished the furnace. When he returned to the workshop a few days later, he was amazed to see the glass was full of glistening star-like shapes that resembled gold.[xiv] The sparkling specks were the result of copper minerals that were crystallized during the cooling process.[3]

2 | In the Venetian dialect, *rosso copo* is the color of roof tiles whereas *rosso da bisse* could possibly indicate the reddish-serpentine fish *bissato*. The term *rosso da bisse* is no longer used by the Venetians, leaving many respected Murano glass historians to assume its meaning.

"Perhaps someone could rebuff this story and say it was just a creative little tale that derived from the imagination of this tradition but, instead, this story has all the grounds of truth because it is based on the phenomenon that happens every day in workshops of our conterie."[xv]

By the mid-1700s, Miotti's discovery received its highest accolades. *"No other producer attained the likeness of big, sparkling specks as that of the avventurina of Miotti,"* described Zanetti. Extremely popular, avventurina was shipped throughout Europe and used on beads, necklaces, snuff bottles, plates, buttons, rings, brooches, perfume bottles, drawer pulls, walking cane handles, stemware, letter openers, mosaic tablets, trinket boxes, and a variety of other decorative objects.

Although very popular, Miotti's avventurina could not be mass produced. During this

3 | The result of *avventurina* is characterized by a slow cooling process. Once the glass technician sees that the composition is ready, he turns off the furnace and closes all the openings except for the central opening which is needed to observe or modify the cooling process over a number of days. (*Vettore Zaniol,* L'avventurina—L'oro di Murano, *Cicero, Venezia, 2004.)*

era, the capacity of crucibles did not exceed fifty kilos.[xvi] Furthermore, the avventurina enamel was unpredictable, sometimes resulting in an inconsistent, non-sellable product which, in turn, forced the Miottis to demand a higher price to cover their losses. Additionally, once the avventurina had evolved, one side of the furnace had to be demolished in order to extract the crucible. Then the crucible itself had to be demolished in order to extract the avventurina from within it. Demolishing and rebuilding the furnace, with no guarantee that the batch of enamel could produce the desired results, was a tremendous risk and expense for each "hopeful" batch.[4]

By 1786, the Miottis lost its monopoly as the sole producers of avventurina, as other enamel fabricators were given the rights to produce it. This is noted in Article 16 of the *Capitolare ossia Matricola dell'Arte Vetraria di Murano Riformata* of 1786.[xvii] According to the article, the production of avventurina was considered the workmanship delegated to only those furnaces producing glass enamels, mosaics, and cane.[xviii]

Although other Muraneses tried to develop avventurina, no one could achieve as much success or quality results as the Miottis.[xix] Since avventurina was known to be difficult to create, few enamel fabricators were interested in attempting to produce it; its unpredictability and cost were risks that few were willing to take.[5] Nevertheless, the manufacturers who did take up the challenge managed to knock off a product of much lower quality and sold it to local beadmakers in large quantities at considerably lower prices than the Miottis.[xx] At the time, the highest quality avventurina was fabricated solely by the Miottis—only they held the secret, understood the scientific enigma and achieved the mastery of this splendid, precious enamel.[xxi]

In 1787, Alvise Miotti, son of Daniele, obtained the privileges from the Inquisitors of

4 | Today's *avventurina* is extracted while it is still in fusion and left to cool in appropriate containers. (*Zaniol*).

5 | The Abate Fanello, in his memoir, stated that only five percent of an entire production of avventurina resulted in good quality. (*Zanetti, page 14*).

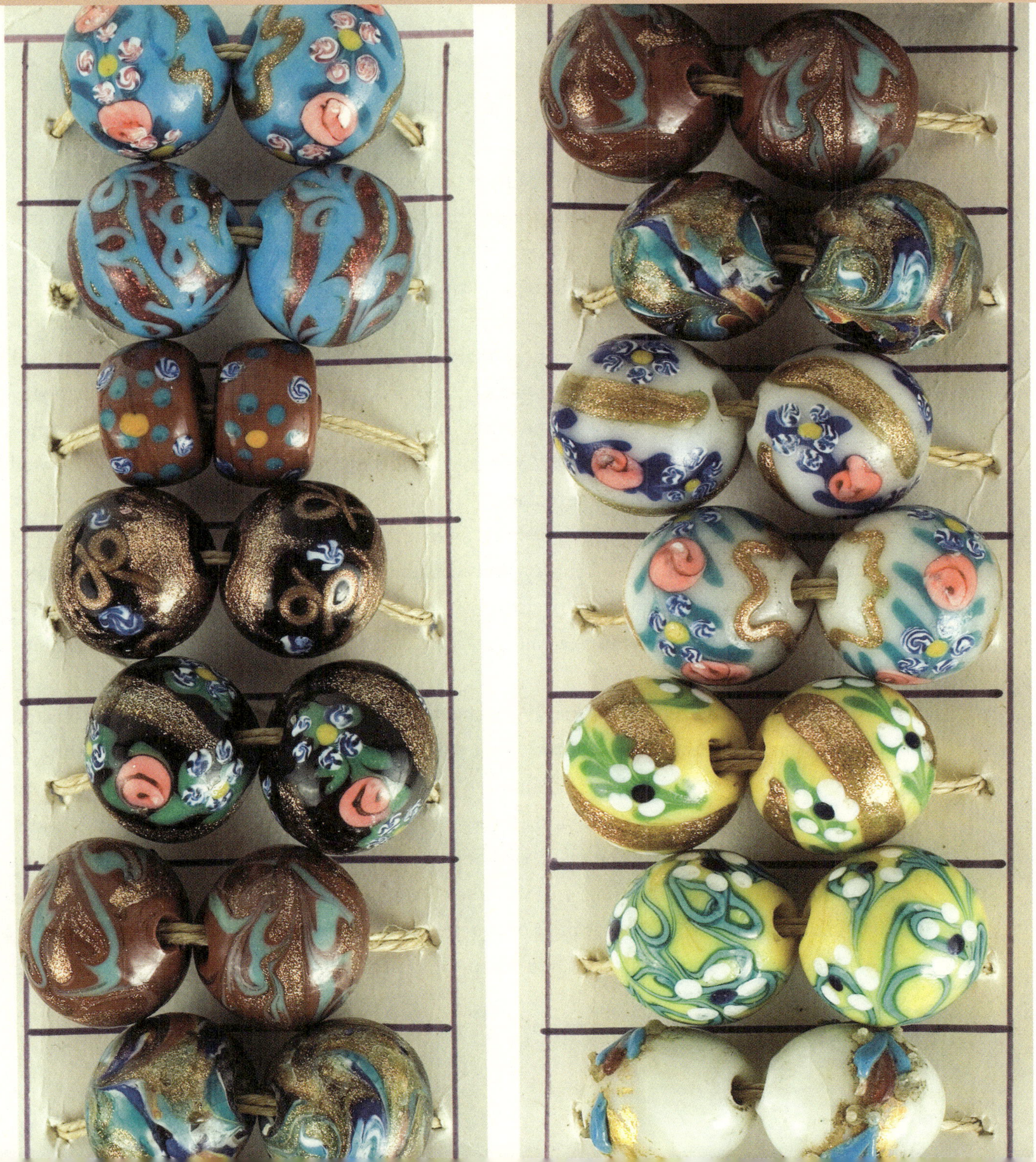

PHOTOGRAPH BY STEFANO PANDIANI;
COURTESY OF THE MURANO GLASS MUSEUM

< LAMPWORKED BEADS
14mm–18mm made in the early 1900s with gildings of avventurina and glass floral decorations. During this early period, the mandrels were quite large (note the size of the bead hole) and dipped in a paste prior to applying the molten glass so that the bead, once cooled, could be easily released.

the State to fabricate avventurina. He then passed the secret on to his son, Stefano. Shortly thereafter, in 1793, Stefano was granted the same privileges that had been passed down through his family for nearly a century.[xxii]

By 1800, the fall of the Republic of Venezia to Napoleon's army provoked a serious crisis for the Murano glass industry, which continued for the first half of the 19th century. The factories that suffered the most were those that produced mirrors, window panes, and objects that were considered luxury items. During this crucial time, however, the conterie industry managed to survive and flourish. The Miotti workshop wasn't as lucky; it closed, thus ending the production of avventurina. Even so, the closing of the Miotti workshop prompted other factories to later revive the recipe.[xxiii]

It wouldn't be until the mid-1800s that avventurina would re-emerge. In fact, the 1800s would be remembered as the century of avventurina, thanks to newer technology such as bigger crucibles and scientific experience. Around 1820, the first recorded documents regarding the rebirth of avventurina emerged from the company Dalmistro-Moravia and Muranese Cavalier Pietro Bigaglia.

In 1825, Francesco I of Austria, Alessandro of Russia, and the King of Napoli visited the Murano workshops and admired some vases that were made using the avventurina of Bigaglia and Dalmistro. In 1826, Dalmistro-Moravia was awarded the silver medal by the *Istituto di Scienze Lettere ed Arti* and Pietro Bigaglia was awarded an Honorable Mention. A jealous dispute between the two workshops emerged, both claiming to be the victors of the re-discovery of avventurina. In 1827, both Dalmistro and Bigaglia received gold medals from the Institute of Veneto for their production of avventurina.

Bigaglia was inspired to continue his quest to produce this most stellar enamel.[xxiv] He went on to win over twenty medals for his avventurina which was used in various glass objects. Bigaglia is credited with fabricating the enamel in colossal fusions, most notably his final fusion, obtained in only one crucible of four hundred kilos.[xxv]

Another merit of Bigaglia was his ambition for commercializing the product and applying avventurina to new uses. He expanded his workshop and collaborated with the most skillful glass artisans and lapidaries who could use it in unlimited ways. Whether it was a small plaque of inlaid work, a tiny brooch, or a fancy goblet or vase, Bigaglia applied avventurina to objects of all sizes and levels of artistry. He successfully established the capability to consistently produce avventurina in mass quantities. Bigaglia envisioned his avventurina to be used in exquisite artistic creations and regarded it as a luxury item worthy of decorating the parlors of royalty.[xxvi]

The Venetian merchants were delighted with avventurina. The effects of its glistening and starry composition were mesmerizing. Whether found in the shadowy, humid and narrow streets of Venice, or under the clouds in an open square, avventurina would always glisten. It needed no special lighting to enhance its appearance and the Venetian merchants had no problem selling it in great quantities.

In 1901, the SVC commissioned two companies, Dalla Venezia and Marinetti, to produce fourteen large crucibles of avventurina.[xxvii] The women of the SVC, many of them lampworkers, were given the task of heating and pulling the avventurina to create *vette* (stringers). The vette of avventurina were used to decorate lampwork beads for nearly one hundred years. The SVC also made conterie cane using avventurina, but the exact date of this production is unknown. A small stockpile of this cane was found in the warehouse by an employee of the SVC in the late 1990s. Hundreds of bead sample cards were also found at this same location, however, none of these cards included beads made with avventurina.[xxviii] Note that in 1868, historian Abbott Vincenzo Zanetti created conterie beads using avventurina. Unfortunately, the production was too costly and was abandoned.[xxix]

The company, Oriago, in Mira (the mainland) produced avventurina in the 1950s, whereas in Murano, the company Dalla Venezia produced it up until the 1980s. Afterward, the production was sold to the factory Bisazza located on the mainland in Spilimbergo. This factory produced avventurina in Italy, as well as in India. The factory located in Spilimbergo closed in 2007, but its production in India continues. Avventurina is now being produced in enormous quantities in China.

After the 1980s, the production of avventurina on the island of Murano ceased. Today, glassworkers in Murano, such as Marco Donà, are still trying to produce avventurina. The following excerpt, taken from an avventurina recipe, is a reminder to the Muraneses of something they all know too well—that following a recipe will not always guarantee a successful outcome and that divine intervention, in the form of prayer, is recommended:[xxx]

"Make sure it is well mixed, turn up the temperature of the furnace, and after ten minutes give it one last stir with a bit of durum semolina. Then close all the openings to the furnace. Leave only the hole in the middle [open] to allow for a bit of air and then go to church and pray for beautiful stars to appear."[xxxi]

Author Vettore Zaniol suggests the Muraneses return to the mentality of the workers in the 1600s and pray to Saint Nicholas, patron saint of glass workers, to intercede on their behalf and help bring back their beautiful, starry avventurina.[xxxii]

CHAPTER THREE *Endnotes*

i The Council of Ten, or simply the Ten, was, from 1310 to 1797, one of the major governing bodies of the Republic of Venice whose actions were often secretive. It was formally tasked with maintaining the security of the Republic and preserving the government from overthrow or corruption. In 1539, the Council established the State Inquisitors, a tribunal of three judges chosen from among its members to deal with threats to state security. The Inquisitors were given equal authority to that of the entire Council of Ten, and could try and convict those accused of treason independently of their parent body. To further these activities, the Inquisitors created a large network of spies and informants, both in Venice and abroad. *(Extracted from http://en.wikipedia.org. last modified in May, 2012).*

ii Vettore Zaniol, *L'avventurina—L'oro di Murano,* Cicero, Venezia, 2004.

iii Abate Fanello, Notizie storico geografiche di Murano, Tipografica Rosa, 1797.

iv Vincenzo Zanetti, *Sull'Avventurina Artificiale,* Venezia, Tipografica del Commercio di Marco Visentini, 1873.

v Zaniol, page 8.

vi Zaniol, page 12.

vii Luigi Zecchin, *Sulla Storia delle Conterie Veneziana,* Venezia, Stab. Zinco Tipografica San Marco, 1955, page 60.

viii Zanetti, page 13.

ix Ibid., page 7.

x The Miottis were experts in fabricating glass enamels such as chalcedony, mosaics, and *lattimo* (a milky white glass used to imitate porcelain). Luigi .Zecchin, *Un Ricettario Muranese dell'Ottocento,* Venezia: *Extracted from Rivista Vetro e Silicati, 1964.*

xi Zaniol, page 8 and Beyersdorfer, *Studien uber dan Aventuringlas,* Reichenbach/Oberlausitz, 1942.

xii Zaniol, page 9.

xiii Zaniol, page 12.

xiv Zanetti, page 11.

xv Ibid.

xvi Ibid., page 13.

xvii Zanetti, page 14 states 1786, whereas Luigi Zecchin, *Avventurina* Vol. 1, 1971, page 76 states 1766.

xviii Ibid., pages 14-15.

xix Giovanni Giacomuzzi made avventurina and also Pietro Bertolini who had a porcelain factory in Murano and worked with enamels for the conterie industry. *(Zanetti, page 15).*

xx Zanetti, sites the *Matricola dei fiolai*, Museo di Murano, page 208.

xxi Zanetti, page 15.

xxii Ibid.

xxiii Ibid., pages 16-18.

xxiv Ibid., pages 18-19.

xxv Zanetti, page 19.

xxvi Ibid., pages 19-20.

xxvii Zaniol, page 27.

xxviii Interview with Luigi Cattelan, employee of the Società Veneziana Conterie, Murano.

xxix In the archive of the Murano Glass Museum there is a sample of these beads with the inscription: Avventurina beads made with cannelle (small pieces of perforated glass cane) and "reduced" (made smooth) in the tube. "First experiment executed carefully by Abbott Zanetti in the workshop of Salviati & C. in 1868." (Zaniol). Zecchin, Paolo. Journal of Glass Studies, La pasta venturina, vetro special Muranese: Corning Museum of Glass, Vol. 47, pages 93-106, 2005.

xxx Photocopy of an old recipe dated 1787 from the archives of Vettore Zaniol.

xxxi Antonio Fabris, Il vetro mirabile: l'avventurina veneziana: Jolly Hotels Magazine, 1988, II, n. 2, pages 22-26.

xxxii Zaniol, page 31.

Behind every able man,
there are always other able men.

CHINESE PROVERB

Producing Glass Cane

(*Canna di Vetro*)

Today's glassworkers, who create glass cane, are collectively called a *piazza*, but for hundreds of years they were called a *muta* (or *mua* in the Venetian dialect). A muta consisted of several workers including a glass master (or *maistro/maestro*), also called the *scagner,* named after the bench (*scagno*) where he would sit and work, the *servento* or *pastoner* (those workers who made the *pastone* (the cylinder-shaped gather of glass), the *conzaureri/consaori*, and the *tiradori* or *tiracanne da ferro*. The *conzaureri* gathered a small portion of molten glass onto the extremity of an iron rod, compressed it, reheated it in the furnace, then attached it to the trunk of the pastone, which was then passed on to the workers who pulled the cane, the tiradori or tiracanne da ferro. The muta worked as a team in a harmonious and synchronous manner.[i]

Using a steel or iron rod (*ferro di canna*), a servento would extract a designated amount of molten glass (depending on the pre-determined diameter of cane) from the crucible (*crogiolo*)

1 | It takes the experience of a skilled worker to pull a cane with no curvature or angularity and maintain a consistent diameter; as such, the *scagner* often took on the role of *tirador*.

and rolled it back and forth onto a steel table, thereby molding the glass into a uniformed, proportional cylinder shape. The execution of rolling and shaping the molten glass onto a table is called a *marmorizzada* (referred today as "to marver"). If the cane had a determined number of layers, the servento had to repeat the process of extracting the molten glass and effectuate a marmorizzada after each extraction. The word marmorizzada gets its name from the flat, steel tables (also known as *il bronzino*) that were once made of marble (*marmo*) or bronze.[ii]

The serventi created the pastone, which was attached to an iron rod and was passed on to the scagner, who sat on his bench and inserted long tweezers (*borsella*) into the center of the pastone, piercing it from the top through to the bottom, creating a perforation/hole throughout its entire length.

After the hole was made, the scagner would take the pastone to the furnace to heat it again. He then executed another marmorizzada onto the bronzino, carefully preserving the hole and the symmetrical pastone.

The conzaureri conjoined a small amount of molten glass onto the trunk of the pastone and now the pastone was ready to be pulled into a long cane.[iii]

Enter the tiradori: workers who pulled and/or ran with the pastone in opposite directions until it was minimized into a thin cane.[1] The corridors of the SVC, for pulling of the cane, were one hundred meters. In order to create a very thin cane, a small amount of glass

> THIS ILLUSTRATION depicts the process of shaping the molten glass into a cylindrical form called the "pastone" (FIGURES 1 – 4). The gather is then pulled to the desired length and laid on top of wooden planks to cool and harden, as shown in FIGURE 5. The wooden planks mitigate the temperature difference between the cold floor and the still-warm glass cane, as direct contact between the floor and the cane could cause thermal shock, resulting in cracks in the cane. In FIGURE 6, the cane is cut into segments and bundled for further processing.

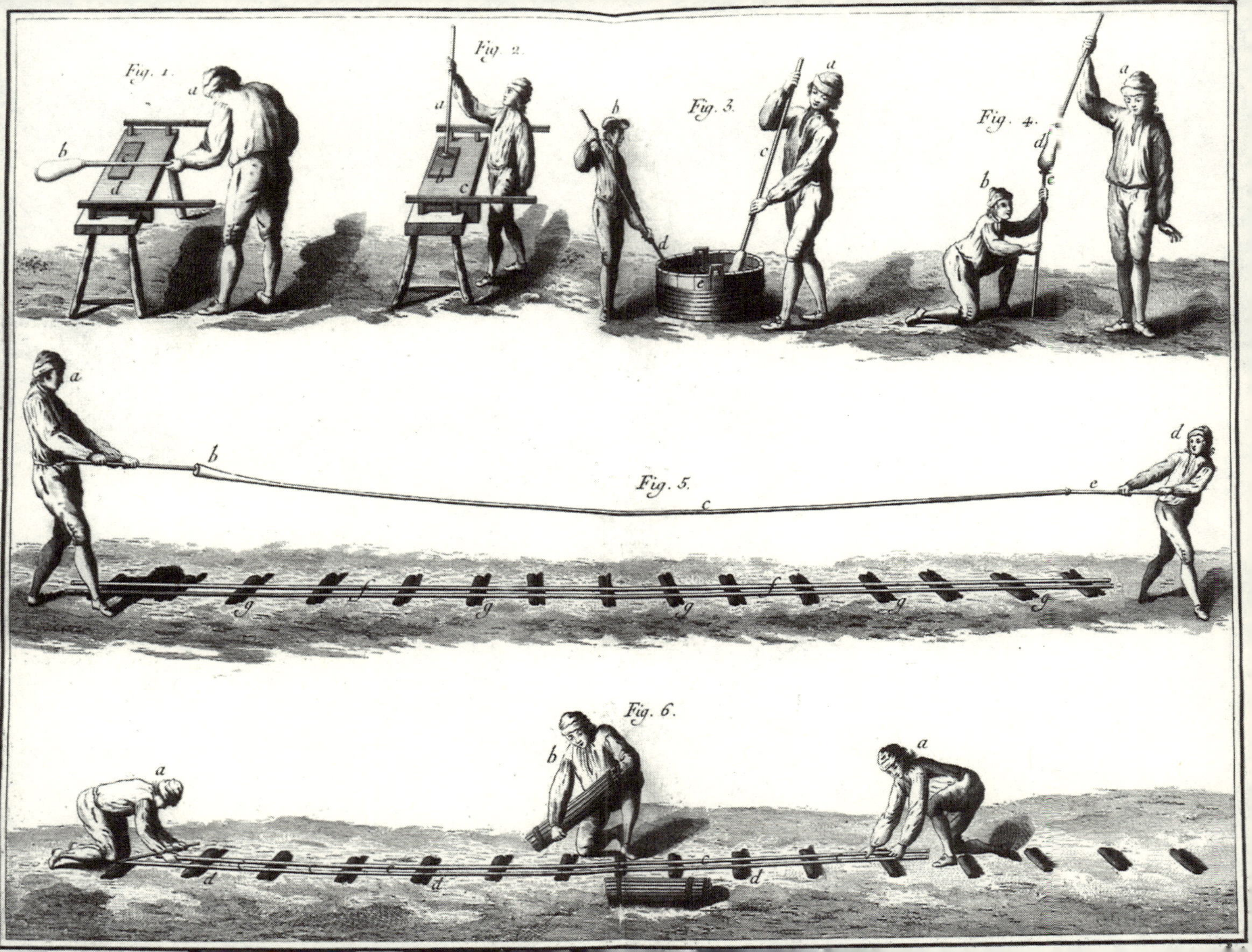
Fig. 1.
Fig. 2.
Fig. 3.
Fig. 4.
Fig. 5.
Fig. 6.

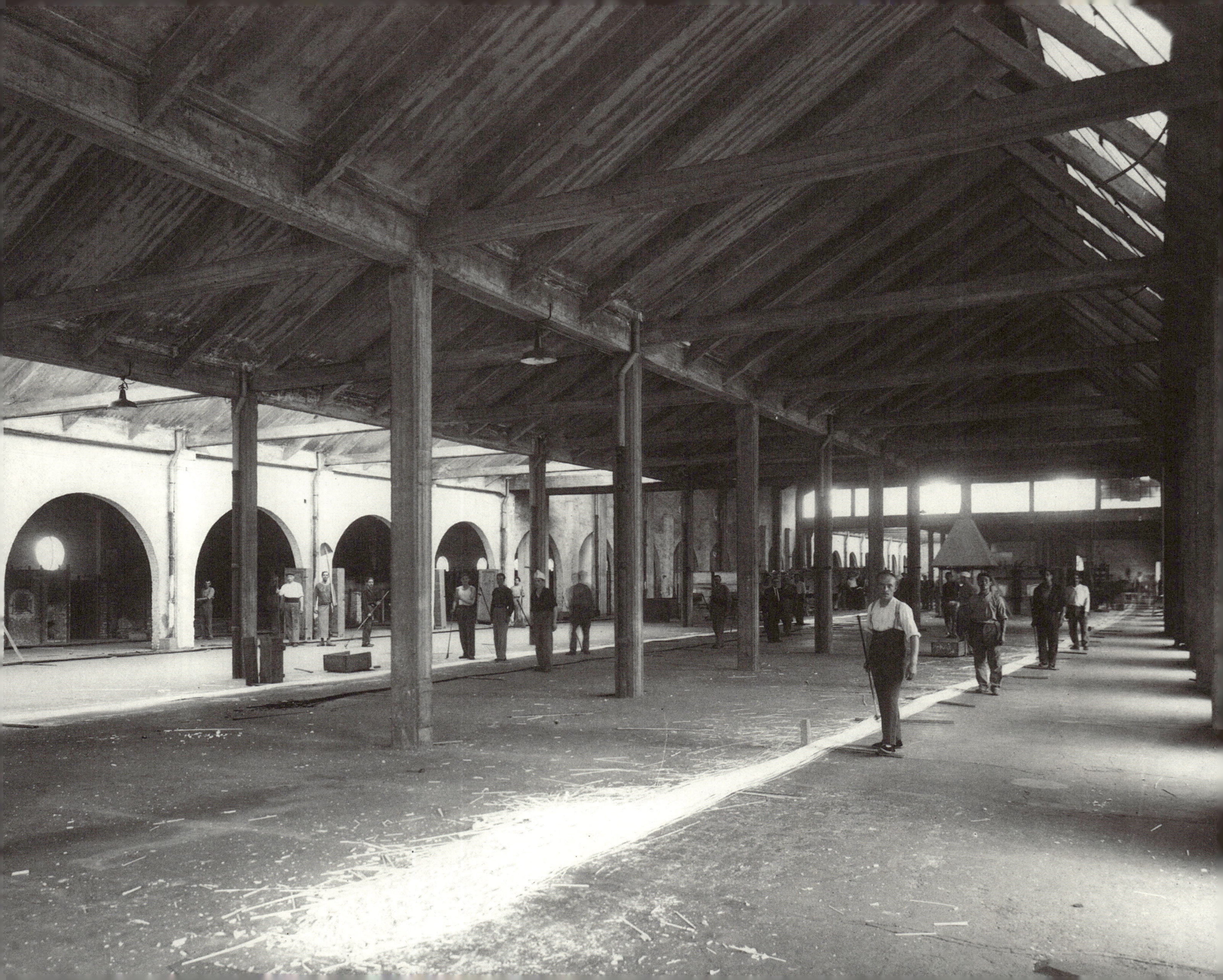

was used to make the pastone and then the tiradori would have to run quickly. The faster he ran, the thinner the glass cane became. Once the cane was stretched to its limit, it was laid onto wooden planks situated along the length of the corridor so that it would not touch the floor and cause thermal shock. The cane, now hardened and stiff, was immediately cut into segments (*cannelle*) of one meter by simply tapping the cane with tweezers dampened in cold water. The cannelle was then gathered into a wooden box (or onto a paddle), cooled, and delivered to the department of the *cernidore* where it was separated according to diameter, color, and quality. However, the larger diameters of cane (those over eight millimeters) were placed into an annealing oven where they would cool slowly to minimize breakage and cracking.

Solid cane, used for making lampwork (a lume) beads, was made the same way as described above except the process of piercing a hole into the pastone was not executed.[2]

Glass cane can be fashioned in a variety of colors, shapes and diameters. It can also have colorful stripes. It can be pulled into cylindrical, square, or hexagonal shapes (*maca*). When glass cane is made with different layers (*coperte*), the innermost layer is called the *sottana*. Beads with a white glass sottana and a coperta of transparent colors are called *corniole*. Perforated cane made of different layers and colors and with a stellar pattern on the outer circumference is called *rosetta* (also known as chevron). The stellar pattern comes from plunging the molten glass into an optic mold made of heat-resistant material such as ceramic, brass or iron. The *rosetta* cane is much different than the cane used for making *conterie* beads; it has more layers and colors and must be ground by hand so that the stellar pattern appears

2 | By the 1980s, the SVC introduced a machine that could mechanically pull the cane to any required length and diameter.

< THE *CAPANNONE* (or *cason canna* in the Venetian dialect) was the area in the factory where the glass cane was pulled. The SVC had two side-by-side corridors each measuring 100 meters in length and 20 meters wide. Looking closely, many of these men are holding metal pipes, indicating that they were the pullers/runners for the glass cane. Situated along the length of the corridor, the wooden planks were used to support the hot cane, preventing it from touching the ground and causing thermal shock.

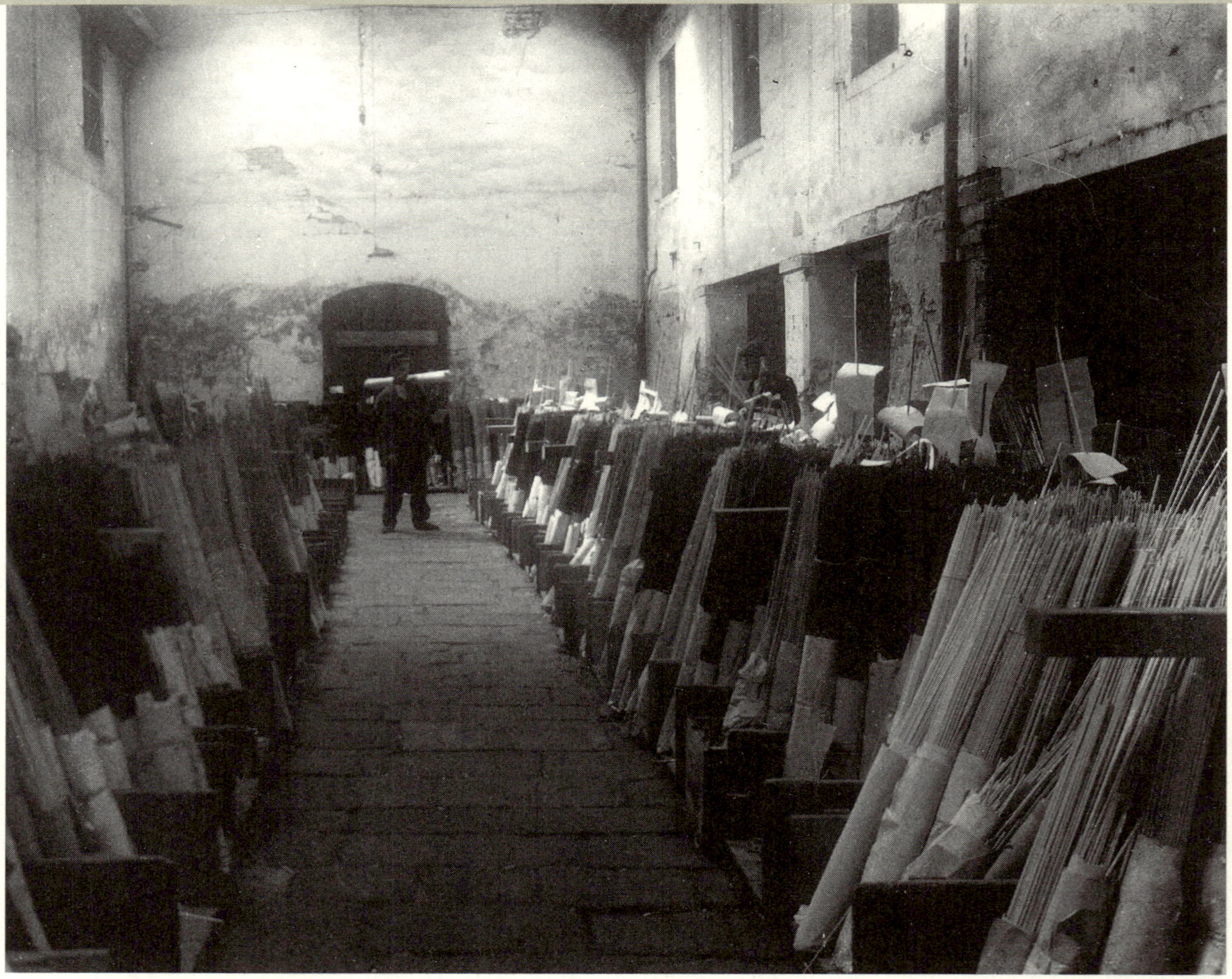

> THE STORAGE ROOM OF THE SVC ACCOMMODATED hundreds of kilos of glass cane. Each glass cane was approximately one meter in length, the diameter varied. It is necessary to first produce perforated glass cane to manufacture conterie (seed) beads, solid glass cane to create lampwork beads, multi-layered/ patterned non-perforated glass cane to produce millefiori (thousand flowers) for the production of mosaic beads, and perforated multi-layered glass cane to fabricate rosetta (chevron) beads.

after consuming the outer layers of the cane. The SVC made perforated glass cane to manufacture conterie beads, solid glass cane used to create lampwork beads, multi-layered/patterned non-perforated glass cane to produce millefiori cane for the production of mosaic beads, and perforated multi-layered glass cane to fabricate chevron beads.

CHAPTER FOUR *Endnotes*

i Cesare Moretti, Glossario del vetro veneziano Dal Trecento al Novecento, Marsilio, Venezia, 2001. The serventi can also be called the pastoner.

ii Moretti, page 53. The verb 'marmorizzar' can be considered as the English word "marver" and the French word "marbre."

iii Astone Gasparetto, *Il Vetro di Muran dalle Origini ad Oggi,* Neri Pozza Editore, Venezia, 1958, page 180.

In art, the hand can never execute anything higher than the heart can imagine.

RALPH WALDO EMERSON

American essayist and poet

(1803–1882)

The Art of the Venetian Lampwork Bead

The production of Venetian lampwork beads dates back to 1528 when Andrea Viador o Vidor (from Friuli, Italy) introduced a new technique to make glass beads. Rather than using a hollow cane to make the margarite or conterie beads, he used a solid glass cane (*massiccio*) which was heated by the flame of a lamp/torch to create a solid bead. The beads could then be decorated with silver, gold, multi-colors, or made into various shapes and sizes. This new form of artistic expression provided limitless artistic value to the Venetian beadmakers. It was during this era that the bead artisan was born.[i]

In the late 1700s, the lampwork bead artisans were called *suppialume*. During that era, the workers used oil lamps fueled by animal fat, in which the flame was regulated by the air of a bellows located next to the craftsman. The stench from the burning animal fat was unbearable, thus, the suppialume were not permitted to work near Saint Mark's Square, nor near the Rialto market, nor anywhere near the historical center where tourists and the elite gravitated. Suppialume who violated this law would lose all of their tools.[ii] As a result of this city ordinance, many suppialume went to live and work in the area of Saint Francesco delle Vigne, a neighborhood populated with commoners and far from the city center.[iii] The craft of making lampwork beads did not require a big factory, physical strength, or several employees. The workers, mostly women, could easily set up a workshop at home or in a small shed.

To make a bead, the bead artist/artisan (*perleri*) sits at a table with a flame lamp (the torch) placed in front of him/her. The perleri takes in one hand a solid glass cane (the diameter and length of this cane vary) and melts it under the flame onto a metal skewer. The molten glass is wound (*arrotolata*) onto the metal skewer.

The beadmakers were commissioned from the Murano glass factories to produce custom designed lampwork beads. Sometimes the factories provided the raw materials for the assignments.[iv] The designs of these beads were infinite, but the most popular designs were the flowered bead (*fiorato*) and the mosaic bead, which was made using several individual pieces of decorative glass cane, cut into thin slices, known as *millefiori* (thousands of flowers). To make a mosaic bead, the millefiori slices would either be directly applied to the skewer of molten glass (using tweezers) or gathered onto it by rolling the molten glass directly onto the slices. Then, the skewer was re-heated in the torch, thereby melting the millefiori slices onto the molten glass, creating one mosaic bead.

> YOUNG GIRLS OF THE SVC produced an infinite number and variety of lampwork beads, but the most popular of these were the fiorato (flowered) beads, still being produced today in Murano and Venice. The two gentlemen in the center of the photograph were the supervisors of this department who oversaw the bead production, assisted the needs of the lampworkers, and announced the breaks and the termination of the day's work.

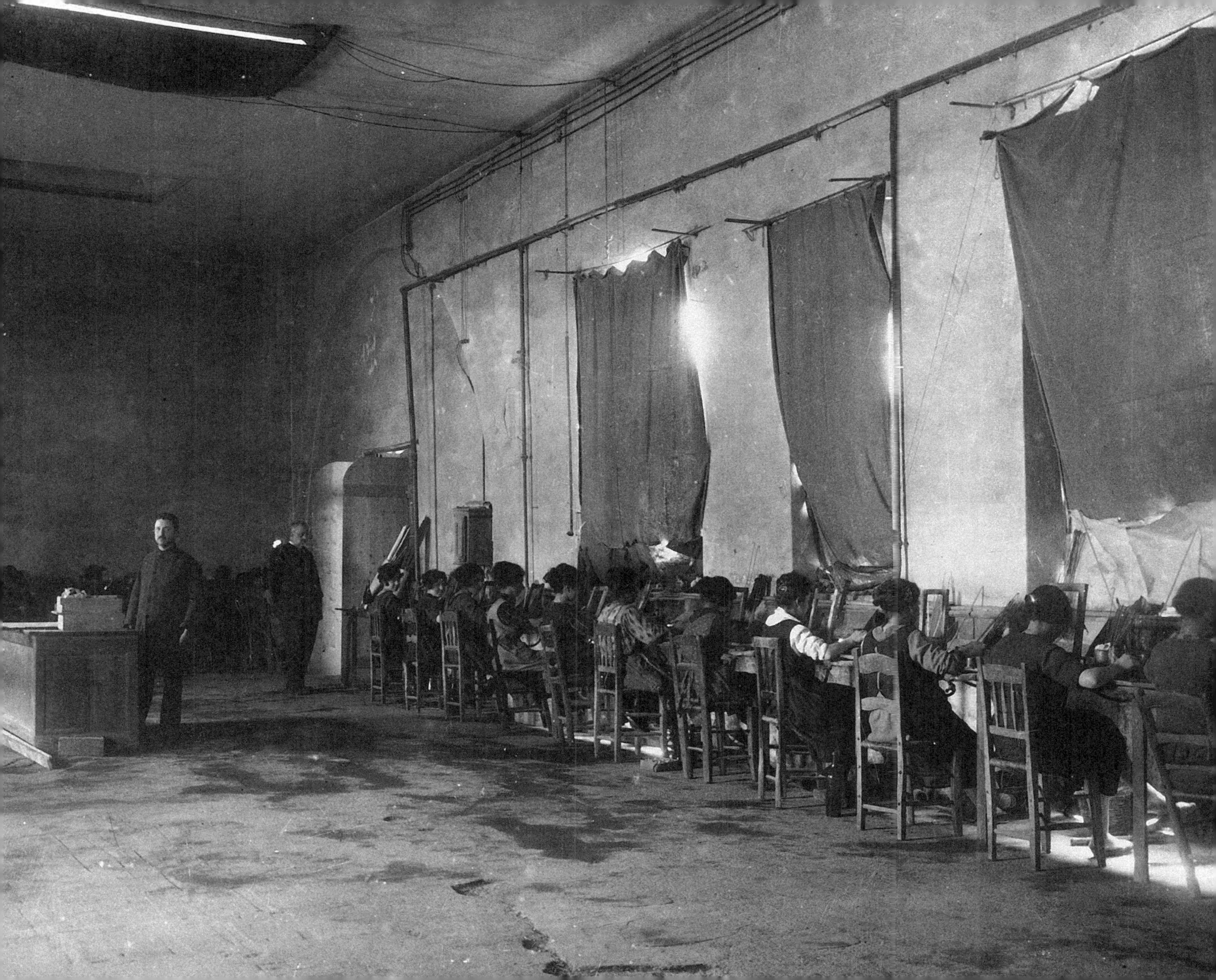

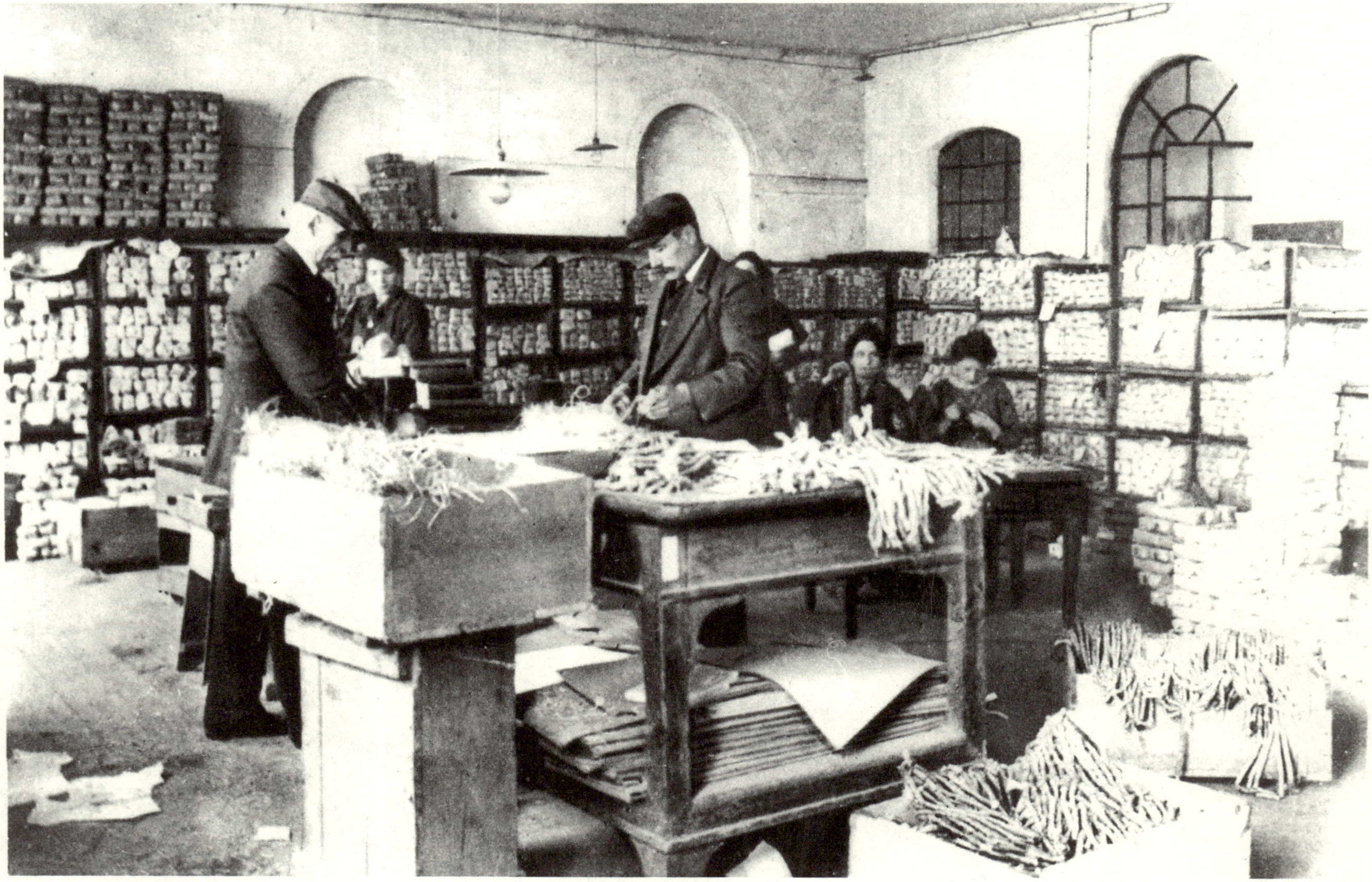

^ IN THE EARLY 1900S, THE SVC employed hundreds of women to occupy positions (such as here in the storage room for lampwork and mosaic beads) that were far removed from the dangers and the sweltering heat of the furnaces. Using the techniques of lampworking, the mosaic beads (commonly known as African trade beads) were made with numerous slices of multi-colored millefiori cane.

Dominique Bussolin, the author of *Les Celebres Verreries de Venise et de Murano,* described the production of the lampwork beads in 1842 and how the Venetians used a bead release on their mandrels: *"The craftsman holds in his right hand a cane of enamel or colored glass and with the door to the contact of the flame, holds in his left hand a piece of iron covered with a hodgepodge composed of strong glue, calce spenta [calcium hydroxide] and soil from Vicenza so that the bead does not stick to the iron skewer. The glass cane, when in contact with the flame, melts instantly and drops onto the iron skewer to make a bead. The shape comes from the creator's will, turning the iron skewer between the fingers and often using provided examples. To execute the decorations and flowers, the creator takes some thin cane of enamel of various colors and brings the point of the cane to the flame of the lamp, melting it above the bead in order to create the drawings."*

The various forms of the beads can be made into perfect shapes and sizes by pouring the molten glass into a metal or brass mold (*il bronzo*). After the bead is formed, it is immersed into a basin that is filled with the ashes of a reed plant which grows in the marshlands of the Laguna. There, the bead anneals slowly, preventing it from cracking or breaking. It wasn't until 1935, with a procedure invented by Ercole Moretti & F.lli, when a copper mandrel was used and, in order to release the mandrel from the bead, the bead would be submerged in nitric acid. The Venetians adopted this method so that the hole of the bead would be left polished and transparent. However, if a bead was gilded in gold, it would not be submerged into the acid, as this would remove the exterior gold embellishments. In this case, the antique method of using a paste, coated onto the mandrel in order to release the bead, would be used to preserve the beauty of the gold gildings.[v]

In 1842, Bussolin tried to persuade the Venetian lampworkers to discontinue the use of animal fat as fuel and to opt, instead, for a new system using hydrogen gas that would provide better control over the temperature and flame of the torch. He patented this invention in 1843, but in a French publication of 1846, he complained that despite the obvious advantages from his invention, the perleri continued making beads using the old system. It wasn't until 1863 (and the lack of beasts to slaughter to provide the oil for the torch) that the Venetian perleri adopted Bussolin's invention.[vi]

Lampwork glass beads were used to create necklaces, earrings, bracelets, rings, and other jewelry. Dozens of young women were hired by the SVC to produce a multitude of beads. The SVC also outsourced assignments to stay-at-home mothers, with a majority of the production occurring in the Cannaregio district of Venice.

Venetian lampwork beads are still being produced, however, it is increasingly difficult to differentiate between them and their imported counterfeit imitations.

Some of the most collected beads in the world were made by the Venetians and their market value continues to appreciate over time. Many Venetian beads are exhibited in museums around the world, such as the Glass Museum of Murano, Italy, and the Picard Trade Bead Museum in Carmel Valley, California.

CHAPTER FIVE *Endnotes*

i Bartolomeo Cecchetti, *Monografia della Vetraria Veneziana e Muranese*, Venezia, 1874, page 266; Giuseppe Morazzoni, *Le Conterie Veneziane dal Secolo XIII al Secolo XIX*, Venezia, Società Veneziana Conterie e Cristallerie, 1953, pages 24-25.

ii Venezia, *Archivio di Stato*, Inquistori di Stato, 97 Perleri.

iii Morazzoni, page 33.

iv *Mille Anni di Lavoro e di Lotte dei Vetrai di Murano e Venezia*, Filcea/Cgil, 1982, Venezia page 28.

v Giovanni Sarpellon, *Venetian Beads, Mosaic Glass and Murrrine*, Palazzo Rota, Venezia, 2003, page 33.

vi Morazzoni, page 55; G.D., Le Tre Venezia, *Perle Veneziane a lume*, Instituto Veneto per il Lavoro, 1933, page 170.

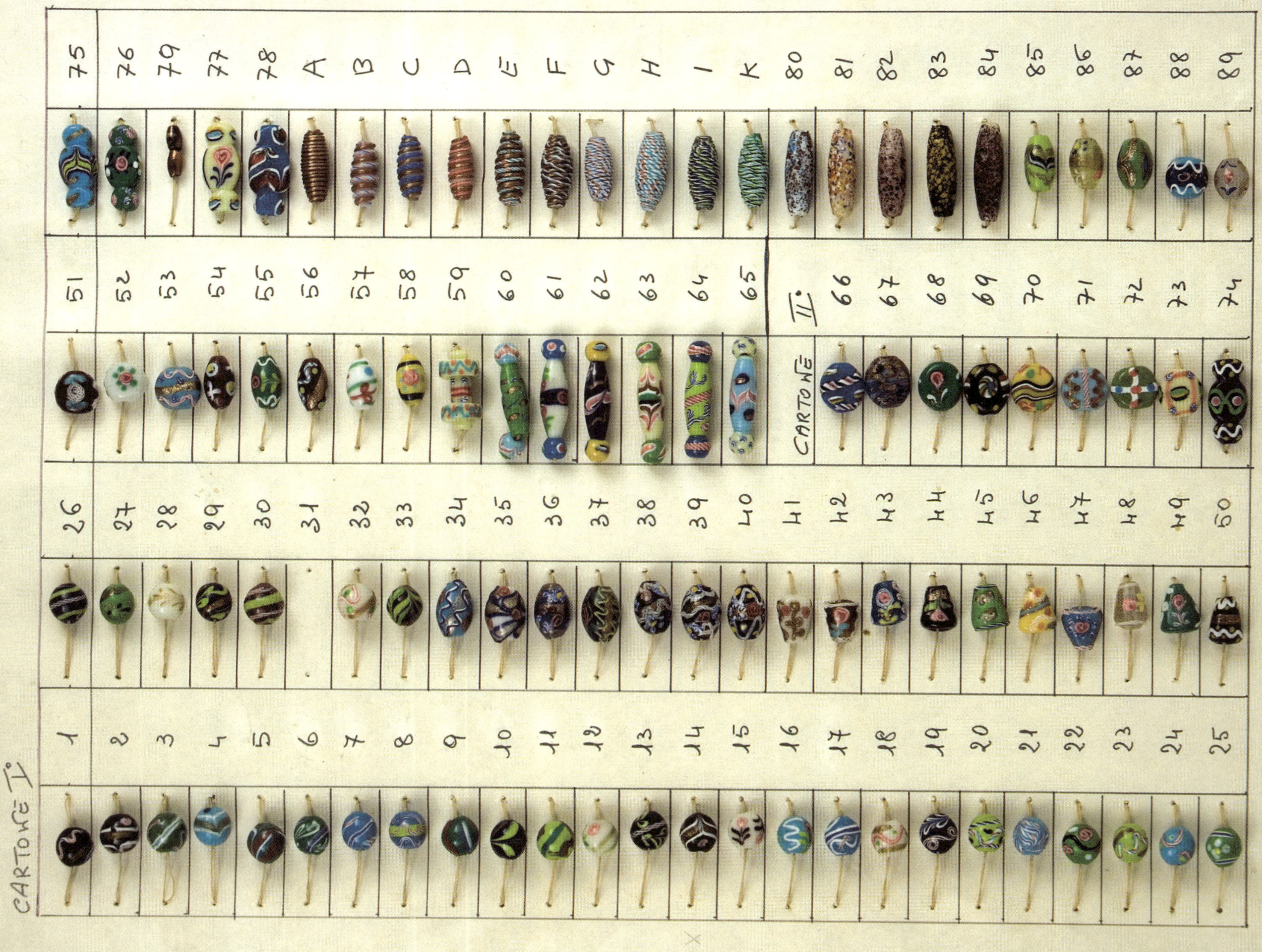

BEAD CARDS COURTESY OF THE MURANO GLASS MUSEUM;
PHOTOGRAPH BY STEFANO PANDIANI

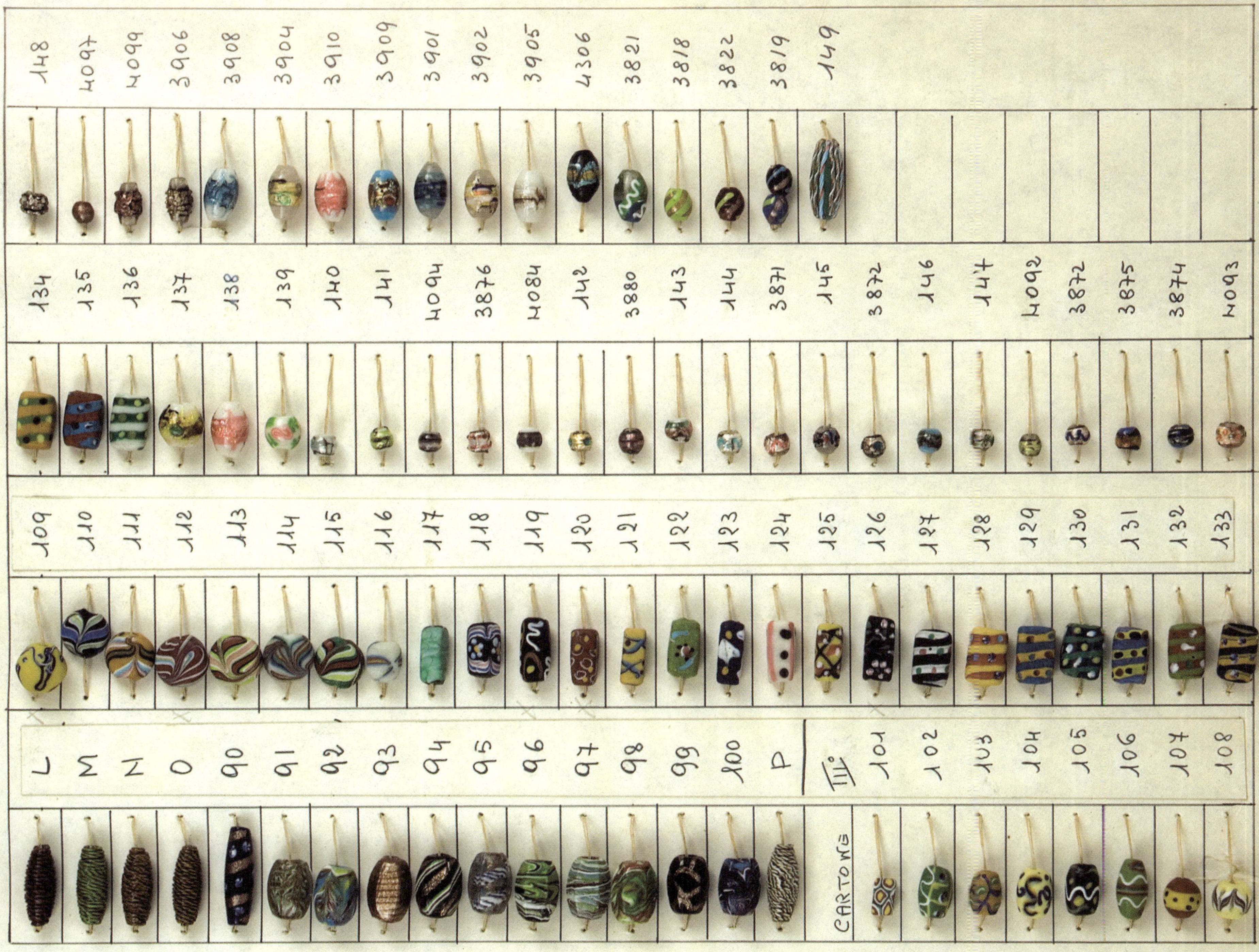
148 4097 4099 3906 3908 3904 3910 3909 3901 3902 3905 4306 3821 3818 3822 3819 149
134 135 136 137 138 139 140 141 4094 3876 4084 142 3880 143 144 3871 145 3872 146 147 4092 3872 3875 3874 4093
109 110 111 112 113 114 115 116 117 118 119 120 121 122 123 124 125 126 127 128 129 130 131 132 133
L M N O 90 91 92 93 94 95 96 97 98 99 100 P III° 101 102 103 104 105 106 107 108

When man has touched wood or stone,
it is no longer wood or stone, but takes on something of man.
An edifice is a dogma, a machine is an idea.

VICTOR HUGO
French poet and novelist
(1802–1885)

Creating Conterie Beads

THE EIGHT STAGES OF PRODUCTION

When seventeen individual manufacturers of *conterie* beads in Venice and Murano joined forces in 1898 to form the Società Veneziana per l'Industria delle Conterie (herein referred to as the SVC), their first order of business was to create glass canes to produce *conterie* beads, or *margarite*, commonly known as seed beads.

The process of creating conterie beads begins after glass has been fused in a furnace, pulled into long, narrow, hollow canes while still hot, and then cooled. Then, the eight stages of conterie production begins, followed by the stringing and packaging of the beads.

Most historical accounts regarding Murano glass production are expressed in the Venetian dialect. The Muraneses were clever when it came to naming the individual stages of production and the job titles of the workers who performed job tasks within each stage. A worker who contributed to the bead-making process was called a *margaritaio*. The process of creating conterie beads was also known as *riduzione*, or reduction. Here, each bead was gradually reduced or scaled down as it was subjected to various operations during the conterie bead production.

In some cases, the names of the production stages are used interchangeably with the titles of the persons performing the job functions. For example, the term *cernitrici* refers to both the work of separating the canes, as well as the person who was doing the work. Additionally, there were many other workers behind the scenes assisting in operating and maintaining the constant flow of productivity. For example, several *porta-massa* were employed to transfer large wooden crates filled with glass canes, cylinders or glass chips from one department to the next. The wooden crate would be balanced between two men with ropes *(lacci)* fastened on each end and attached to a very strong, resistent, yet flexible, acacia branch. Together, two *porta-massa* could carry up to four hundred fifty kilos.[i]

During each stage of production, only one *palato* was used at a time. A *palato* is a large clay crucible of 1.20m to 1.25m in diameter with the capacity to hold approximately eight hundred kilos of molten glass. Each palato batch was marked with a production date, a consecutive number, and color. As each stage was completed, the glass cane from the labeled palato was passed and delivered to the next stage by the *porta-massa*.

The following is the sequence and description of the eight stages of the conterie bead production, the process that reduces glass cylinders into conterie beads:

The Eight Stages of Production

The overall process of transforming glass canes into tiny beads is called the L'Arte del Margariteri, and includes the following production stages:

1

Cernitrici: *Separating the canes according to diameter.*

2

Tagliatrice: *Cutting the canes into small, cylindrical pieces.*

3

Schizzadori: *Separating the whole cylinders from the chipped fragments.*

4

Fregadori: *Filling the holes of the cylinders with the siribiti compound.*

5

Tubanti/Arrotondamento: *Rounding and smoothing the sharp and jagged edges of the cylinders to become homogeneous beads.*

6

Cavaroba: *Unclogging and cleaning the bead holes of the siribiti compound.*

7

Lustradori: *Polishing the beads.*

8

Governadori: *Separating the beads according to size.*

The eight stages were followed by these processes:

Impiraresse: *Stringing the beads.*
Impaccatura: *Packaging the beads.*

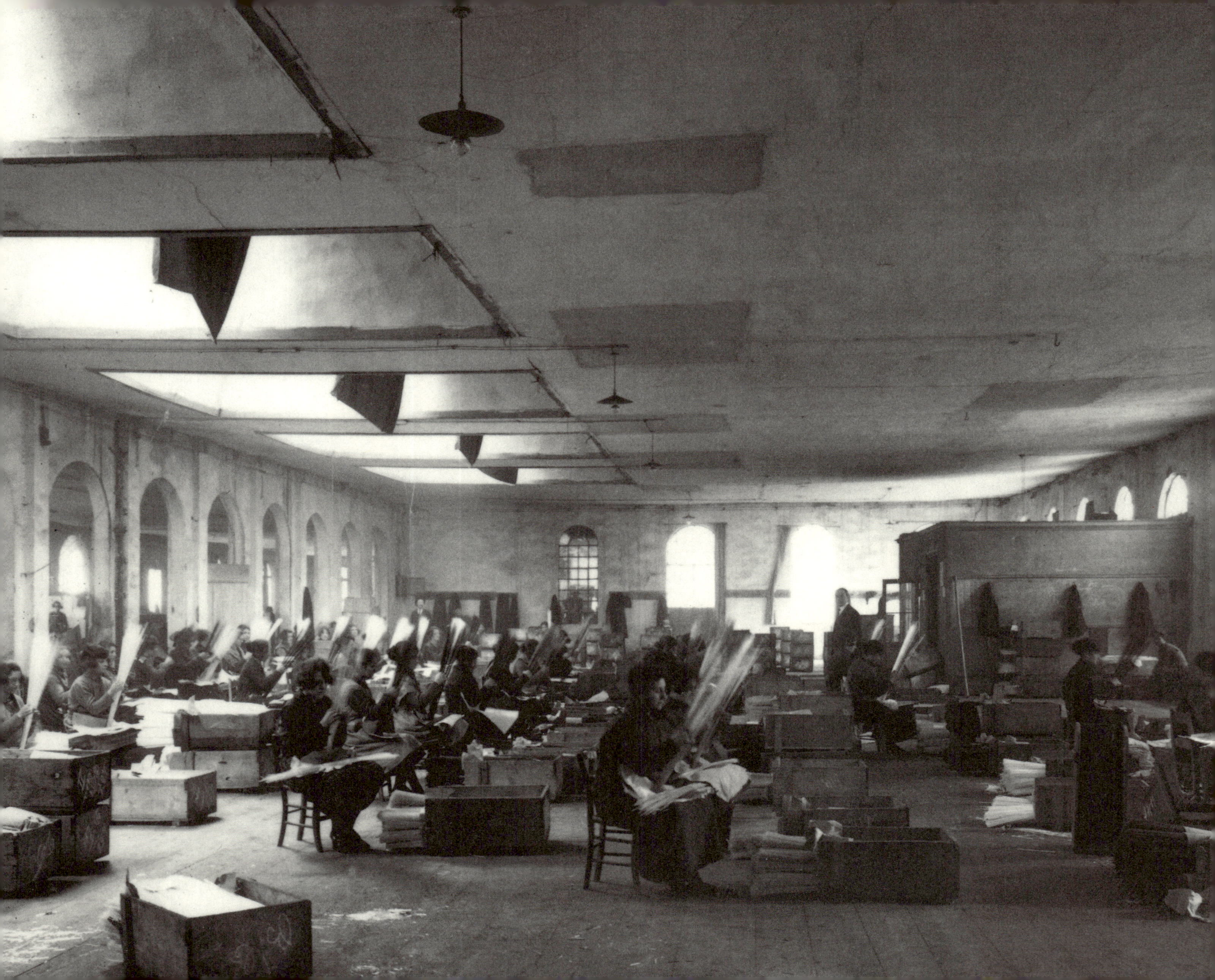

ONE

Cernitrici

Separating the canes according to diameter

When glass cane was pulled by hand, the resulting cane varied in diameter. The first stage in the conterie bead production was handled by women, the *cernitrici*. Hundreds of women were employed at the SVC to perform the task of dividing the one-meter canes (*cannelle*) according to diameter. During this process, defective cane (for example, those that contained *grumi/grotti* which were sand granules or raw un-fused elements), or those with irregularities in diameter, were identified and removed from the batches. (The grumi/grotti were later cut from the cane and re-fused in a crucible). The cernitrici developed remarkable dexterity and precision in handling the cannelle. Typically, she took a given quantity of canes, sat on a low stool or chair, and set the ends of the canes on her knees (which were protected with a thick padding of packaging paper lest she rip a hole in her garment or skin). She then separated and divided the canes according to diameter, each finger (*indice, medio, anulare, mignolo*) represented a specific diameter of cane where the thinnest cane was sorted near the baby finger (*mignolo*) and the thicker cane near the index finger (*indice*). The women worked in such rapid succession that they appeared to be playing a harp. The canes were placed according to diameter into narrow, wooden crates (called *pain*) which were situated around her. Glass canes that were mechanically pulled were too long to fit into the standard 1.05m pain and were placed in an open-ended, three-sided box called a *sbocco*. By the mid-1950s, only a few cernitrici remained employed (as opposed to hundreds in the early

< IN THE EARLY 1900S, THE SVC EMPLOYED HUNDREDS OF WOMEN to work in the various stages of seed bead production. In this photo, the workers in the Cernitrici Department are actively separating the glass cane according to diameter. The arched entries on the left lead to the Cutting Department, the next stage in the bead production.

1900s) when an automatic machine replaced her. By this time, the only canes needed to be divided were those that were pulled by hand, such as the *corniole* (with two layers) or the stripped cane (*rigata*). The sorted canes were ready to be passed on to the *tagliatrice*.

TWO
Tagliatrice
Cutting the canes into small cylinders

After the glass canes were separated, they were transferred (by the porta massa) to the *tagliatrice* to be cut into small cylinders. In the 1700s, this process was performed exclusively by hand and by men. Equipped with a steel chisel, the tagliatori would cut the canes on a small bench or tree trunk (*soco* in Venetian dialect). The tagliatori would gather the canes with one hand and place their ends on an anvil. The other hand would hold the chisel and strike the canes repeatedly, which fell in small pieces into a container.

Around 1822, Captain Cavalier Marino Longo invented the first machine for cutting the canes into small cylinders. However, this machine proved to be both dangerous and impractical, so it was not used. A second cutting machine was invented by Giovanni Sola, but this too was deemed impractical. Finally, in 1867, Carlo Romiti developed a machine powered by a steam engine that was favored and adopted by many bead factories. Early on, young men and boys operated these machines. By the early 1900s, these semi-automatic machines, which numbered approximately one hundred twenty, were operated exclusively by women, the *tagliatrice*.[ii]

> THE QUANTITY OF GLASS CANE NEEDED TO CREATE LAMPWORK BEADS was considerably less than the cane needed to create conterie beads (seed beads). For this reason, we see only a few workers (the Cernitrici) separating the cane according to diameter. Look closely on the right—the two porta massa are carrying a trunk between them, supported by a strong yet flexible branch of an acacia tree.

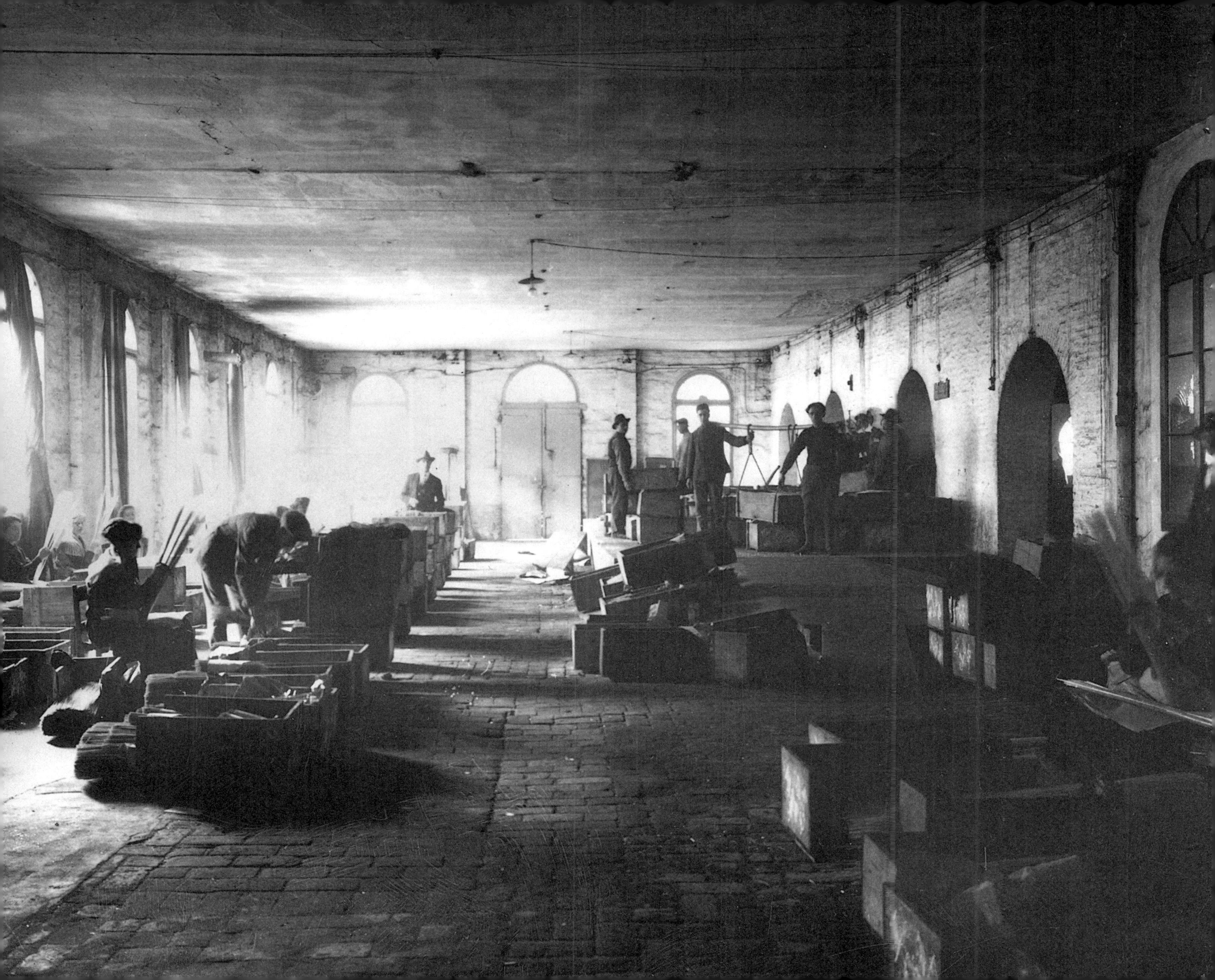

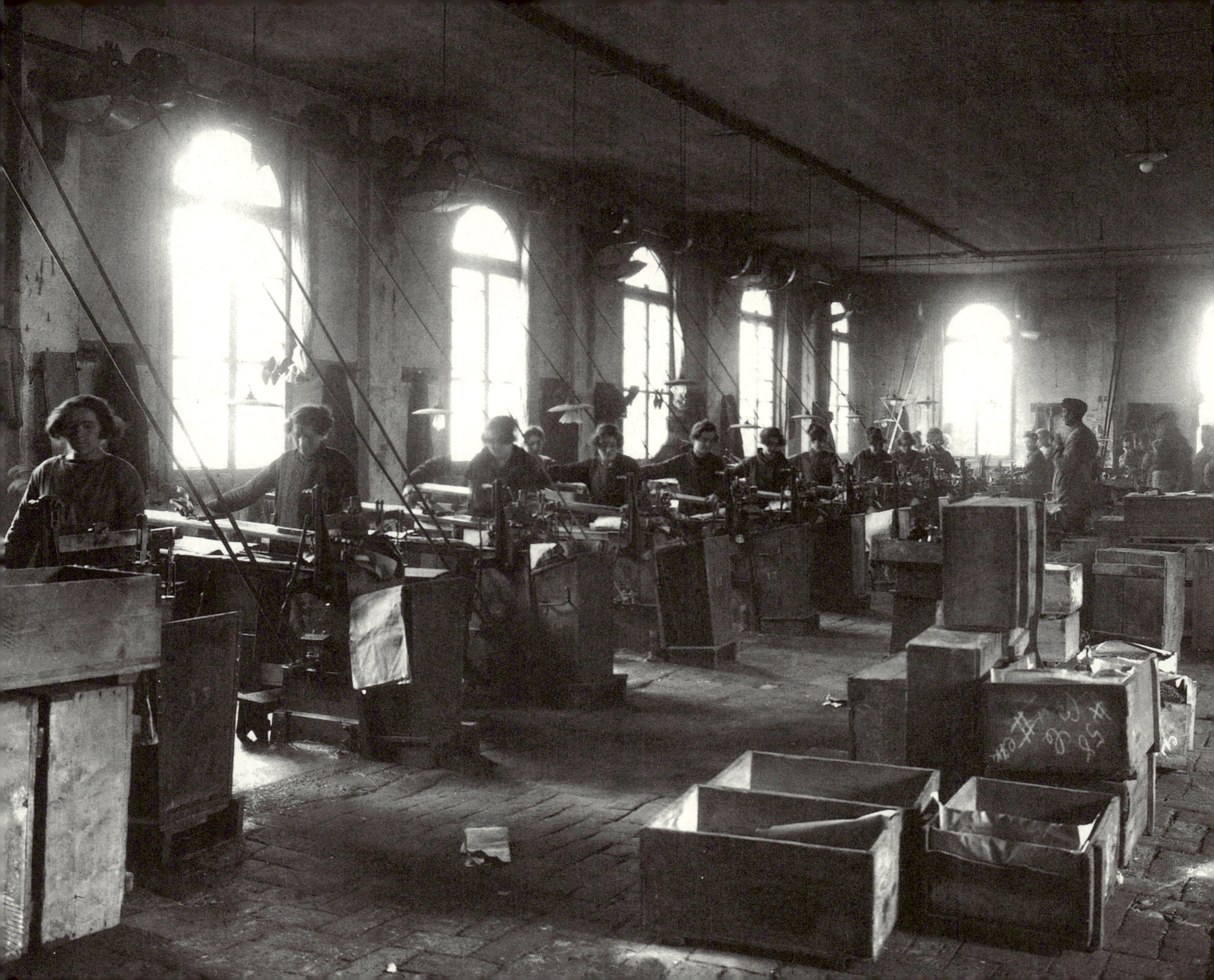

Assisting the tagliatrice were approximately sixty *sbrizzadore* and thirty *filatore*. The tagliatrice were given a *sbrizzada* (handful) of canes by the young female sbrizzadora. Each sbrizzadora was responsible for providing assistance at two machines (or two tagliatrice). The number of canes that were cut varied according to the cane's diameter. The sbrizzadora would place the canes onto a flat surface; their ends would then be fastened and secured with a very large rubber-lined clip called a *molletta*. In fact, this machine was called the "*macchina a moletta*". The molletta would then be gently pushed forward by the tagliatrice toward a single iron V-groove roller (*rullo*) that would guide the canes and serve as a mandrel to hold and position them for cutting. In the 1930s, an automatic machine replaced the sbrizzadora.

The V-shaped corrugations on this roller would correspond to the diameter of the cane that was being fed into the machine. If thicker diameter cane was being processed, then the iron rollers that were selected for the machine required wider grooves to accommodate the canes. Conversely, if thinner diameter cane was being processed, then the iron roller required narrower grooves.

Immediately after passing through the iron roller, the canes passed between two smooth rubber rollers, rotating in opposite directions to feed the canes forward. Then the canes would be cut by a set of upper and lower tempered steel blades. The upper blade was called the *ferro da tagio*, and the lower blade was called the *scarpeo*. The lower blade had teeth-like indentations, again corresponding to the diameter of the cane, on which the glass canes rested and worked in conjunction with the upper blade. The upper blade would administer a

< HERE IN THE CUTTING DEPARTMENT, the Tagliatrice were women who operated a semi-automatic machine to cut the glass cane for the production of conterie beads. Approximately one hundred twenty of these machines were in operation in the early 1900s. The fourth girl on the left (closest to the window) was the Sbrizzadore, who was responsible for replenishing the glass cane for two machines/two Tagliatrice.

1 | The following is the daily production of the tagliatrice, known as her *tasca giornaliera:*

EACH TAGLIATRICE COULD CUT
- 86 kilos per day of glass cane 1.8mm in diameter;
- 96 kilos per day of cane 2.0mm;
- 120 kilos per day of cane 2.2 mm;
- 140 kilos a day of cane 2.4mm;
- 160 kilos per day of cane 2.6mm;
- 350 kilos per day of the larger diameter glass cane 2.8-3.0mm.

three-point contact load, at sixty degree angles, to deliver three clean strikes to the exposed length of cane.[iii]

The precision of this machine, and its finely designed blade, allowed the SVC greater production, less waste, and ultimately a more perfect cut. In fact, in the early 1930s, this machine was so technically advanced that it was executing seven hundred twenty strikes per minute.[1]

The upper blade itself was made by industrial artisans, the Beniamino Donà family of Murano, who have been blacksmiths and tool smiths since 1865. The lower blade (the one with the teeth) was manufactured by the blacksmiths of the SVC and measured approximately twenty four centimeters long and six centimeters high. The number of teeth on the lower blade varied according to the diameter of the glass cane. The corrugated roller and the lower blade were considered a set because the grooves in the roller had to match the indentations of the lower blade. The rollers were all made within the SVC and were stored together as a set (or *muta* in Venetian dialect).

It was the responsibility of the *filatore* to sharpen and change the blades. Each filatore was responsible for four cutting machines. Depending on the hardness of the glass, it was necessary to sharpen the blades every ten to fifteen minutes. To sharpen the blades, the filatore used industrial oil and a special stone found in Candia, Greece. The bravura of the filatore was to sharpen the blade precisely; if he sharpened the blade too hard, the blade would heat too fast, become dull, unproductive, and would require frequent replacements.[iv]

Once the canes were cut, the tiny glass cylinders would fall into a container. A small percentage of the glass pieces were found to be imperfect. These broken and chipped fragments were called *schizzi* and would have to be eliminated in the next phase of production by the *schizzadori*.

> THE SCHIZZADORI DEPARTMENT didn't require many workers. By the early 1900s, the SVC had devised a mechanical procedure for separating the glass chips and fragments (the *schizzi*) from the whole, intact cylinders. Note the large wooden crates labeled "SVC".

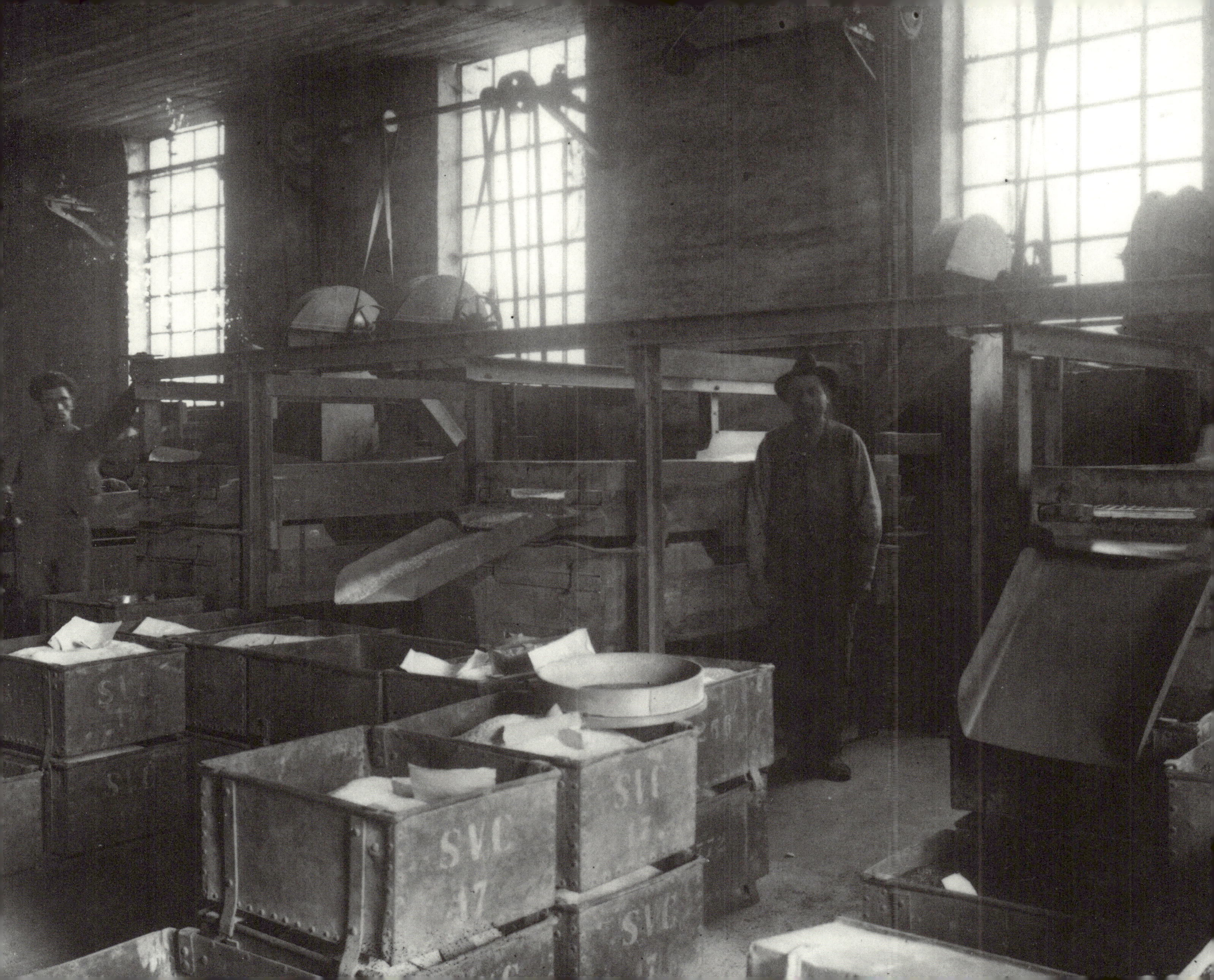
SVC
17

THREE
Schizzadori
Separating the whole cylinders from the chipped fragments

Separating the defective pieces of cylinders was accomplished using sieves (*crivelli*) made of metal. The sieves contained holes which were smaller than the diameter of the cylinders so that the broken pieces would fall through these holes, leaving the whole cylinders in the sieve. The schizzadori would take the glass cylinders from the container and pour them into the sieve. He would then shake the sieve, allowing the broken fragments (or schizzi) to fall into a tub while the whole cylinders remained in the sieve. The schizzi were later re-fused as the SVC recycled everything. By the early 1900s, the SVC modernized this department and devised a mechanical procedure for separating the schizzi from the whole cylinders. The beads were now ready for the *fregadori*.

FOUR
Fregadori
Filling the cylinder holes

The fourth step in the reduction/production of the conterie came from the *fregadori*, where the holes of the cylinders were filled with a compound (called *siribiti*) to prepare them for the *tubanti/arrotondamento* stage. It was necessary to fill the holes of the cylinders with this compound to prevent them from closing or shrinking while undergoing the heat of the furnace during the *tubanti/arrotondamento stage.*[V]

To fill the holes, the fregadori used the siribiti, which was made of calcium hydroxide (traditionally called slaked lime) and fine wood charcoal dust. The wood charcoal was crushed into

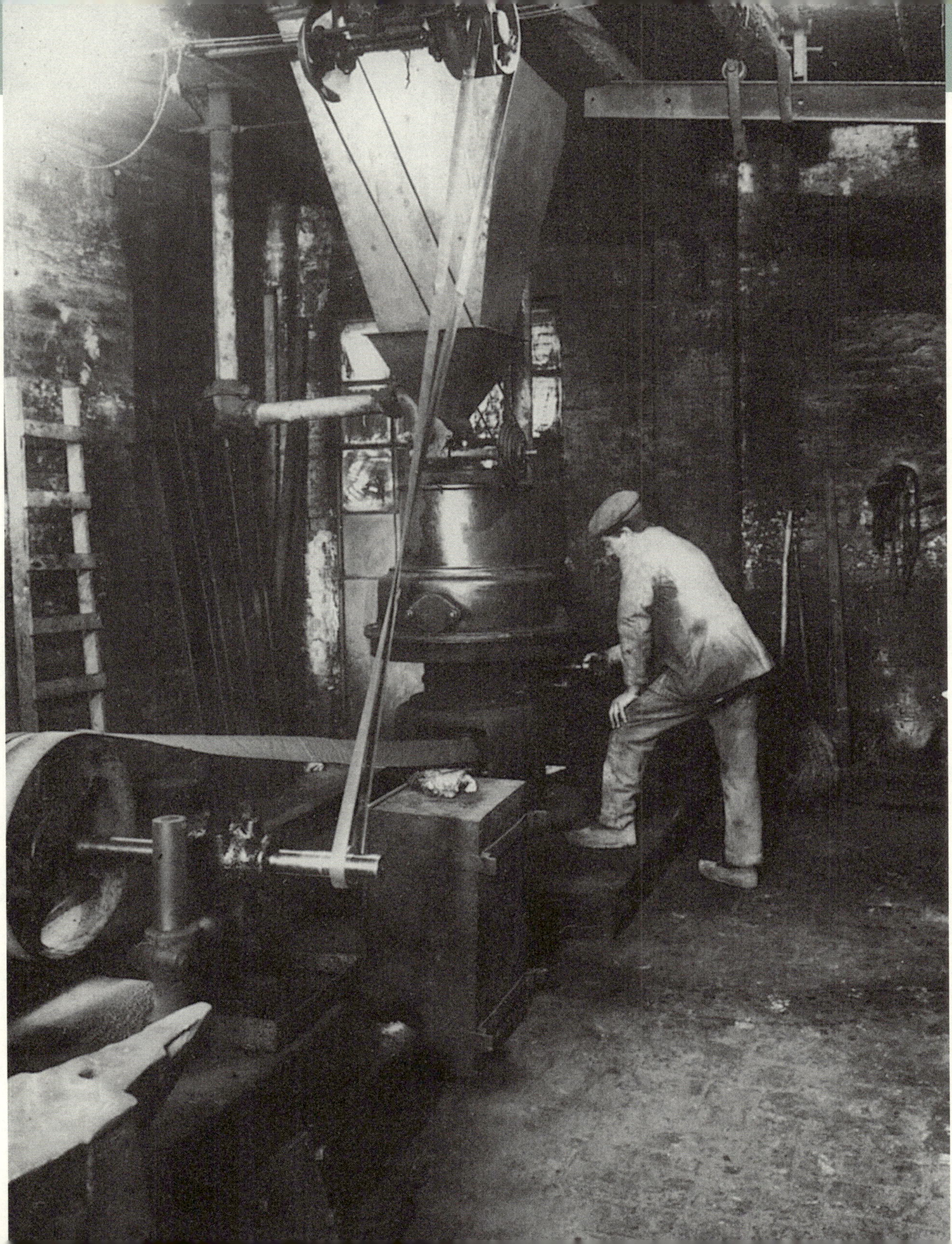

< COVERED FROM HEAD TO TOE IN CARBON DUST, the Fregadori (also known as the *frangi carbone*) was responsible for operating a machine that could crush chunks of charcoal into a fine powder. The SVC invented this grinding machine in the 1920s and continued to operate it until the 1980s. The carbon dust was an essential ingredient in the siribiti compound which was used to fill the holes of the glass cylinders prior to undergoing the heat of the furnace to prevent them from closing/shrinking.

a fine powder by the *frangi carbone* who, by the end of the day, was black and covered with coal dust. It was the responsibility of the frangi carbone to pour chunks of charcoal into a grinding machine and collect the charcoal dust. The blacksmiths of the SVC invented and built this grinding machine in the early 1920s. It wasn't until the late 1980s that the SVC found a distributor on the mainland who sold charcoal dust, thus eliminating the need for the machine and the worker.[vi]

The siribiti was dampened with water and then mixed together with the glass cylinders. In the mid 1800s, the fregadore mixed the cylinders with the siribiti by hand, but by the 1900s, and until the SVC closed in 1992, the fregadori performed this task by using an industrial-size dough mixer, the same kind of mixer found in a local bakery. Once the holes were filled with the siribiti, the cylinders were ready to be passed onto the *tubanti/arrontondamento* to be rounded and made into beautiful conterie beads.[vii]

FIVE
Tubanti/Arrotondamento
Rounding the cylinders

The glass cylinders, having sharp and jagged edges from cutting, progressed to the next stage to round and smooth the edges, called the tubanti/arrotondamento. In addition, certain colors of glass, such as ruby, red, and amber, needed to be re-fired in order for those tonalities to appear.[viii] To obtain the desired homogeneous quality, smoothness, and optimal tonality, it was necessary for the cylinders to be subjected to a second application of fire (the first being the fusion of glass). The stage of tubanti/arrontondamento required appropriate furnaces in a spacious locale that was separated from the other operations of the factory because this operation emitted sand, dust, powder, as well as noxious fumes.

Until 1817, the rounding of the hollow cylinders was called *ferrazza/ferraccio* (for smaller pieces) or *spiedo* (for larger pieces). During the ferraccio process, only a few kilos of cylinders could be placed on a copper or iron tray at once to be heated in a reverberating furnace (a chamber or kiln), where the glass cylinders were heated indirectly by a flame deflected downward from the roof.

In 1817, Luigi Pusinich, who came from a family with a long history of beadmaking, invented a new and faster way to round and smooth the cylinders using a copper drum (*il tubo*) that was inserted into a small furnace (*fornacino*). While the drum was in the furnace, the tubanti (or his helper, the *garzoni*) would continually rotate it with a manual crank to stir the cylinders inside (to prevent them from sticking together). By the mid 1900s, the drum was rotated mechanically and could hold approximately nine to twelve kilos. The Pusinich method was universally adopted in all the Murano bead factories as it was an operation that resulted in more perfect and appealing beads.

The Pusinich drum is shaped like the bottom of a cannon, resembling a small barrel or bicone. The first drums were made of copper and could contain only a small amount of cylinders, approximately nine kilos. A few years later, Captain Cavalier Longo invented a drum made of clay.[ix] While the drum was modified over the years, and redesigned by various mechanics with other materials (such as cast iron), the tubo and its original application continues to be credited to Pusinich.[x]

Circa 1985, a new system of drums and ovens was built. All of the drums used by the SVC were made of 4mm sheet metal. Manufactured by the blacksmiths of the factory, they had the capacity to hold 100-120 kilos of glass cylinders. During its final years of operation, the drums were made on the mainland. When sand was added, the total capacity of these drums was 350 kilos, thus a mechanical crane (electric jack) was required to empty it.

To begin the process of arrotondamento, a one-part mixture of glass cylinders (already filled with siribiti) was added to two parts sand. The sand was essential so that the cylinders would not melt and stick together when subjected to heat. The sand came from the beaches of Bacan, an area near Murano which is located in front of the island of Saint Erasmo. The sand had to be dried and filtered before it could be used to round the cylinders. If the sand was humid, more time was needed for the arrotondamento process. As such, the damp sand was spread across the floor near each tubante's work space. Extended on top of the sand were eight square, metal ferraccio to receive the hot beads. The heat from the hot beads (cooling in the ferraccio) would indirectly dry the sand. Using a sieve, the sand was purified of shells and sea creatures, as it wasn't uncommon to find live crabs and clams in the sand.[xi] In the 1980s, the workers of the SVC had the idea to build an oven that could dry the sand. This oven (almost as big as a house) was adopted and manufactured on the mainland for the SVC. The tubanti also added a small amount of powder called *patussa* to the smaller drums. This powder (used to improve the luster and brilliancy of the beads) was the residue of previous labors deposited all around the tubanti's work area and found on the window sills, the wooden beams, and on top of the furnaces. The patussa was collected once a year and put into a storage container called a *conca*.[xii]

The cylinders and the dry sand were united in a metal container using a triangular-shaped spout called a *piria*. From the piria, the cylinder/sand mixture was poured into the drum. A

> THE ARROTONDAMENTO PROCESS (performed by the Tubante) occurred on the upper floor of the SVC. The "rounding off" or smoothing of the glass cylinders was necessary as the edges were sharp and jagged when the cane was cut. Arrotondamento also enhanced the tonality of certain colors such as red and amber. A large drum (tubo) was filled with one part of glass cylinders to two parts of sand (as seen in the foreground), which was extracted from the Venetian lagoon and introduced into an oven. The Tubante then manually rotated the tubo using a crank.

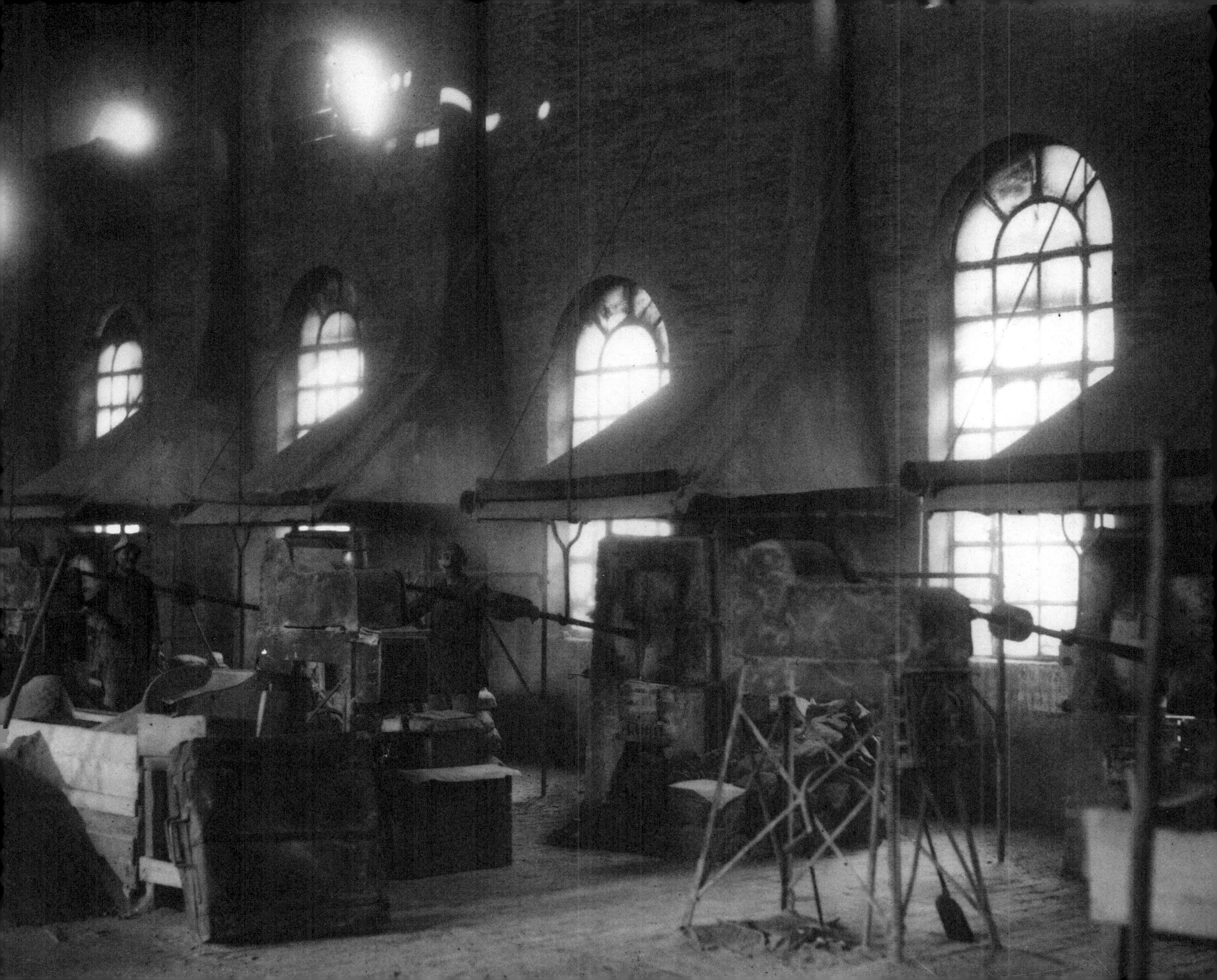

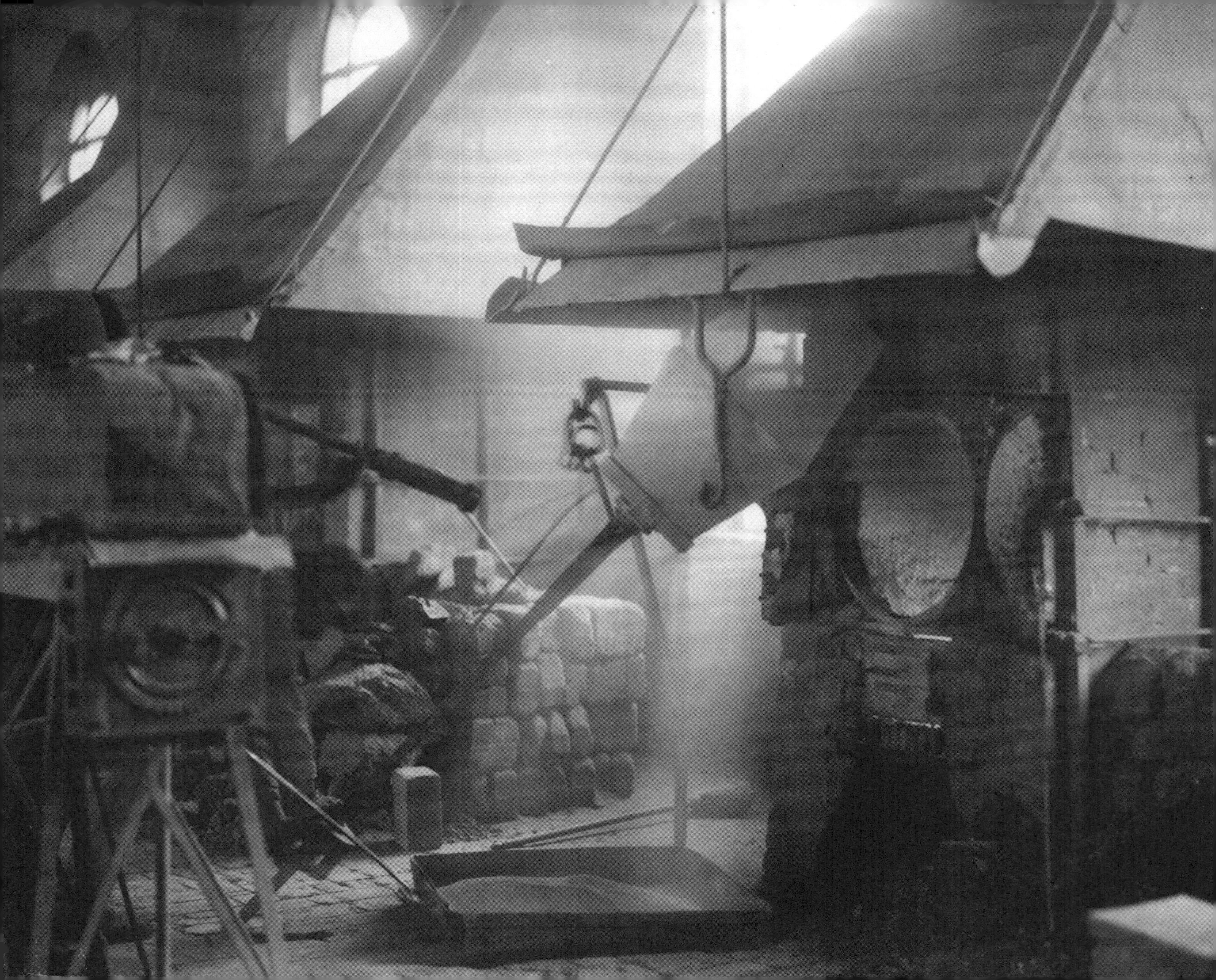

wheel-shaped guide with a center hole was placed on top of the drum. A long iron staff was inserted into that hole until it reached the back wall of the oven. Incorporated in the back of the oven was a mandrel holder (*cojon*) which would hold the iron staff in place. The drum was introduced, secured into the furnace, and then continually rotated.[xiii]

Since all the beads must be heated evenly to have the same quality and tonality as the preceding batch (*cotta*), the tubanti sampled each batch during the cooking process. To do this, he removed a spoonful of the beads while they were still in the furnace, inspected them, and then decided if they were ready for the next stage of production or if they needed more cooking time. This was the most critical moment in the production of the conterie because if the beads cooked for too long, or not long enough, the tubanti risked losing an entire cotta. Depending on the color and size of the beads, it took approximately twenty to thirty minutes for each cotta. Done correctly and with expertise, the result was perfectly round beads, with no rough or sharp edges, and with uniform tonality, quality, and brilliance.

The SVC had sixteen to twenty standard drums in operation at any given time. Each tubanti was responsible for operating two drums simultaneously. Each worker, including the tubanti, worked with and was responsible for one palato at a time. Each palato could contain anywhere from 300-600 kilos of glass cylinders.[xiv]

Once the tubanti was satisfied with the quality of the beads, he would pour the hot contents into the ferrazza/ferraccio where they were left to cool. As each batch was emptied from the incandescent drum, a big cloud of sand, dust, ash, and calcium hydroxide particles would fill the air, as well as the smoldering heat. In order for the hot beads to cool and temper evenly, the

< BY THE MID-1900S, the incandescent tubo was extracted from the oven using a crane. When the tubo was released, the hot beads would empty into a metal container, known as the ferrazza (as shown below the tubo).

high mound of conterie beads was then spread out evenly and leveled with a tool similar to a garden hoe, called the *paeta*, by the garzoni. Although the charcoal dust and sand was burned during the arrotondamento, not all of it escaped through the chimneys. The tubanti and garzoni wore masks while working, however, they still inhaled noxious fumes and particles, either from their own ovens or from the ovens that were situated around them.[xv]

The tubanti inspected the beads as they were left to cool. If the cotta was perfect in appearance, and an exact match to the previous cotta, then the tubanti carved an "X" into the bead batch. It was the bravura of the tubanti to consistently produce each batch exactly alike in appearance and tonality. If, however, the cotta appeared to be discolored or defective in shape and size, the tubanti carved a circle into the bead batch. The beads that were given an "O" grading were either sold as *buratini* (beads of the same diameter but of various colors) or as *bulgari* (beads of various colors and various diameters.)[xvi] At fifteen kilos per drum and twenty to thirty minutes per cotta, just one drum could produce about 275 kilos of rounded beads per day. The tubanti could produce an average of 500 kilos of beads per day.[xvii] Some colors were very difficult to produce, such as the transparent colors. When working on transparent beads, or beads of a large diameter, the tubanti could only put in ten kilos of cylinders and sand in the drum.[xviii]

The arrotondamento of the beads was undoubtedly the most intricate of the beadmaking processes due to its many variables, including flame temperature, cooking time, and the proportion of sand to beads. Every aspect of the tubanti operation influenced the outcome and quality of the finished product. The roles of the filatore and the tubanti were the two stages in the reduction of the conterie where a single mistake or miscalculation could ultimately affect the day's production. Prior to the reduction of the conterie, the role of the glass master was also dependent on human capability. Until the 1950s, the canes were pulled by hand, allowing a greater margin for error, as opposed to the mechanically-pulled canes.

"The operation of the tubanti is the most laborious and most accountable of all stages in the production. He is a worker who, for 14 hours a day, must stay in front of an ardent fire to increase the flame and feed the furnace. He must bend his arm in a perpetual rotation like that of a motor, extracting and returning the incandescent tube, which is an enormous weight, into the furnace at least 40 times in the course of a day and who absorbs and inhales the most harmful fumes of carbon dust and calcium. For all of this, the tubanti is paid between 2 – 2.5 franchi a day. He can be equated as the unhappiest laborer. What I would like most, and I say this with all sincerity, is that if it were possible, is to have this man replaced with a machine or at least improve the conditions." (Bartolomeo Cecchetti, *Monografia della Vetraria Veneziana e Muranese,* Venezia, Tip. Antonelli, 1874, page 130.)

After the beads were cooled, the next step in the process of the conterie was to remove the remaining siribiti from the bead holes and to give the beads their first cleaning.

SIX
Cavaroba
Unclogging the bead holes

After the arrotondamento of the beads, the siribiti compound was comprised only of calcium hydroxide powder since the charcoal was burned. As such, the beads required unclogging in addition to removing the surrounding sand. This stage of production was the first stage of cleaning and was accomplished by the *cavaroba,* who gets his name from the Venetian dialect *cava roba,* meaning "to take things out."

In the 1800s, the beads were unclogged by hand and given their first cleaning. The beads were agitated in a sack (*saccoccia*) with wheat bran and then filtered with sieves. By the early 1900s, the SVC employed a hexagonal-shaped machine whose tumblers were filled with beads and rotated very slowly on all six sides. As each side hit the surface, the remaining siribiti and sand from the bead holes would be released. Once the beads were unclogged, they were ready for the next stage of production, the cleaning and polishing by the *lustradori*.[xix]

SEVEN
Lustradori
Polishing the beads

In the early 1900s, the SVC invented a *lustradori* machine to polish the beads using wheat bran. This process consisted of two stages. The first stage was done with an electric tumbler where the beads were mixed with bran. After approximately thirty minutes (depending on the color of the beads, with black being the most difficult color to clean and polish), the beads were emptied from the tumbler and then moved to the second stage involving another machine that separated the bran from the beads. Fabricated within the SVC factory, this machine consisted of one wooden receptacle and one metal chute located on either side of a big metal spout. The opening of the spout could be regulated according to the quantity of the beads. An electric blower was installed outside this machine. Once the beads were poured down the spout, the

> IT IS NOT KNOWN WITH CERTAINTY but it has been suggested by several Murano historians that the women in this photograph are cleaning, polishing, and smoothing out/lightly grinding the mosaic beads (also known as African trade beads) by using water, sand, and perhaps other materials and tools.

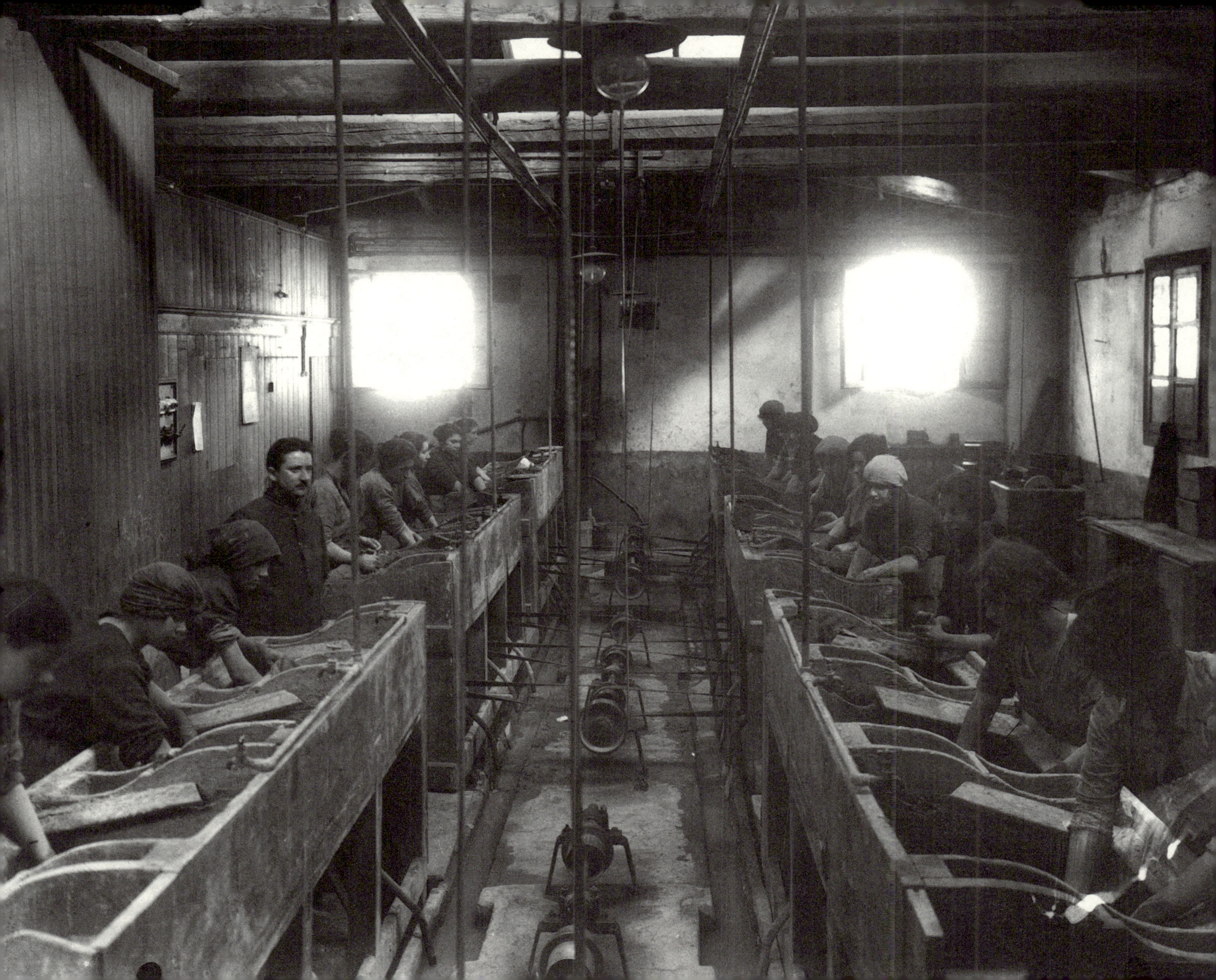

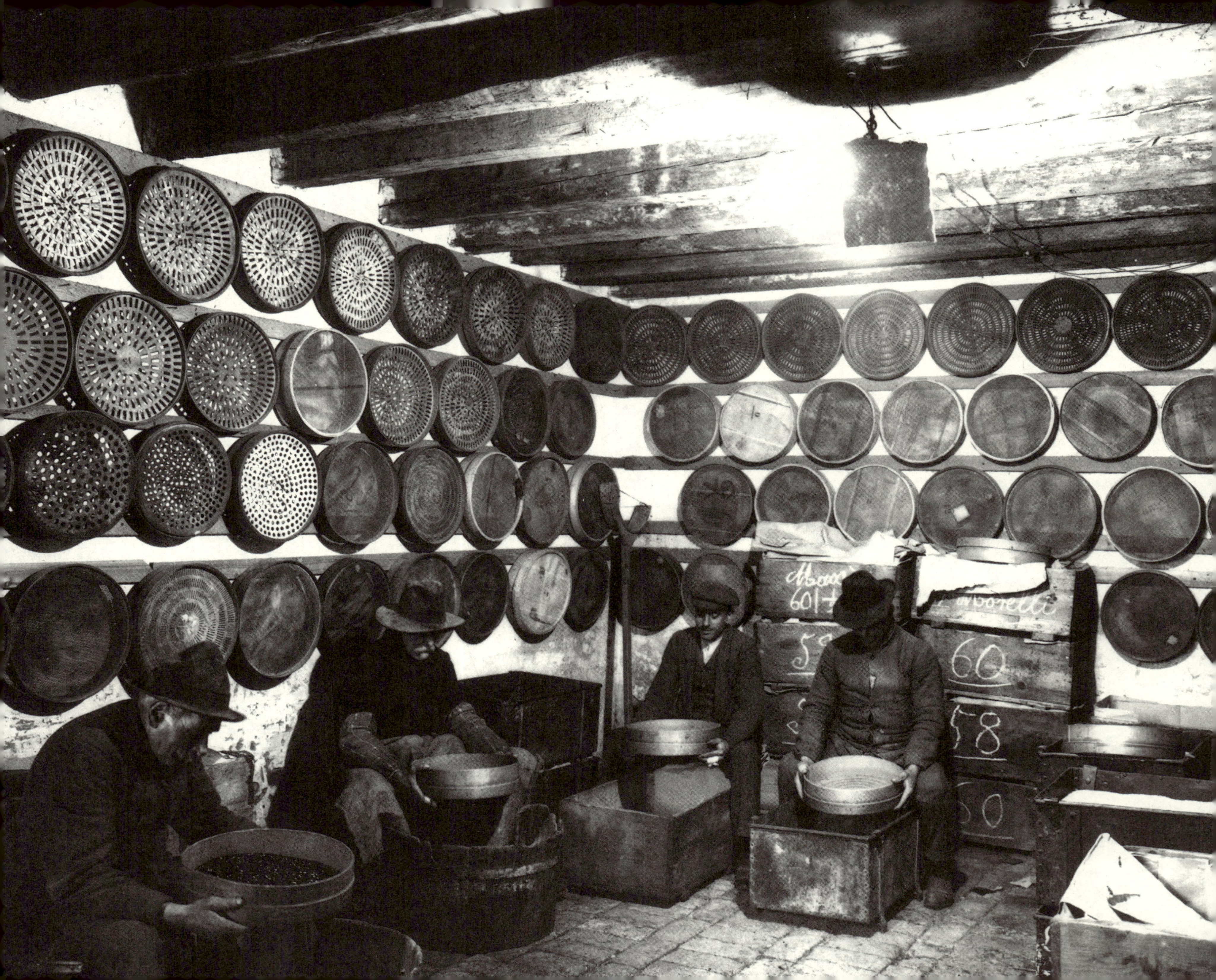
60
58

force of the blower would separate the bran from the beads and, in doing so, ultimately polish and clean them. The power of the blower would drive the bran into one receptacle while the beads (heavier than the bran) would be blown into an opposing container. After polishing, the beads were placed in metal crates and transferred to the *governatori* to be separated according to size.

EIGHT
Governatori
Separating the beads according to size

The job of the *governatori* was to separate the "bad" beads from the "good" beads and to divide the beads according to diameter. The bad beads were those with no holes (called *orbe*, meaning blind) or those that were *storte* (distorted in shape). The orbe and storte beads would be refused in a crucible.

In the 1800s, the governatori would place the beads on a smooth wooden tablet. Holding this tablet at an incline and moving it slightly, the perfectly round beads would run rapidly down the tablet and end up in a bin, while the irregular beads remained fixed on the tablet.[xx] Later, the beads were separated by placing them in sieves with holes of differing diameters and then shaking the sieves by hand. By the 1950s, the SVC invented a machine to separate the beads according to size. The sieves (*crivelli*) were made of sheepskin bound in wooden frames. Stacked on top of each other, several sieves would be placed onto an electric vibratory machine, called the

< USING SIEVES OF VARIOUS HOLE DIAMETERS, the Governatori, in the early 1900s, were employed to manually separate the beads according to size. This operation also separated the whole beads from the partial/broken beads.

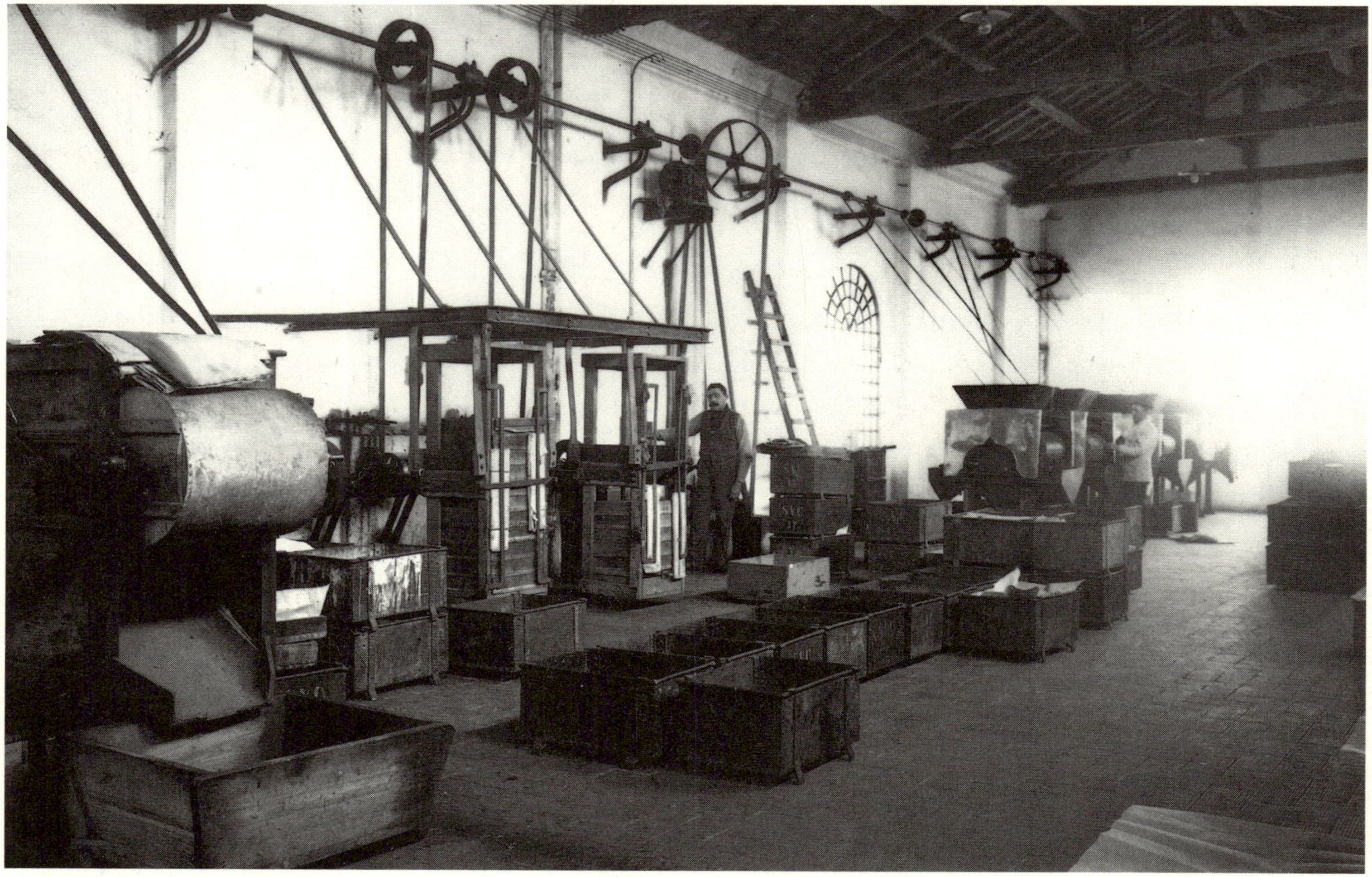

∧ BY THE 1950s, THE SVC INVENTED A MACHINE TO SEPARATE THE BEADS according to size using an electric device called the Carrettine. Several sieves of differing diameters were stacked. The beads were then poured into the top sieve and as the Carrettine vibrated, the beads would fall into the appropriately-sized lower containers. To the far right of the Carrettine is the Macchina degli Orbi (Machine of the Blind) used to separate the beads with/without a hole.

> MANY CONTERIE BEADS WERE TREATED WITH PAINTS AND CHEMICALS by the Silver and Luster Department to create a variety of tonalities and textures such as gun metal, mother-of-pearl, satin finish, and silver-lined. Note the "short-order cook" hats on these workers.

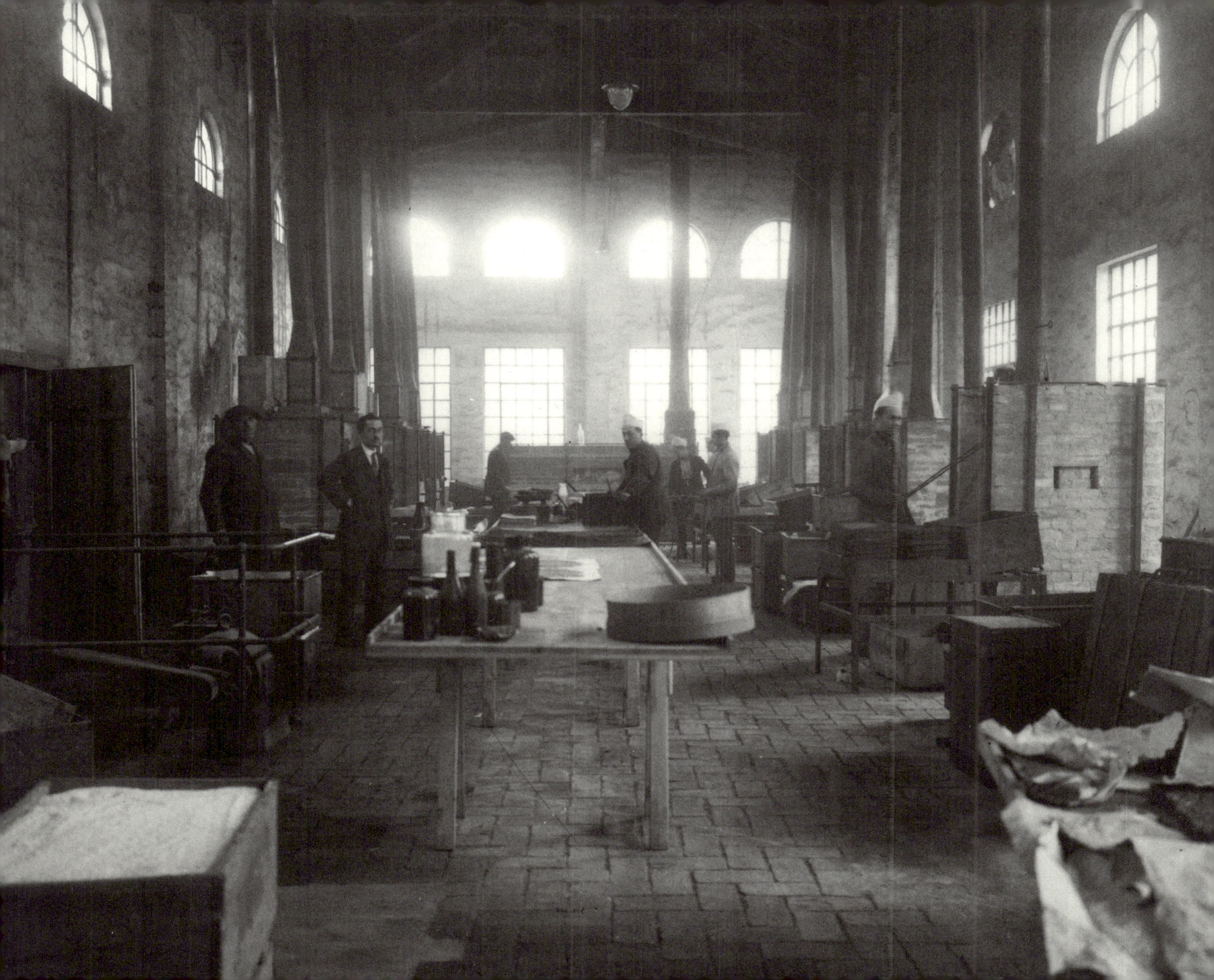

carrettine. All the beads, large and small, were poured into the first top sieve and as the machine vibrated, the beads would fall downwards and collect into the appropriate sieves according to their size. The smallest diameter crivelli was on the bottom.

After the beads had been polished and separated, they were ready to be strung. Some of the clear, transparent beads were transferred to the Luster and Silver departments to be treated according to the requests of the client. The Luster department applied many interesting tonalities and colors to the beads, such as gun metal, fuchsia, and mother-of-pearl, using paints and other chemicals. The Silver department tumbled the beads with silver nitrate making the beads look like sterling silver. The silver nitrate would attach itself to the beads inside and out.[2] The outer surface of the beads would be polished off, leaving only the silver finish on the internal part the bead. Next, the beads were ready to be sold, shipped, or have them strung by the *impiraresse*.

2 | Silver nitrate is a poisonous colorless crystalline compound, AgNO3, that becomes grayish black when exposed to light in the presence of organic matter and is used in manufacturing photographic film, silvering mirrors, dyeing hair, plating silver, and in medicine as a cautery and antiseptic. *(The American Heritage® Dictionary of the English Language, Fourth Edition copyright ©2000 by Houghton Mifflin Company. Updated in 2009.)*

POST PRODUCTION
Impiraresse
Stringing the beads

Many of the beads were sent out of the SVC factory and distributed to women in the poor, residential areas of Venice, in particular the Castello district. It was the task of the *impiraresse* to string the beads using micro-fine needles. The gauge of these needles depended on the size of the bead hole.

The impiraresse strung the beads into groups of *mazze* (hanks) which were composed of dozens of strands, according to the orders that came from the factory. The stringing was done with silk, linen, or cotton threads, depending on the quality of the beads and the request of the

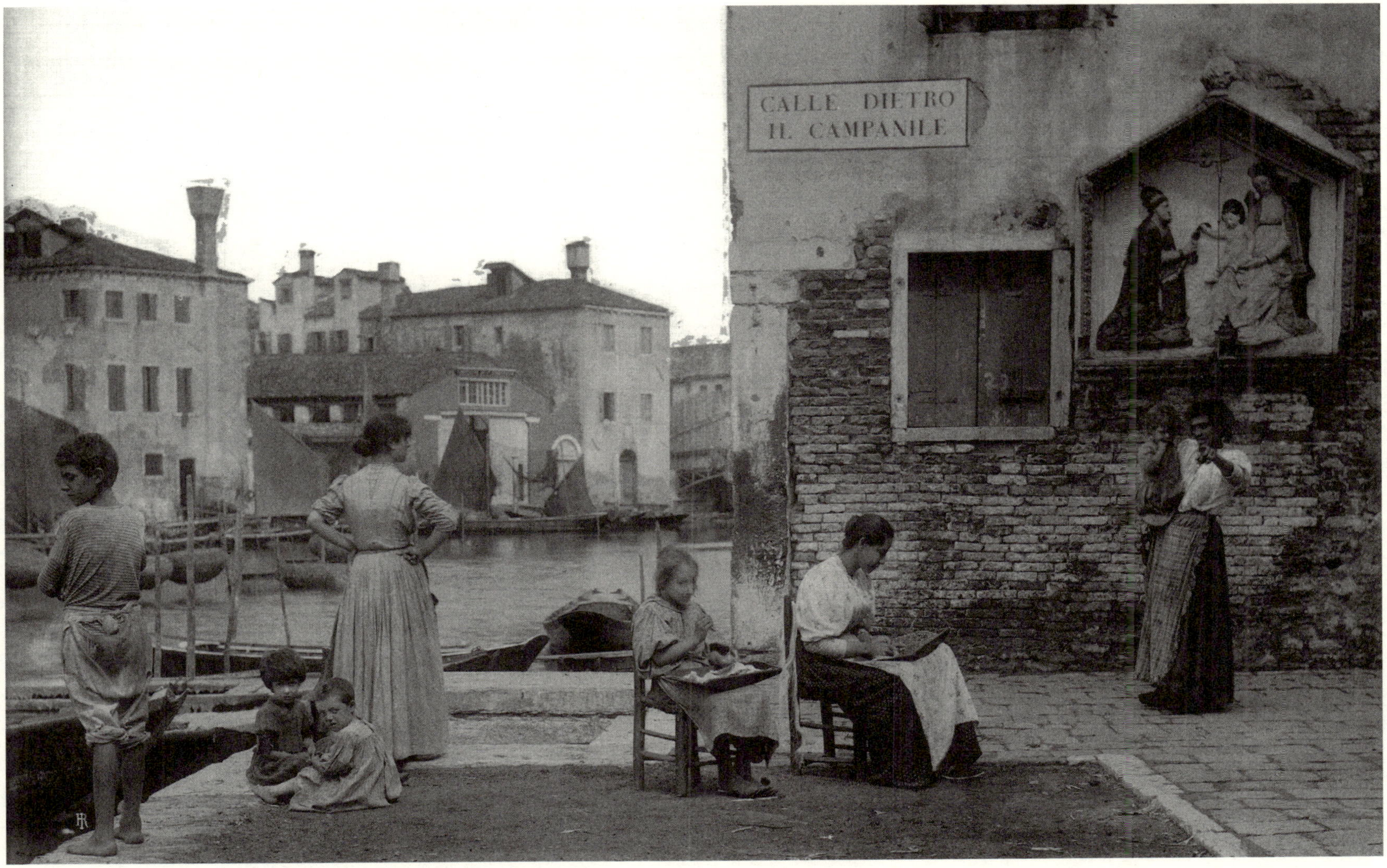

∧ THE SVC OUT-SOURCED WORK TO HUNDREDS OF WOMEN AND GIRLS CALLED THE IMPIRARESSE, who were responsible for stringing the conterie beads onto threads. The majority of these workers lived in the Castello district. Taking advantage of the natural lighting and fresh air, these Impiraresse are working in an open area on the island of San Pietro di Castello near the street Calle Dietro il Campanile ("Street Behind the Bell Tower"). Note the sculptural relief next to the street sign. It depicts the baby Jesus giving the keys to the kingdom of heaven to San Pietro (Matthew 16:19).

customer. The impiraresse had to return the strung beads to the *mistra* (the woman who represented the impiraresse on behalf of the factory), who allocated the work assignments.

POST PRODUCTION
Impaccatura
Packaging

Once the beads arrived in the warehouse of the factory, they were divided either by hanks or by weight: half a kilo and one kilo. To satisfy the American clients, the beads were separated by weight in pounds (instead of kilos). The strung hanks were wrapped in paper packages. It was the *impaccatura's* job (mostly women) to package current orders for shipment, while the remainder of the beads were stored as inventory. In the 1970s, the SVC purchased a machine to handle this task. This machine was previously used for packaging and sealing bags for hard candies. In 1992, the last year of the SVC, approximately 450,000 kilos of beads were sold with much more remaining in the inventory.[xxi]

CHAPTER SIX *Endnotes*

i Interview with Iginio Costantini, *filatore* (blade sharpener) in the Cutting Department of the SVC from 1955-1990.

ii Vincenzo Zanetti in Gasparetto, page 198; Giuseppe Morazzoni, *"Le Conterie Veneziane," Venezia*, 1953, pp. 53-43.

iii Interview with the manufacturers of the blades, Muranese family Donà.

iv Interview with Iginio Costantini.

v Vincenzo Zanetti, *Guida di Murano e delle Celebri Sue Fornaci*, Venezia, 1866, pp. 20-37.

vi Interview with Iginio Costantini.

vii Gasparetto, page 198; Paolo Zecchin, "La Nascita delle Conterie Veneziane," *Journal of Glass Studies*, Vol. 47, 2005, page 85; interview with Iginio Costantini.

viii Domenico Bussolin, *Guida alle Fabbriche Vetrarie di Murano*, Tip. Andrea Santini e Figlio, Venezia, 1842, page 14.

ix Angelo Bassani, *Atti dell'Istituto Veneto di Scienze, Lettere ed Arti*, "Mutamenti Tecnologici nella Conteria Veneziana nel Primo 800: Il "Tubo" Pusinich e Altre Innovazioni," 2002-2003, pp. 410-415.

x Morazzoni, page 53; Gasparetto, page 198; Bussolin, pp. 20-21, Bassani, pp. 434-445.

xi Interview with Iginio Costantini.

xii Ibid.

xiii Gasparetto, page 198.

xiv Interview with the late Franco Mian—*tubanti* of the SVC.

xv Interview with Iginio Costantini.

xvi Interview with Luigi Cattelan, Director of Production for the SVC.

xvii Interview with the late Franco Mian.

xviii Ibid.

xix Bartolomeo Cecchetti, *Monografia delle Vetraria Veneziana e Muranese*, Venezia, Tip. Antonelli, 1874, pages 130-131.

xx Bussolin, page 23, Zanetti, page 35.

xxi Cattelan.

A person's a person, no matter how small.

DR. SEUSS

American writer and cartoonist

(1904–1991)

Children in the Workforce

In the 1700s, in order to own a glass factory or even be an employee, you had to be able to prove Muranese lineage. As such, it was common to find extended family members working together.

"The Art is composed of two different branches. One of which is the Owner of the Factory and the other are the Workers. In order to be considered in one of these two branches, one must prove the legitimate birth of Muranese origin and must have ancestors recorded in the book called Libro d'Oro [the Book of Gold] *of Murano."*[i]

The owner of the factory had the highest position. The workforce included one or more glass masters and a few helpers, the *garzoni*. The garzoni of the factories could not be admitted until reaching the age of ten.[ii]

A garzoni in training would undergo a five-year apprenticeship, known as the *servitù*, before being hired in a glass factory. During this period, the garzoni was required to work full time. Moreover, during these five years, if his apprenticeship was interrupted for any reason (even if he transferred to another factory), he would lose credit for all of the time he accumulated as an apprentice. If he chose to re-enter the profession, he would be required to restart his servitù from the beginning.[iii]

The employment structure in the factories allowed room for advancement. Following the five-year apprenticeship, the garzoni would register as a legal *Garzonetti*. He worked in this capacity for another six years, with at least four of those dedicated to the activities imperative to the functions of a factory. Upon completion, he qualified to take the *Prova* (the Test). If he passed, he could rise to the level of a glass master.[iv]

In the 1700s, the Prova was a rite which was undertaken with the utmost solemnity. Chancellors, ministers, judges, and aristocratic delegates were present for the examination. The Prova would determine whether or not the aspiring glass master possessed complete mastery of the trade. Present during the Prova were friends of the candidate, relatives, work companions, and even enemies, each trying to influence the outcome of the test. In 1766, the Chief Magistrate imposed entrance only to candidates and Prova evaluators, which consisted of a representative of the Doge (the ruler of Venice), various governmental officials who oversaw the practices of the glass factories, two glass masters, and a few highly-trained workers of the factory. During the Prova, even the assistants in the factory were strictly forbidden to speak or communicate with the candidate by any means. Early on, it was not uncommon for judges to be offered bribes—such as prayers, money, and invitations to meals—to influence their decisions. Eventually, the bribes were deemed unethical and it was declared that they were to be eradicated.[v]

> IN THE EARLY 1900s, the SVC hired many boys and young adults to work in the factory. Times were tough, food was scarce, and many families lived in poverty, (yet the only robust person in this photograph is the boss/owner of the factory as seen on the right). Note the worker on the far right with the rope around his shoulder; this is evidence that he was employed as a *porta massa* (the porter/carrier of the mass quantities of glass). The rope was used to wrap around and hold each end of a wooden trunk as it was carried between two men to the various departments during the production of the conterie beads.

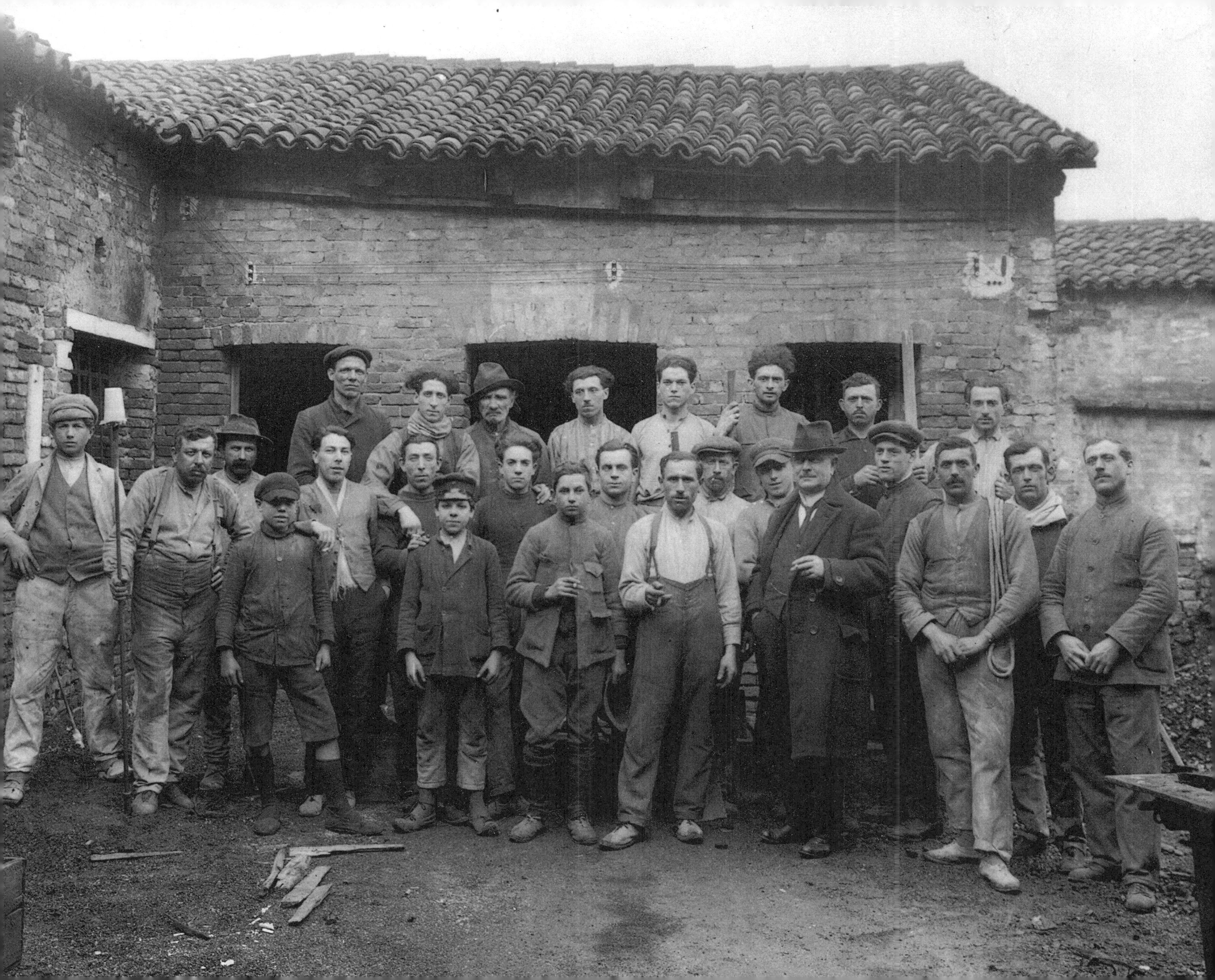

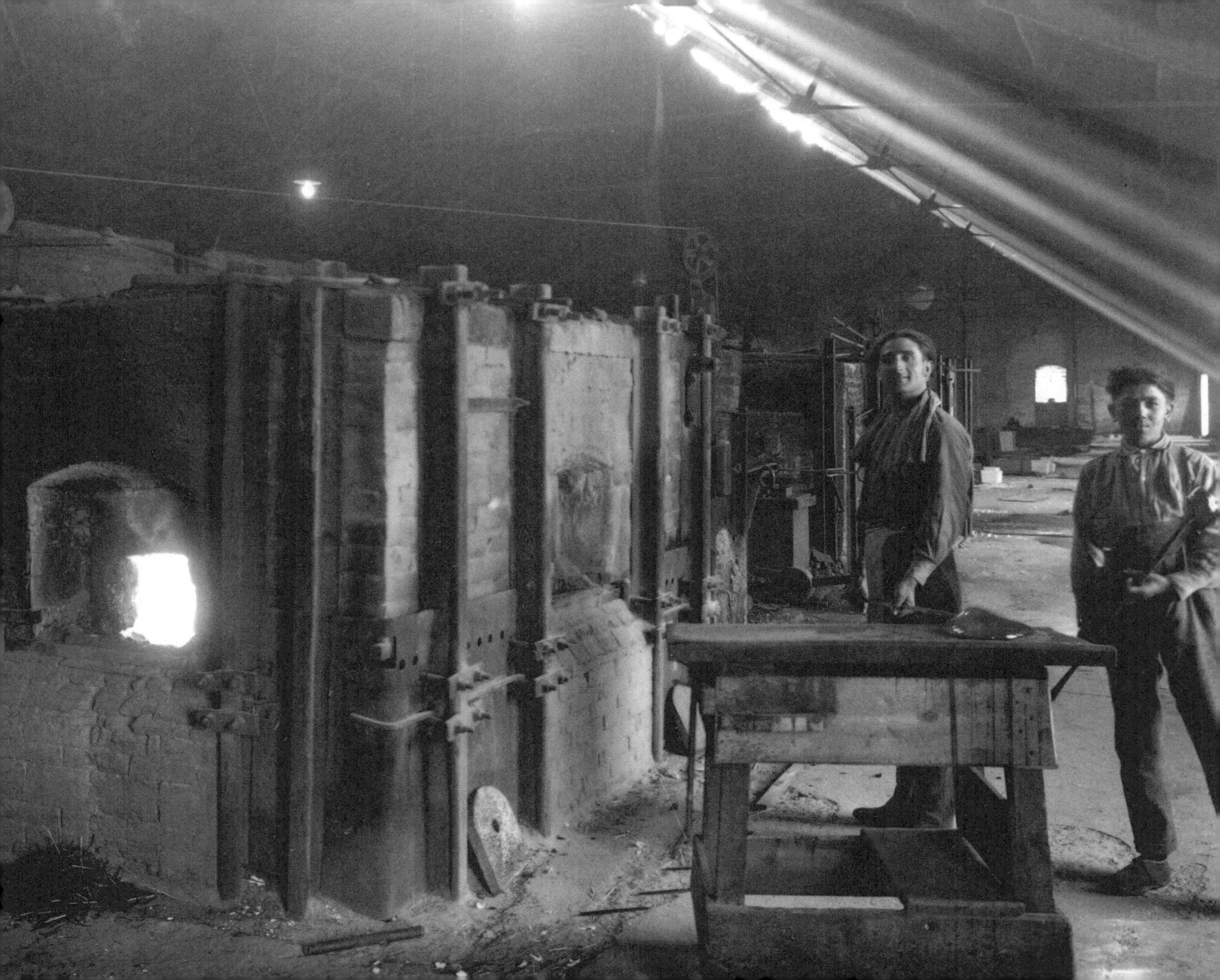

Within a factory, children worked full-time in numerous industrial occupations. In 1779, it was noted that there was an overwhelming presence of 1400 women and children working in Murano glass factories.[vi]

Murano glass historian and author, Vincenzo Zanetti, noted that in the 1800s, a ruling increased the age of admission for a garzoni from age ten to age thirteen. This allowed the garzoni to become educated in academics, Italian culture, and moral and religious principles which had been neglected in the former system.[vii]

The November 1876 edition of the *Giornale degli Economisti* newspaper included a report of women and children working in the manufacturing industries of Venice without legal guidelines, even though the factories enforced a separation of the sexes within each department. The article draws attention to the fact that many tasks in these industrial establishments were occupied exclusively by women and adolescents.

Women and children worked the day shift and had Sundays off, in addition to all the national and ecclesiastical holidays. Generally, the work shifts were from eight to twelve hours a day, allowing no time for studies.

< WITH THE EXCEPTION OF THE THE YOUNG APPEARANCE OF THESE TWO GLASSWORKERS and the introduction of methane gas, little has changed in the Murano glass factories over the past one hundred years. The ovens continue to be made of refractory bricks, the shape and size of the glory hole and door (laying on the ground) remain almost unaltered, the technique of extracting the molten glass using long steel blowpipes is still practiced, and the table (*il bronzino*), used for shaping the molten glass (as demonstrated by the glass master), remains an essential apparatus used every day in the Murano glass factories.

"Glass factories, the conterie industries, and other similar industries, always had a number of male children working, but these children occupied secondary operations that were not dangerous. Numerous women, however, were employed in operations that were complementary to the factory, such as the stringing of the beads at home by the Venetian impiraresse."[viii]

Following the unification of Italy, there was an increase in technology and industrialization. Prior protective restrictions regarding the employment of children were no longer observed; hiring them became especially desirable for economical and political reasons because children could be paid lower wages and were more submissive. In 1886, the first child labor law in Italy was established, which set the duration of the work day to "only" eight hours for children from ages nine to twelve, but in practice, this law was widely disregarded.

"In the glass industry, one of the unhealthiest environments, an increase in the percentage of its workforce comes from adolescents. The children are given jobs for which they are not qualified and must work under difficult conditions such as severe subordination—suppressing them from the more specialized workers—those who are strongly bound to the belief in a profession that has been handed down from generation to generation."[ix]

Finally, in 1902, after much uproar and two hundred fifty assemblies, the Socialist party proposed child labor laws which they presented to the Trade-Union Headquarters. They argued that the existing laws led to physically weaken women and children due to the excessive abuses in the workforce. Although the Socialists agreed that children working in the factories were useful and contributed financially to the poor families of Murano, they proposed laws limiting a workday to eight hours for children between the ages of twelve and fifteen, and eleven hours a day for children over the age of fifteen. They also proposed a twelve-hour day limit for women over the age of fifteen and a one to two-hour break for everyone, depending on the duration of the work schedule.

"Moreover, a weekly rest of 24 hours is mandatory for women and children under the age of fifteen. The socialists want to bring the minimum age limit of children to fifteen years old and to reduce the workday to a maximum of 11 hours instead of 12. Also, the maternity leave must be extended to eight weeks—four weeks before and four weeks after the delivery."[x]

Furthermore, the child labor laws mandated the prohibition of males under the age of fifteen from working in dangerous and unhealthy conditions and forbade them from nocturnal work.[1]

"Therefore, by reason of a careful consideration, it can be seen to reconcile the industrial interest with the protection from excessive and harmful exploitations to the health of women and children."[xi]

Moreover, a 1907 law stated,

"Women and children under fifteen years old must have a medical booklet which certifies they are healthy and capable of working for the job they are applying. This booklet must indicate the date of birth of the child and if they've been vaccinated. For children under the age of fifteen, the booklet must also indicate if they've attended elementary school and if they've passed their exams—except in the case of intellectual incompetence where a certificate from the school is required."[xii]

1 | Nocturnal work is considered from 8 p.m. until 5 a.m. from October 1st through March, and from 9 p.m. until 5 a.m. during the other months.

Requests for Child Work Permits in 1925

"The child, Iolanda Giusto (daughter of Giulio), born in Murano on July 3, 1912, must be considered for the work permit. In fact, having a father who abandoned the family, she could not complete her elementary studies due to economic reasons as well as have to share the caregiving of her younger siblings. Presently, the support of the family (composed of seven persons) is provided by the sister of the above mentioned, who is only fifteen years old and whose occupation is cutting cane for the Società Veneziana per l'Industria delle Conterie. It should be taken into consideration that her income is not continuous because the work in the factory is not continuous and the pay for a worker her age is limited."[xiv]

"A booklet for permission to work is requested for Inda Pustetto (daughter of Eliodoro) born in Murano on May 9, 1912. The aforementioned child obtained a promotion in the academic year 1920-1921 with votes 50/80. After 1921, she no longer attended school due to illness and needs of the family. The conditions of the Pustetto family are very poor and it should be added that there are six siblings, the oldest, who is just fourteen years old, and the smallest one is just four. It should not be forgotten the difficulties the family presents, with many shortages and illnesses. Attached is a medical certificate for the aforementioned requesting that Pustetto is able to receive a work permit."[xv]

"Guido Vianello (son of Giulio) obtained a promotion up to the fifth grade and is the son of a very-invalid of war and can no longer attend school due to the conditions of the family. Angelo Ragazzi (son of Gabriele) obtained the promotion of the third grade in July of 1923 and after such date has no longer attended elementary school due to a malaria infection as seen from the enclosed medical certificate. He is from a poor family. Algerio Pizan (son of Giuliano) attended four years in the first grade without obtaining a promotion. He comes from a numerous family of very poor conditions. In view of the above cases, it is requested that the three children are given permission to obtain a booklet for the permission to work."[xvi]

By the early 1920s, exceptions to the law opened the door for many families to request work permits for their children. To receive a work booklet, it was necessary for a family to prove the following two conditions:

1. A greater workforce—where there must be no doubt the child must abandon his studies because the family's finances do not allow him to attend school or for other exceptional and serious circumstances of character, or;
2. Extreme poverty—of which it is absolutely necessary to give an occupation to a minor in order to put him in a position to satisfy the most elementary requirements of life.[xiii]

At the glass factories, workers were only hired during periods of high customer demand. As such, it wasn't unusual for a factory to operate for three months and then be closed for the next three months. Faced with the daily threat of losing one's job, father and son would seek jobs at opposing factories to cover any subsequent unemployment. In the event that the father or son lost his job, at least one would remain employed to maintain a steady flow of income to support the family. In cases when the father was a Glass Master, his son could work in the same factory since a Glass Master rarely lost his job and if he did, he would be quickly hired at another factory.

"In the early 50s it was easy to find work in the factories," explains Muranese Iginio Costantini. Born in 1939, Costantini began to work full time at the age of twelve. *"I was twelve years old at the time, but there were kids working in the factories at the ages of eight, nine and ten. We were all working illegally because you had to be at least fourteen years old to work and in possession of a work booklet. Many kids came from Burano looking for work. Most of us came from poor, needy families.*

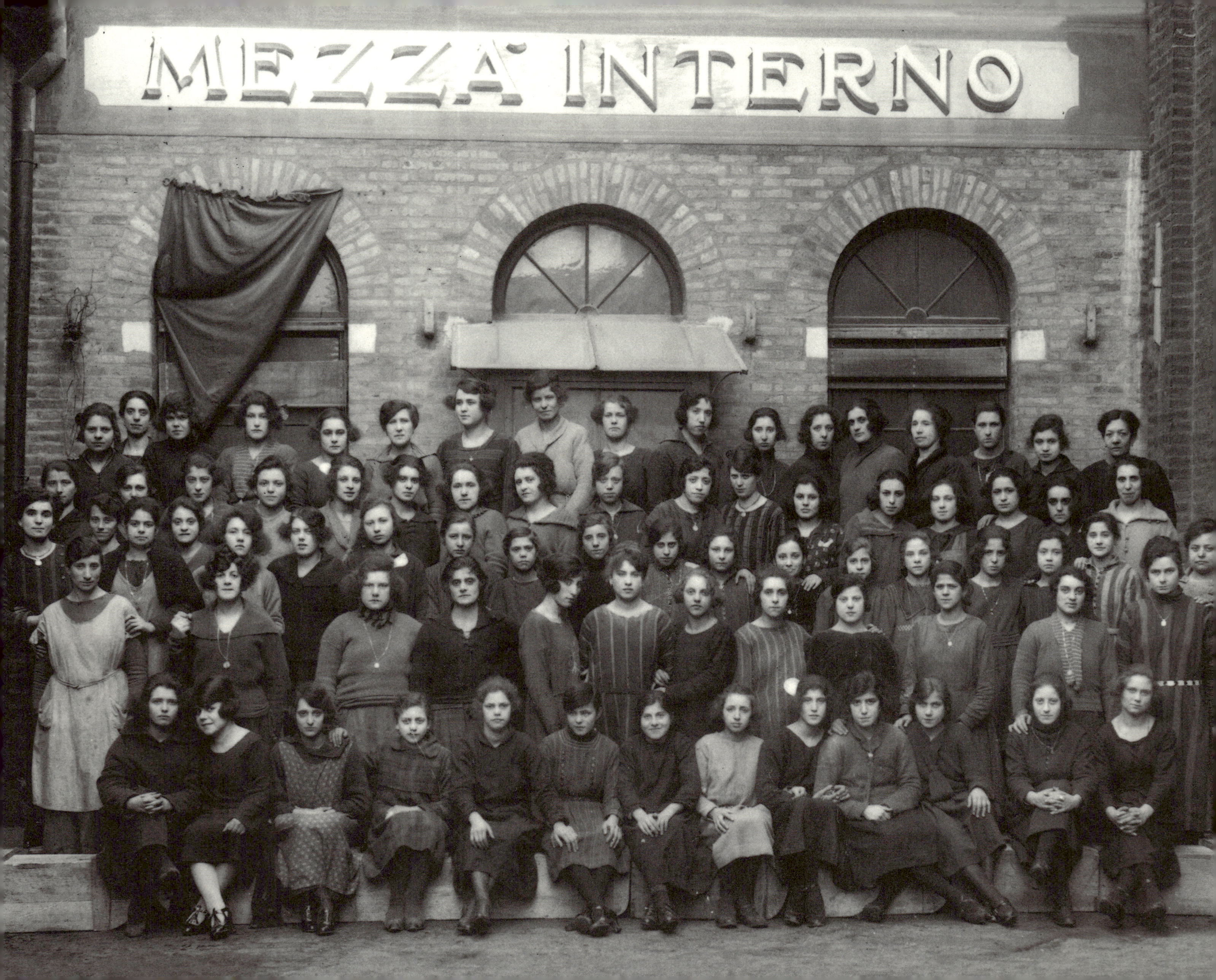
MEZZA' INTERNO

We would stand outside a factory and wait for the owner to call us in. We'd move from factory to factory looking for work. Most of the factories were small, so if a crucible cracked, we'd have to wait for days before it got replaced and production could continue. So we'd go from factory to factory waiting outside until someone would hire us for the day."

Costantini was a typical garzoni. He worked up to forty-eight hours a week, including Sundays. *"All of my pay, which was a misery, went to my mother. I never saw a dime except for the days I worked on Sunday. This was called the 'mesata' in Venetian dialect. We could buy whatever we wanted with that money—toys, candy. We would work on Sundays from 7 a.m. to 1 p.m. We had only a half of day each week for free time."*

"I went to work in the factory at age eleven," recounted Franco Mian (now deceased), born in Murano in 1946. *"There was so much misery at that time . . . I'd say 95 percent of my classmates were working in the factories. If you needed money, you had to work in the factory. There were kids younger than me working. We were all illegal and when word got out that an inspector was going from factory to factory to catch children, we would escape or hide. We hid in the straw, under boxes, behind supplies. If we got caught, we'd get fired and the factory owner would get a fine. At that time, I worked sixteen hours a day because I found two jobs in the factory—one during the day and one during the night. No one stayed at home. You had to go out and work. Hundreds and hundreds of workers arrived each day, every forty minutes, on the ferry boat from Burano.*[2] *We called them the 'Children of Attila.'*[3] *We all worked as often as we could because we were very poor. And all of my pay went to my mother . . . every penny of it up to three months before I got married. I was proud to work and bring home the money."*

2 | According to the personal research of Muranese Vittorio Visam, born in 1932, there were 1,800 Buranelli arriving to Murano each day looking for work.

3 | Mian jokes about calling the kids from Burano, the 'Children of Attila' because near Burano is the island of Torcello where legend has it that Attila the Hun once lived there.

< HUNDREDS OF WOMEN AND YOUNG GIRLS were hired to work at the SVC (not all are present in this photograph). Looking closely, many of these girls could possibly be sisters. The arched windows were designed specifically to allow natural lighting in the factory.

The rapport between the owner of the furnace, the glass masters, and the subordinate workers had always been one based on great respect. In fact, there were written rules based on this relationship where the glass master (*scagneri*) and the serventi must give "total obedience" to the boss of the factory (*Capo Fornace*).[xvii]

"We were obedient children," recounts Costantini. *"We were more mature than the kids today. We worked closely with adults and we were serious, disciplined, and had great respect for our elders."*

Muranese Sereno Serena, born in 1930, recalls the attitude and respect the children had for their superiors in the glass factory. When faced with an angry glass master, *"We would bow our heads in complete obedience and humility. We would never talk back."*

"There were nice Masters and there were mean Masters. The mean ones would slap you around or burn you with a hot poker," explained Mian. Costantini agrees. *"A good crack on the head was what happened to us if we ever got out of line. We were always on our best behavior."*

Children continued to work in the glass factories until the 1960s. Even today many accomplished glass masters will attest that they began working in the sweltering furnaces at a very young age. Economic crises, wars, and poverty all contributed to the need for manual labor, even if it meant a child had to forgo his or her education for the greater benefit of the family.

Murano glass factories no longer hire children, nor are the workers required to take a test to prove their mastery in the trade. During the summer months, the workers' hours are reduced due to the heat in the furnace. Most Murano glass factories are closed during the month of August; during this period, the ovens are turned off and the factory undergoes a general maintenance and cleaning.

i Il Capitolare dell'Arte Vetraria Muranese of 1766 cited in *Mille Anni di Lavoro e di Lotte dei Vetrai di Murano e Venezia—un Popolo di Verieri,* A cura del Sindacato Vetrai di Murano FILCEA/CGIL, Venezia, 1982, page 29.

ii Ibid.

iii Ibid.

iv Ibid.

v Giuseppe Morazzoni, *Le Conterie Veneziana,* Società Veneziana Conterie e Cristallerie, Venezia, 1953, page 11; and A. Pancotto, *La condizione dei Garzoni a Venezia dalla fine del sec. XVI alla fine del sec. XVII,* 1945-46.

vi Cecchetti Bartoloemo, Vincenzo Zanetti and E. Sanfermo., *Monografia della Vetraria Veneziana e Muranese,* Venezia, 1874 cited in *Mille Anni di Lavoro e di Lotte dei Vetrai di Murano e Venezia—un Popolo di Verieri,* A cura del Sindacato Vetrai di Murano FILCEA/CGIL, Venezia, 1982, page 30.

vii Vincenzo Zanetti, *Guido di Murano e delle Celebri Sue Fornaci,* 1866, page 224.

viii G. Tonolo, *Giornale degli Economisti,* November, Padova, 1876 cited in *Mille Anni di Lavoro e di Lotte dei Vetrai di Murano e Venezia—un Popolo di Verieri,* A cura del Sindacato Vetrai di Murano FILCEA/CGIL, Venezia, 1982, page 30.

ix L. Dalle Nogare e L. Finocchi, Nascere, *Sopravivere e Crescere nella Lombardia dell'800,* Milano, 1981, page 159 cited in *Mille Anni di Lavoro e di Lotte dei Vetrai di Murano e Venezia—un Popolo di Verieri,* A cura del Sindacato Vetrai di Murano FILCEA/CGIL, Venezia, 1982, pp. 30-31.

x Ibid.

xi *Gazzetta di Venezia,* Marzo 22, 1902.

xii Archivio del Stato Celeste, Busta N. 310 , del 1912-1921.

xiii Estratto da bollettino N. 14 Atti Ufficio della R. Prefettura di Venezia, 6 Aprile, 1924, from Ispettorato dell'Industria e Del Lavoro.

xiv Archivio del Stato Celeste, 5 January 1925.

xv Ibid.3 June 1925.

xvi Ibid. N. 2958, 21 September 1925.

xvii Ibid. Busta N. 310 from 1912-1921.

Humility is not cowardice. Meekness is not weakness.
Humility and meekness are indeed spiritual powers.

SWAMI SIVANANDA

Indian philosopher

(1887–1963)

The Venetian Impiraressa

The word *impiraressa* (or plural, *impiraresse*) is derived from the Venetian dialect *piron* and the ancient Greek word *peiron*, meaning to string or to thread.

The occupation of an *impiraressa* was to string loose beads onto threads. Once strung, the flowing appearance of the beads became more attractive than if they were left unbound in a crate. Stringing the beads also helped to identify the broken beads, the defective beads such as those without a hole (*perle orbe*, meaning "blind beads"), and the *storte* (distorted or irregular), as well as to eliminate the dust which was sometimes found in and around the beads.[i]

The beads would be delivered directly to the home or storage space of the *mistra/maestra* by means of a transport boat, the *Peata*, which was used exclusively in the Venetian laguna.[1] The *mistra* (or plural, *mistre*), was the intermediary between the impiraressa and the factory. The mistra was responsible for dividing the beads amongst the impiraresse according to the work assignments given by the factory. Just as the impiraressa was responsible for the quantity and quality of her work, the mistra was responsible for the all the assignments given to her by the factory, sometimes facing criticism and scrutiny. As such, the mistra had to manage the inventory of beads, commission the work, distribute the necessary threads that corresponded to the assignments, and trust the impiraressa would string the beads properly and return the finished product by a pre-determined date.

The beads had to be strung according to the specifications of the factory. The long strands measured approximately forty-two centimeters, and the short strands measured thirty-two

1| The *Peata*, also known as the *Piatta* (meaning "flat") was the major cargo boat used in the canals of Venice for centuries. It was used mostly for transporting construction materials such as stone, bricks, columns, and wood pilings. It was designed with a flat bottom to transport the maximum capacity of cargo, as well as optimize

(Continued...)

the navigation when the tides were low. The Peata, made of oak wood, was constructed in the shipyards on the island of Burano and could be made in various dimensions, carrying a burden of 1,000 to 12,000 kilos. Typically, the Peata was 15 meters long and 3.4 meters wide. It was navigated by two men, the *peatèri,* who either rowed (when the tides permitted) or punted with long, heavy ores into the shallow and muddy waters. The Peata was cleverly designed with wide foot ways along the sides (the *'nerve'*) enabling the peatèri to punt at the bow of the boat, push downwards, and walk forward as the boat advanced. The method of punting, pushing, and walking forward was called, *'paràndo'* and gave the peatèri the power and momentum to advance the boat. No longer constructed, the historical Peata is a true symbol of the master shipbuilders of the Venetian Lagoon. Models of it can be found at the Museo Storico Navale in Venice. (*Http://www.vogaveneta.altervista.org*)

> THE PEATA Transport Boat.

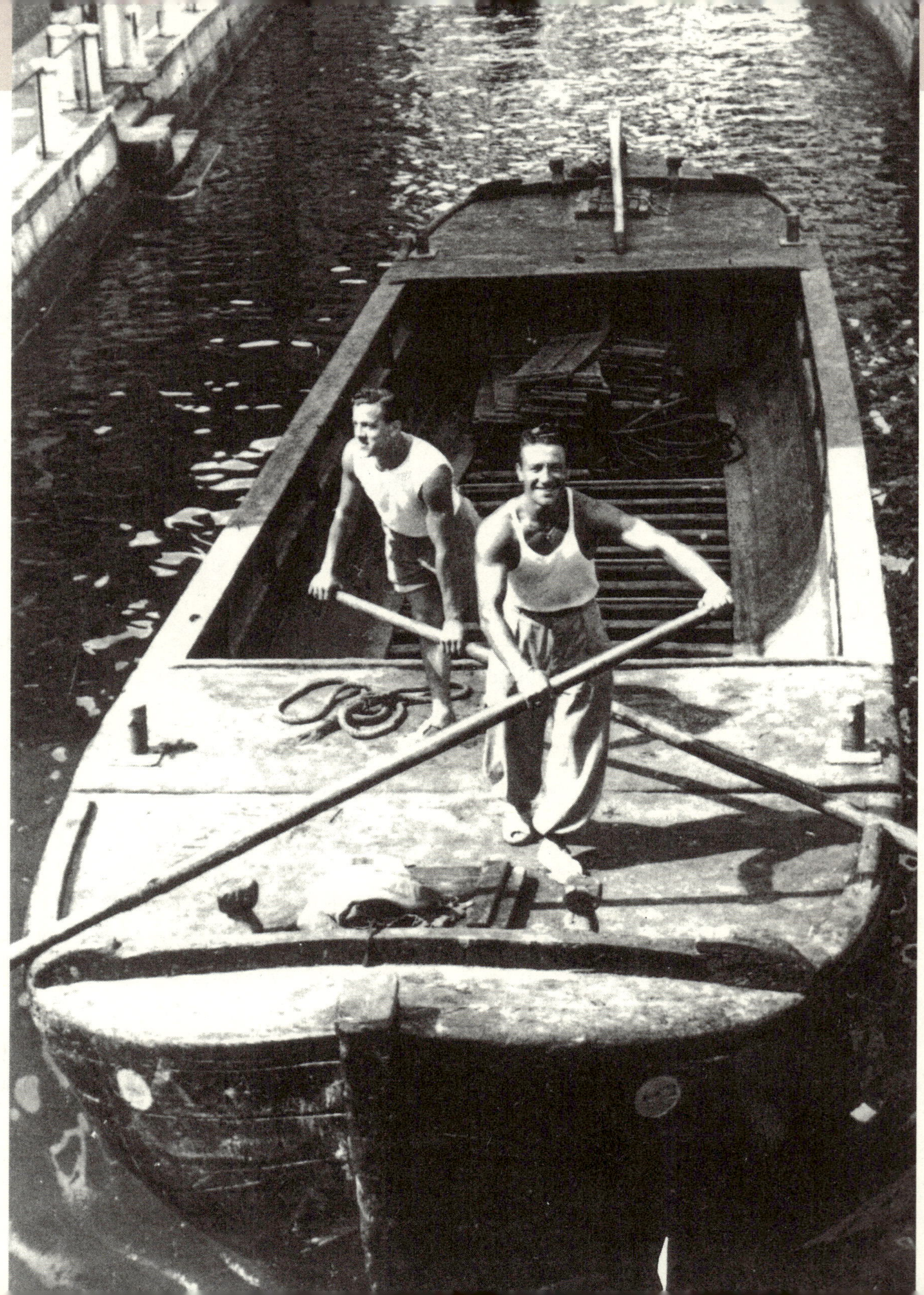

PHOTO COURTESY OF STEFANO DA VILLA

centimeters. A *colana,* for example, consisted of five strands of beads. A *mazzo* consisted of four *colane,* and a *mazzo intiero* consisted of two hundred forty strands. A *giardineto* (a little garden) was made up of multi-colored strands.[ii]

The job of the impiraressa didn't demand much concentration or intelligence, but it did require much patience, endurance, energy, and good eyesight. She was paid "under the table" while her mistra was a registered employee of the factory, thereby receiving pension benefits and a salary. The mistra also received a percentage for every mazzo made by the impiraressa. On account of this disparity, there was little harmony between the impiraresse and their mistre. The mistre also hosted workshops where they taught bead stringing and paid their students while they learned.

The impiraressa needed very few tools to work. She needed the hair-thin needles (approximately eighteen centimeters long and, at times, less than ½ mm gauge), an envelope to store the needles, and silk (*sedète*) and linen (*assète*) threads.[iii] The chair that she used would sometimes have its back legs cut shorter than the front, giving her knees a lift, thus allowing her more control and balance of the *sessola.* The *sessola,* which rested on her lap, was a wooden, oblong, concave receptacle used to contain the beads. During the colder months, the impiraressa would put a heater (*scaldino*) under her chair to keep warm. The scaldino was made of terracotta and could burn a few pieces of coal. The scaldino was also the culprit of many jokes because it wasn't uncommon for the long skirts and aprons of the impiraressa to catch on fire, sending the poor Venetian woman jumping and shouting in the air.

It was profitable for the impiraressa to become more skilled in handling more needles. The most skillful impiraresse could handle up to forty to sixty needles in one hand. The more assignments she could complete, the more money she would earn. The impiraressa was not paid at the moment of consignment, but instead would have to wait for every three or four consignments before being paid. When the impiraressa was finished with her assignments, she would deliver the strung beads (and any remaining beads) to the mistra, who would then weigh the beads for accuracy and check for any loss, inspect the work, and record the completed assignments for future payment.

The impiraresse were tireless, meek, unassuming figures, located mostly in the residential Venetian districts of Castello and Cannaregio. The impiraresse from Castello specialized in stringing the smallest beads while the impiraresse from the Cannaregio district specialized in stringing the larger beads, in addition to weaving fringes on a loom, stringing flowers onto metal wires, designing jewelry, and making lampwork beads. In the late 1800s, there were more than two thousand impiraresse and most were working in Castello. Needless to say, it is impossible to know exactly how many impiraresse were working because their employment was never officially documented.[iv]

However monotonous the occupation of an impiraressa, she required stamina to sit for long hours, in addition to stable hand/eye coordination. To begin her work, dozens of needles needed to be strung, arguably the most tedious and aggravating part of the job. She would then place numerous needles onto her first three fingers, and then snap her fingers, forming a fan (*ventaglio* or *palmeta*) of needles. While holding the needles tightly in one hand, she would immerse them swiftly and repeatedly into the wooden sessola so that the beads would fall rapidly onto the flexible needles. The other hand would assist in guiding the beads onto the needles by lightly pushing them towards the needles. The beads would then slide down the needles and onto the threads.[v]

> ON THE FAR RIGHT ARE TWO VENETIAN WOMEN (*Impiraresse*) stringing beads on the street Calle Sarasina, located in the lower district of Castello. In the center of the street, with its doors open, is a typical *capitelli* (shrine/temple). The capitelli are religious expressions of Chrisitan art and devotion, decorated with images and/or statues of Jesus Christ, the Blessed Mother, saints, angels, flowers, candles, picture frames of lost loved ones, lace tablecloths, and so on. They are used for prayers, reciting the rosary, remembering the dead, or for giving thanks for the end of the plague or an epidemic. Numerous capitelli can be found all over Venice. They are reminders of God's presence. (Circa 1894–1897.)

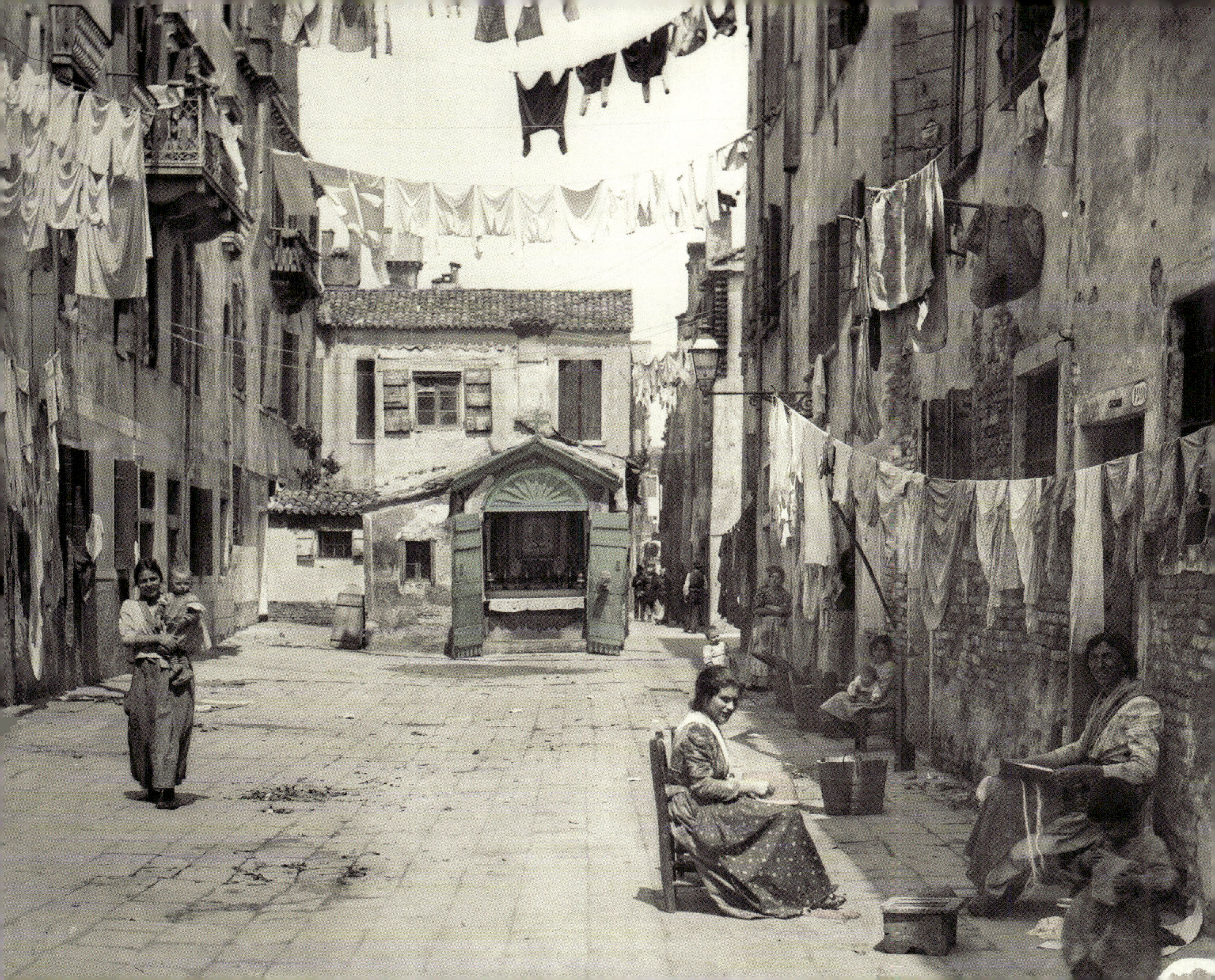

The impiraressa was responsible for returning the same weight of beads that were given to her by the mistra; heaven forbid she should lose some beads on the ground due to clumsiness or a mishap with the children or pets playing around her. Often times she would place an old sheet under her chair to catch any fallen beads and/or set apart the defective beads such as the *storte* (irregular), the *strete* (too narrow of a hole), the *fondi* (chipped), the *orbe* (no hole), the *spolvero* (dirty) or the *buratini* (the bead of a different color).

If interrupted by household chores or family, her momentum and productivity would suffer. In effect, the children of the impiraresse became responsible for many household chores and errands. The children assisted with the shopping, preparing foods, caring for the grandparents and younger siblings, hanging the clothes out to dry, and so forth. Ultimately, as the impiraressa strongly held together her needles, it could be said that she also held together her family and provided an income, however meager.

Many of the impiraresse agree that they were overworked and underpaid, but they also agree that they were given a chance to earn an income. Many of them lived in miserable conditions and any money they could earn, while staying at home, was better than starving. Commonly, this was the only work for which an impiraressa could be qualified.

"Since 1902 she [the impiraressa] literally never moved from her streets. She was a healthy bride with many children but was occupied with the management of the house, supporting her husband (a cheerful liar and almost permanently unemployed mason), his father, the scheming and moody mother-in-law, and the children that came in with hunger like a wolf. She had organized in the shed of the house a rudimentary laboratory of conterie and beads from Murano. Her production paid very little lira from the wholesalers but sufficient enough to put on a pot of soup every day and feast two times a week on bisato [a serpentine fish] or cuttlefish with

polenta." (Ugo Facco Delgarda, *Morte dell'impirarperle,* 1917, page 346.)

It is unclear how much money the impiraresse actually earned. Some say they earned one lire per day (less than a penny) working from dawn to dusk. Others claim they earned forty to sixty cents per day. In any case, despite the fact that the extra income provided an occasional movie or fish soup, at any time in history, the impiraresse have described their wage as a *"paga miseria"* (miserable pay).[vi]

In the early 1900s, author Ugo Ojetti described an area in Castello where outside every door there existed *"five or six impiraresse sitting in a circle stringing beads—the wooden sessola resting on their knees was filled to the brim with beads that seemed like a treasure. Every street had its color and the housewives would socialize while taking the beads from the factory. One street sparkled of diamonds, one shimmered of rubies, and another was all sapphires."*[vii]

The impiraressa's good fortune was being born in Venice, a city arranged around small squares, with serpentine canals that enveloped the narrow streets. The close proximity of the housing in Venice was ideal for the impiraressa, allowing her to sit in front of her house, or in a square, and work endless hours alongside the neighboring women. Aunts, uncles, cousins and in-laws generally lived nearby or even resided in the same house, sharing their resources and lending a helping hand. In order to collect the beads, the impiraressa did not have to travel far, or pay for public transportation; all she needed to do was walk to the storage shed of the mistra, pick up five or ten kilos of beads, and then walk home. The children could be left unattended to play in the streets or the squares.

Perhaps the only disadvantages of working in a city such as Venice were the dark and humid streets. Nevertheless, Venice, a socially colloquial city, proved to be the perfect birthplace for the impiraressa. The impiraressa was able to enjoy the company of other women, stay at home, earn a small wage, and continue her duties as wife, mother, and caregiver.

The impiraresse were also fortunate to be given the chance to work during a period in history when glass beads were shipped to all nations around the world. Millions of glass beads have passed through the hands of the impiraressa. Although her job was low-paying, her contribution to the SVC and the history of beads cannot be underestimated or overlooked. Over time, the role of an impiraressa became a recognized symbol in the streets of Venice. In the late 19th century, her work was appreciated by many and her character admired as noble.[viii]

The impiraressa gave the final touch and beauty to the conterie beads. Using fine, flexible needles and threads, the impiraressa transformed lifeless beads into strands of pendulous gems. Observing their beauty, the strands would appear as sparkling diamonds or rubies as she would dangle them before her eyes. It is easy to imagine how one could weaken under the spell of such beauty, the cascading jewels of the laguna.

The impiraressa needed the beads to survive and support her family, but in retrospect, also the bead factories needed the impiraressa to complete the full circle of the conterie production. Beads are designed to be strung and the impiraressa was a testament to this design. Without the conterie beads, Venice would have never witnessed the unique occupation, figure, and contribution of the impiraressa.

Ilde Torcellan was born and raised in Murano in the year 1913. At age nine, she began to work as an impiraressa. In 2007 she died at age ninety-four. When interviewed, despite her advanced age, she was healthy, hospitable, and bright. She remembered the days when there was little food on the table, when the men in the family were without work, and when families and relatives all lived in the same house. She recounted her story as an impiraressa with clarity and affection:

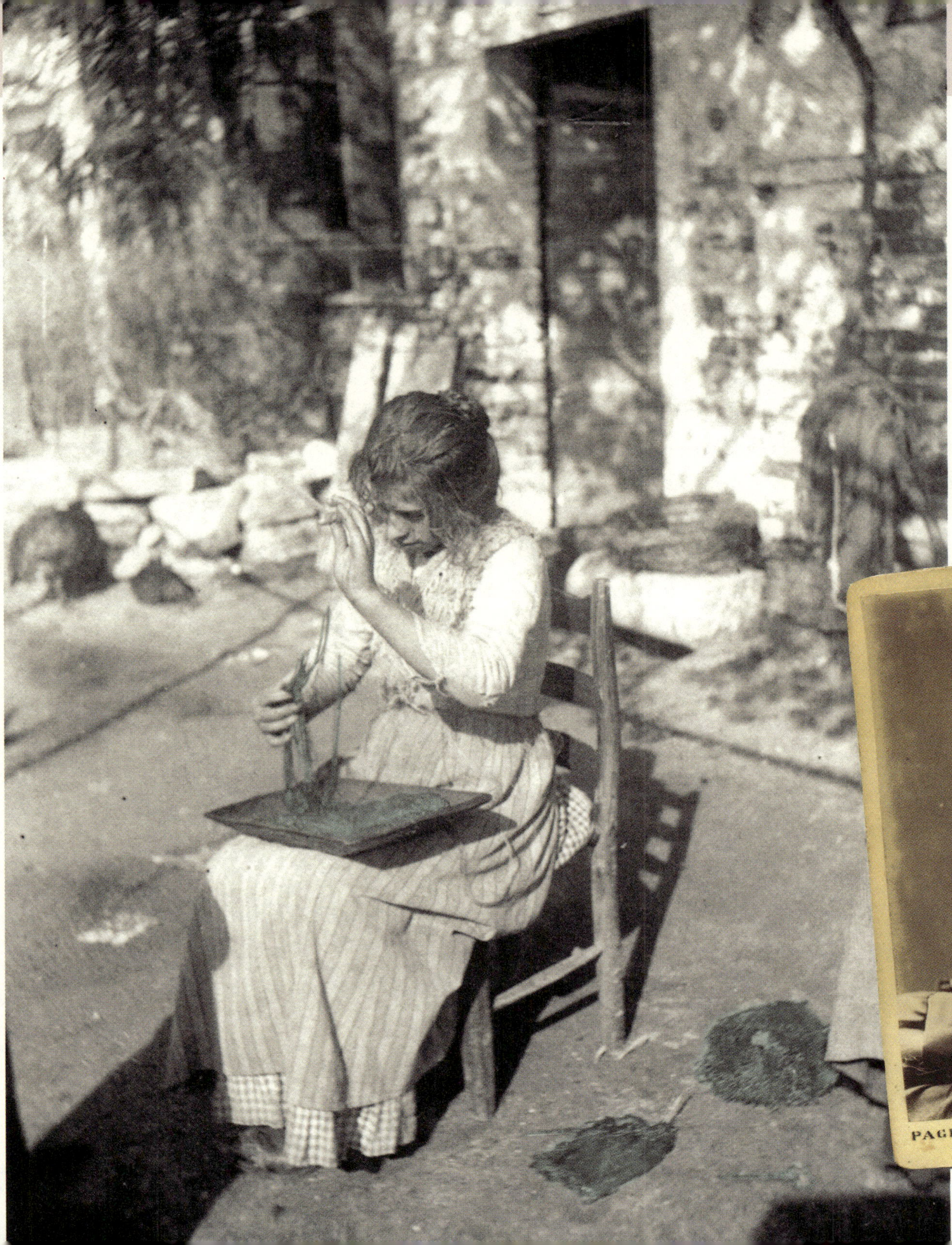

< A YOUNG IMPIRARESSA sits outside on a sunny day "working the sessola," stringing conterie beads. Several hanks of beads and her scissors are located on the ground. Circa 1895–1914.

V PORTRAIT OF LUBA circa 1874, illustrates the usage of conteire beads as a fashion adornment during this era.

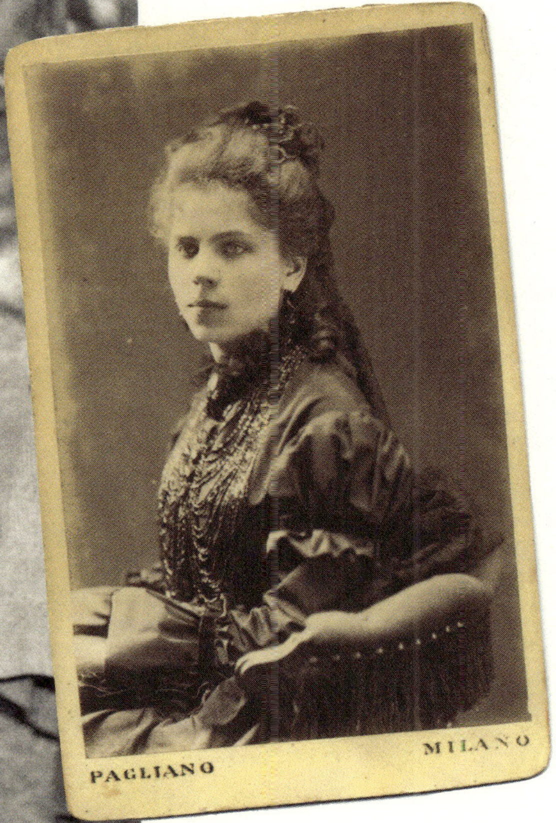

"The youth today, none of them has learned to do this work. Not in my case. I was born into it. My parents always told me, 'Get some needles! Get the sessola! Learn! Learn!' and that's how I started. There was me, my mother, my grandmother, other relatives...we all worked."

Although the work was tiring, Signora Torcellan enjoyed her days as an impiraressa where she could sit outdoors in front of her house and socialize with friends. After several years of experience, she was capable of handling sixty to eighty needles.

"The older women had more experience so they could handle more needles," she explained. *"I was able to string with eighty needles in one hand. But, oh Maria Vergine, how many hours I worked each day! We sat for many hours each day which caused back aches. Even today my knees ache from having a sessola full of beads on my lap."*

"I would earn five lira [a few cents] for twenty masse [strands]. We were all so poor. Many people couldn't find work. My husband would work for one month and then be off for the next three. I would stay at home, string beads and take care of the children. Sometimes if there was a big order I'd be up with my family until midnight stringing beads. Then we'd wake up at five o'clock in the morning and start all over again. Oh, San Benedetto, it's a miracle I'm still here. The kids today could never do what we did."

Loss of eyesight is a common lament and consequence for the impiraressa. The hair-thin needles had to be strung, yet the eyes of these needles were so microscopic they were nearly invisible to see. The impiraressa had to strain her eyes in order to pass the thread through the microscopic eye of the needle. She devised clever ways to thread the needles, but regardless, stringing the needles was a tedious task in itself.

"I used to thread all the needles for my parents and grandparents," continued Signora Torcellan. *"The poor souls eventually lost their eyesight and could no longer see the eye of the needle. I was younger and could do it for them. Today I can hardly see. I'm half-blind. This is what happens when you string beads."*

Whenever there was a demand for their services, the impiraresse wouldn't hesitate to work. They were very poor and there was never a guarantee they would have another chance to work. The factories closed during the summer, weakening the demand for the services of the impiraresse. Notwithstanding, Signora Torcellan quips that during the summer with no work,

"I would never create a purse or a necklace because I was so sick and tired of seeing all the beads."

Signora Laviana Ventura, born in 1929, was the owner of a warehouse and laboratory that the SVC once used for its beads and beadmaking. Her experience working as a mistra helped launch her own bead business in the late 1950s. By the 1960s, her company was manufacturing and exporting thousands of Venetian glass beads to the United States of America.

"The impiraresse were not women who were employed in businesses outside of the home. They were the poorest of the Venetians and, consequently, the less educated. They lived in miserable conditions. The more miserable the area, the more likely to find an impiraressa. There were very few gentlemen in those days and you would never find an impiraressa near San Marco's Square."

"The beads from the SVC were transported in wooden crates by boat and it would take the men a few hours to get from Murano to Castello. For an impiraressa to make the trip to Murano to get the beads would be as if she were to take a voyage across the sea. It never happened."

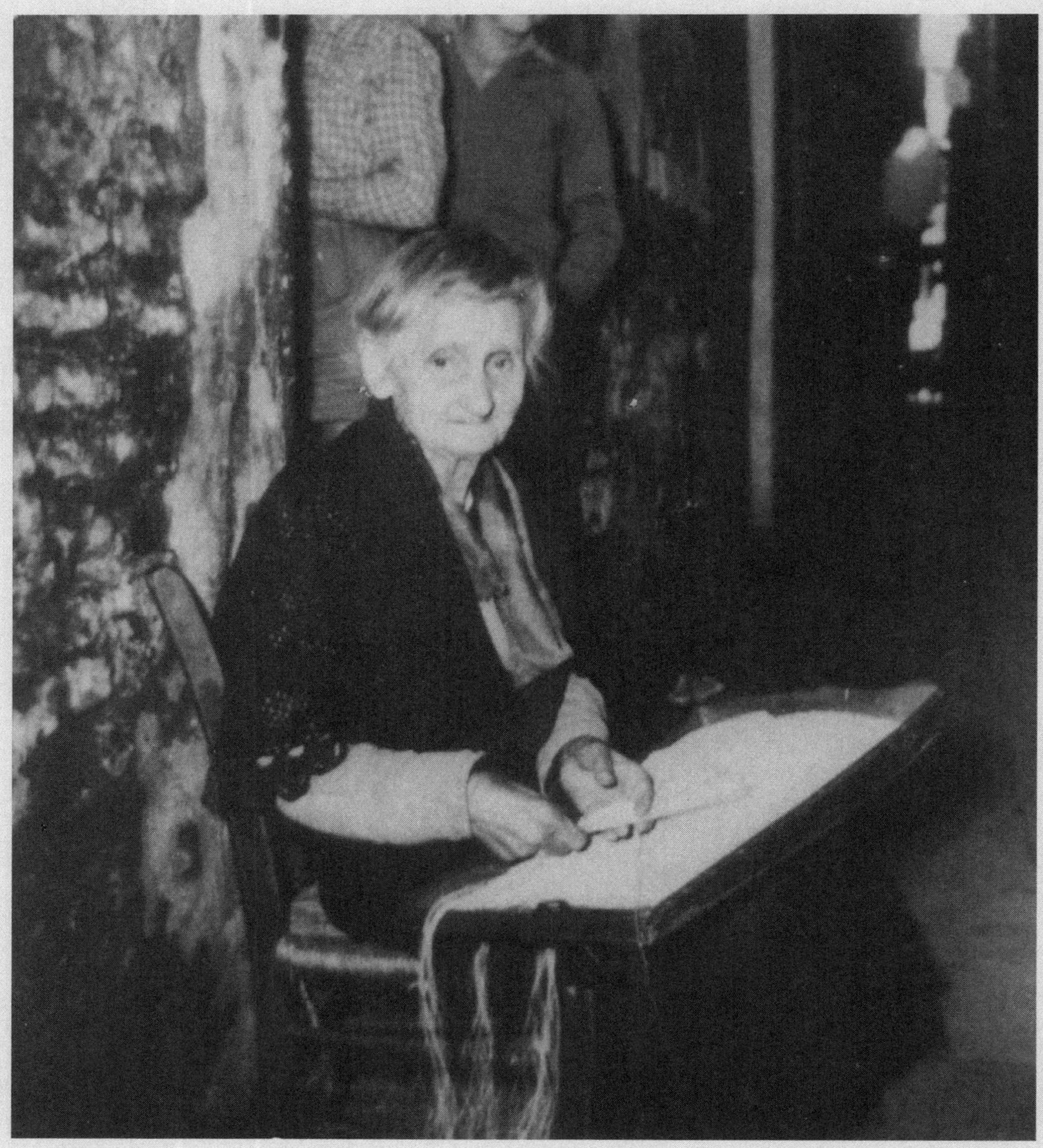

PHOTO COURTESY OF THE DANIOTTO FAMILY

—*La Signora Impiraressa*—

Sitting in front of her house, situated on a long, dark, humid street (calle) in lower Castello, the impiraressa, Signora Amelia Buranella, probably would have considered herself lucky to have lived past the age of forty. Born in 1873, Amelia began working as an impiraressa at a very young age and continued to do so until her death at age ninety-five. She survived infant mortality, two world wars, numerous epidemics, and was age fifty-five before the discovery of antibiotics. Like many Venetians during her era, Amelia lived without electricity, indoor plumbing, and gave birth (at home) without anesthesia. Raised on a poor man's diet of polenta and beans, Amelia spent her lifetime—nearly a century—stringing countless conterie beads.

Although she earned very little, Amelia was able to work at home and raise four healthy children. Her great-grandchildren remember her well. She began stringing the beads at sunrise and would end at sunset. During the winter months, she would place a small coal-burning crock (*lo scaldino*) under her chair to keep her warm. She was a kind and witty woman, enjoyed her work, and would cleverly challenge her children to a game of "Who Can String the Needle First?"

Amelia was a typical impiraressa. The wooden sessola filled with conterie beads, her wool shawl, and the hair-thin needles in the palm of her hand with the long threads were all characteristics of the Venetian impiraressa. Amelia died of natural causes in 1968, leaving behind eighty-five years of experience as an impiraressa.

NOBODY GROWS OLD MERELY BY LIVING A NUMBER OF YEARS. WE GROW OLD BY DESERTING OUR IDEALS. YEARS MAY WRINKLE THE SKIN, BUT TO GIVE UP ENTHUSIASM WRINKLES THE SOUL.

SAMUEL ULLMAN
American businessman, poet
(1840-1924)

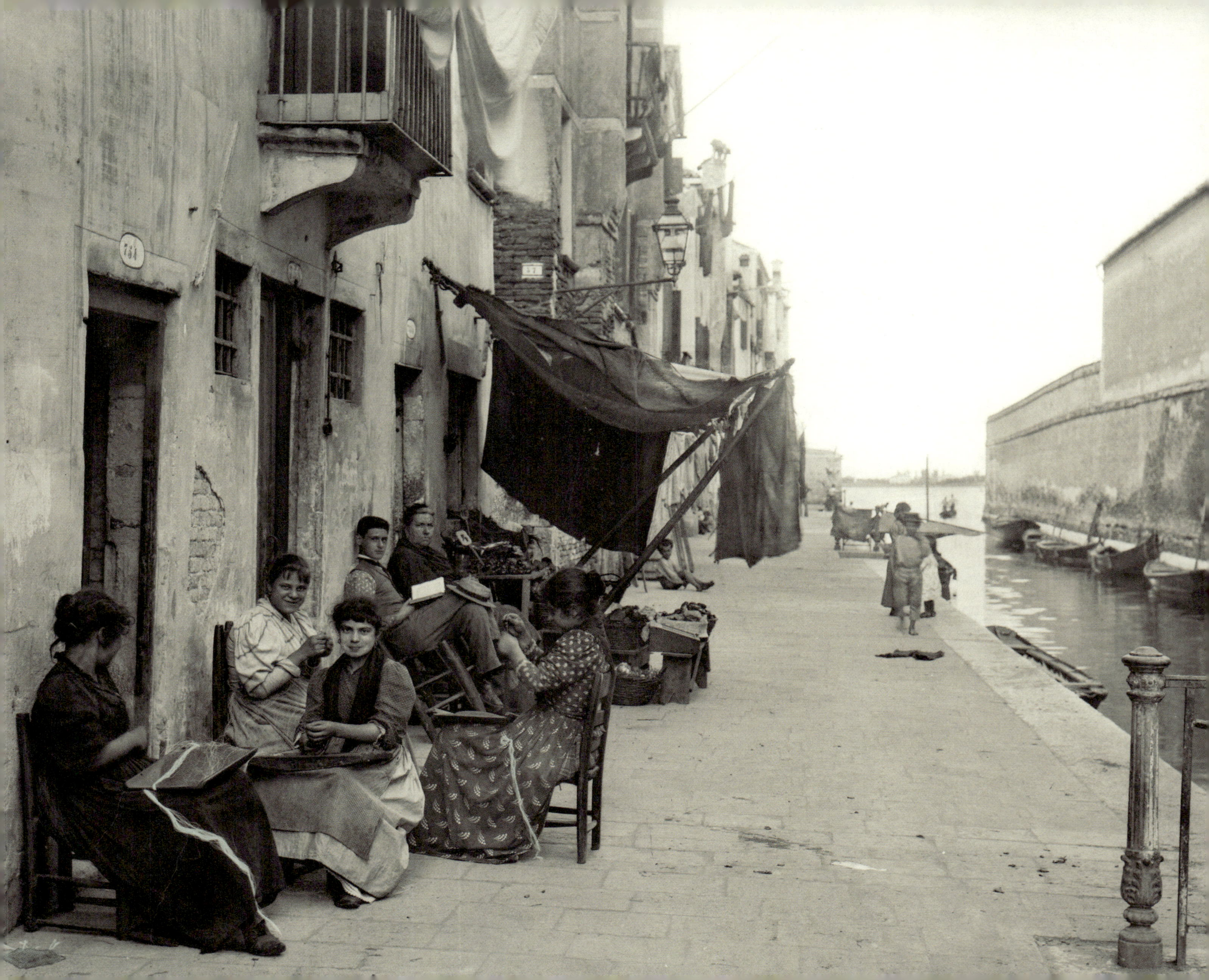

In the book, Morte dell'impirarperle, (Death of an Impiraressa), author Ugo Delgarda speaks of an impiraressa who *"never put a foot on the mainland, never boarded a train, never saw a live horse or cow, and who never even saw the new bell tower of Saint Mark, inaugurated in 1912."* [ix]

Signora Ventura affirms, *"The impiraresse were so poor that they lived and died in the same neighborhood. They never moved. They never went far from home. Some never even went over a bridge. The reign of the impiraressa was right here, in lower Castello."*

Madame de Stael, French novelist, describes Venice very poetically in the early 1800s: *"The silence is profound in this city where the streets are canals and where the sounds of rowing is the only interruption of the silence. It is not in the country because one does not even see a tree; nor is it a city because one does not hear any movements; nor is it even a ship because it does not advance: it is a place where storms make it a prison in which at certain moments one cannot go out of the city nor out of the house. This is Venice, where the common people have never gone from one district to another, who do not know Saint Mark's square, and for whom seeing a horse or a tree would be a true wonder."* [x]

"The mistra provided the initial needles and sessola to those impiraresse who were just starting out," explains Signora Ventura. *"After that, the impiraressa had to provide her own needles. At that time, the needles were very expensive and the impiraressa couldn't afford to lose them. She had to keep the needles in a secure envelope made of leather. I remember a certain Bullo whom I knew personally. He sold needles to all the impiraresse. It became a big problem for the impiraresse when he died because he was the only one who made the needles."*

> FOUR YOUNG IMPIRARESSE SIT TOGETHER along the embankment of San Giuseppe in lower Castello. Note the sessola full of beads. (Circa 1894—1897.)

"Once the beads were strung, we called them 'le lunghe.' If a friend came by your window and asked what you were doing that day, you would say, "I have to do 'le lunghe' which meant you had to string beads. I also remember the phrase, "working the sessola." It was common to ask, 'Are you working the sessola today?' In fact, I remember when I was a child we would all go to the church of San Pietro di Castello to see a movie on Sunday afternoon. The film was one of those sad films where everyone is crying. I remember an old lady was in attendance. At that time, a movie cost only two or three lire. Then, during the film, the old lady stood up, shook her finger at the movie screen, and yelled, 'Oh no you don't! I'll be damned if I must work the sessola day after day only to come here to see a film that makes me cry!' and she walked out. I'll never forget that."

Each sessola had markings engraved on the sides to indicate the required lengths of the strands: forty-two centimeters or thirty-two centimeters.

"Most of the women weren't educated during those times ... it was necessary to have the measurements engraved on each sessola ... plus no one had a measuring tape, we were so poor," explains Signora Ventura.

The late Venetian Lucia Gavagnin, born in 1925, remembered fondly the impiraresse. *"I remember my grandmother had a boat located right here on the bank and it would be full of wicker baskets ... full of these colorful bouquets and flowers. The boat would take the baskets to Murano to the factory. There was a basket full of roses, a basket full of lilies, a basket of tulips, every flower imaginable. There was nothing more beautiful to see. Our streets were lined with wooden crates full of every color imaginable. It was a very lovely sight to see all the women working. We used to make Forget-Me-Not bouquets, flowers and leaves in all sizes. Everything was exported. I have wonderful memories. It's a shame this is a lost art but the kids never wanted to learn the trade of their elders. After the war [WWII], everything declined. And then, when we had the high water of 1966, many people lost everything, including beads and necklaces. Here we were these poor women stringing beads with an abundance of beads at our fingertips. A strand of these beads today would cost a fortune and here we had them in abundance and overflowing."*

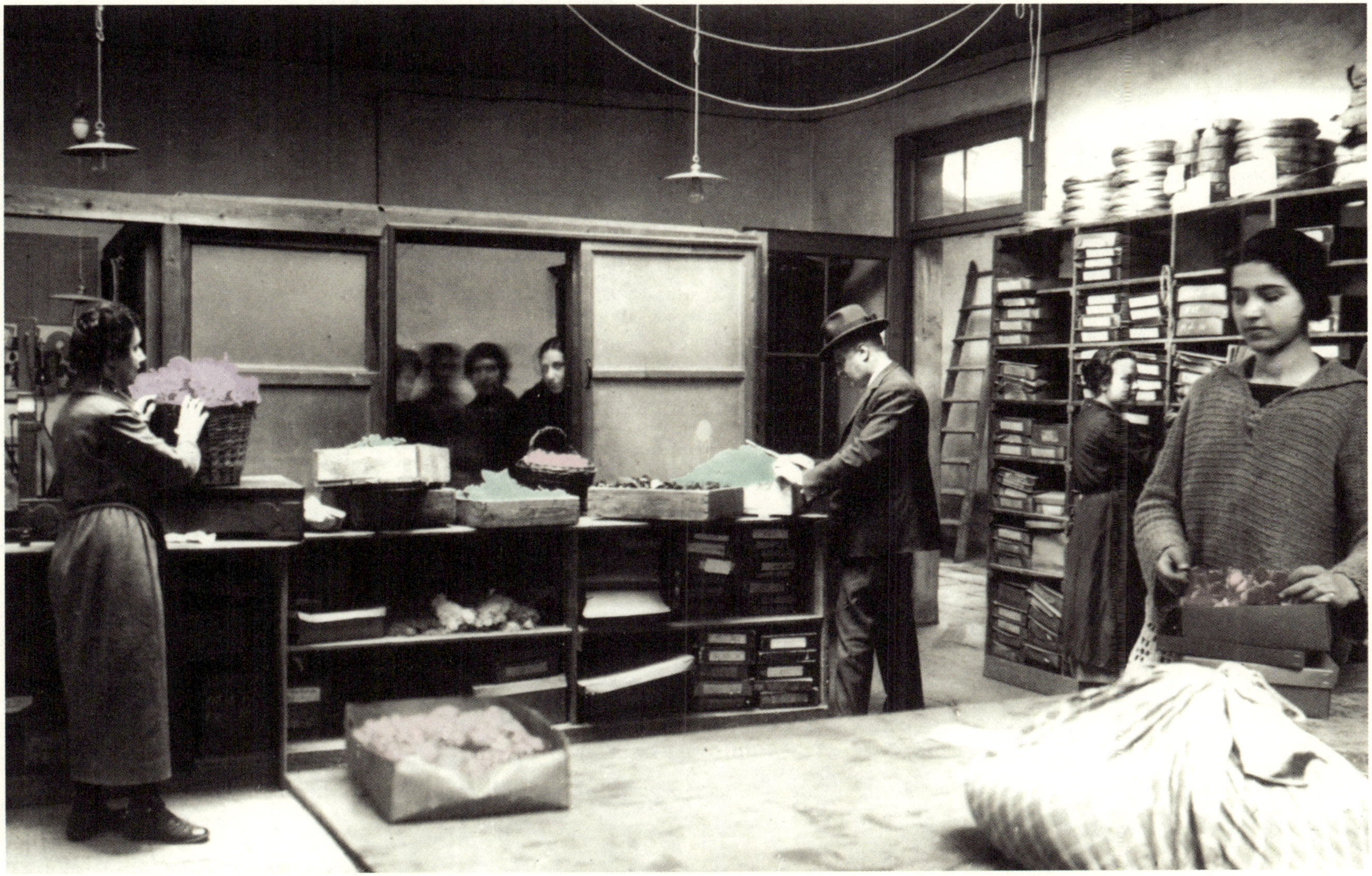

Λ THE MISTRE delivering their assignments in the factory for inspection. They gather here perhaps in anticipation, apprehension and pride as they wait for their beaded flowers (strung on wire) to be approved or scrutinized.

2| A very common row boat with a flat bottom diffused in the lagoon. It is often mistaken for a gondola.

Author Irene Ninni, described a similar scene in the Venetian Laguna in 1893: *"One can see a sandoleto*[2] *on which sits a common woman bearing a naturally majestic aura, surrounded with crates and boxes of beads made of every shape and color glistening in the sun as if they were gems. One would say it is a queen unknowing of her treasures, while for the Venetian woman it is her income, her every resource. And notwithstanding this simple industry, it is divided in two different categories: that is to say, the impiraressa de perle—called man d' opara in tondo e in fin, [worker of the round and fine], and the impiraressa de pive [longer glass beads] or man d' opara in grosso, [worker of the larger beads] which is considered less prestigious of the two."*[xi]

"The impiraresse were everywhere ... in front of every door," recounted Signora Gavagnin. *"Secomarina [lower Castello] was the zone where most of them worked. There was one impiraressa whom I'll never forget. She was able to string beads using over fifty needles in one hand. With just a snap of her two fingers, she was able to open up the fifty needles perfectly creating a fan (ventaglio) and holding onto it securely, she dipped the needles rapidly into the sessola. The bravura was keeping the needles together. When her hands came up, all fifty needles were strung! You should have seen her work. She was incredible! She left everyone in awe. And the beads were the fine ones, the smallest, the size of a grain of sand."*

The impiraresse lived mostly in the Castello district while the *perleri* (the artisans who manufactured lampwork beads) came from the district of Cannareggio.

"I have no idea why Castello was given the job of stringing the smallest beads and Cannareggio was given to do the lampwork beads," ponders Signora Ventura. *"But I'd guess ninety percent of the impiraresse came from Castello and ninety percent of the perleri came from Cannareggio."*

Over time, and especially with the closing of the SVC, the occupations of mistra and impiraressa would become extinct.

CHAPTER EIGHT *Endnotes*

i Irene Ninni, *L'impiraressa,* Venezia, 1893.
ii Ibid.
iii Ibid.
iv Comune di Venezia, *Rilievo degli abitanti di Venezia 1869 per Religione, Condizioni, Professioni, Arti e Mestiere,* Venezia, 1871.
v Mario Sutto, "Figure di Venezia: Impiraressa," cited in *Le Tre Venezie,* Venezia 1926, pp. 43, 44.
vi *Il Secolo Nuovo,* August 6, 1904.
vii Ugo Ojetti, *Cose Viste,* Secondo Tomo., Milan Treves, 1925 page 132.
viii Ibid.
ix Delgrado, page 347.
x Madame de Stael-Holstein, *Corinna Ossia l'Italia,* Napoli; 1810, pp. 51, 52.
xi Ninni

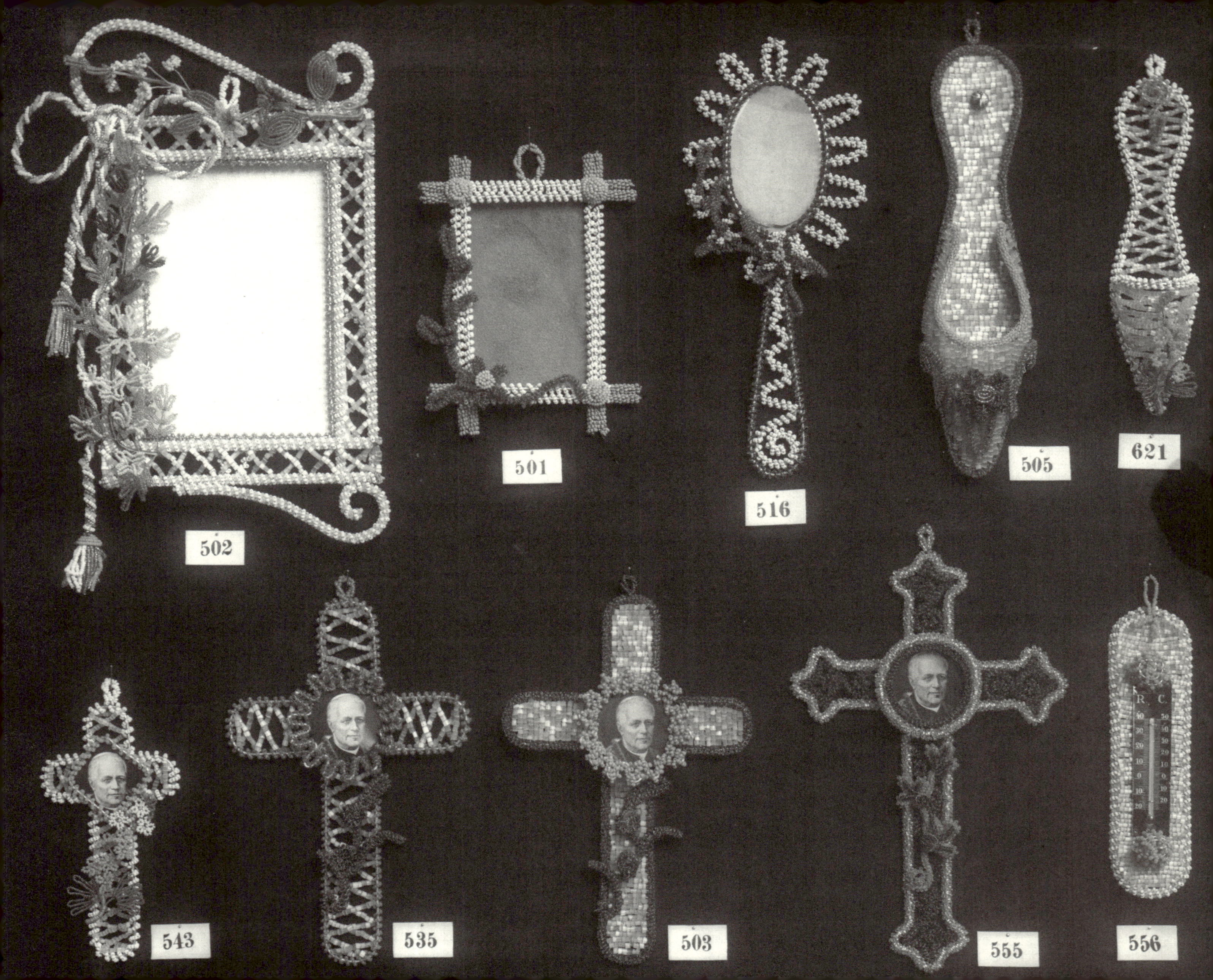
502
501
516
505
621
543
535
503
555
556

< IT HAS BEEN SAID that some of these beaded objects were gifts to the Roman Catholic Church perhaps during a Papal visit. The beaded crosses have a photograph of the patriarch of Venice, Giuseppe Sarto, who later became Pope Pius X from 1903–1914. The beaded slippers depict Papal slippers, a historical vestment traditionally worn by a pope during high religious ceremonies. (1925)

> BEADED BASKETS AND FLOWERS. Note the variety of beaded flowers — Lily of the Valley, leaves, and vines. (1925)

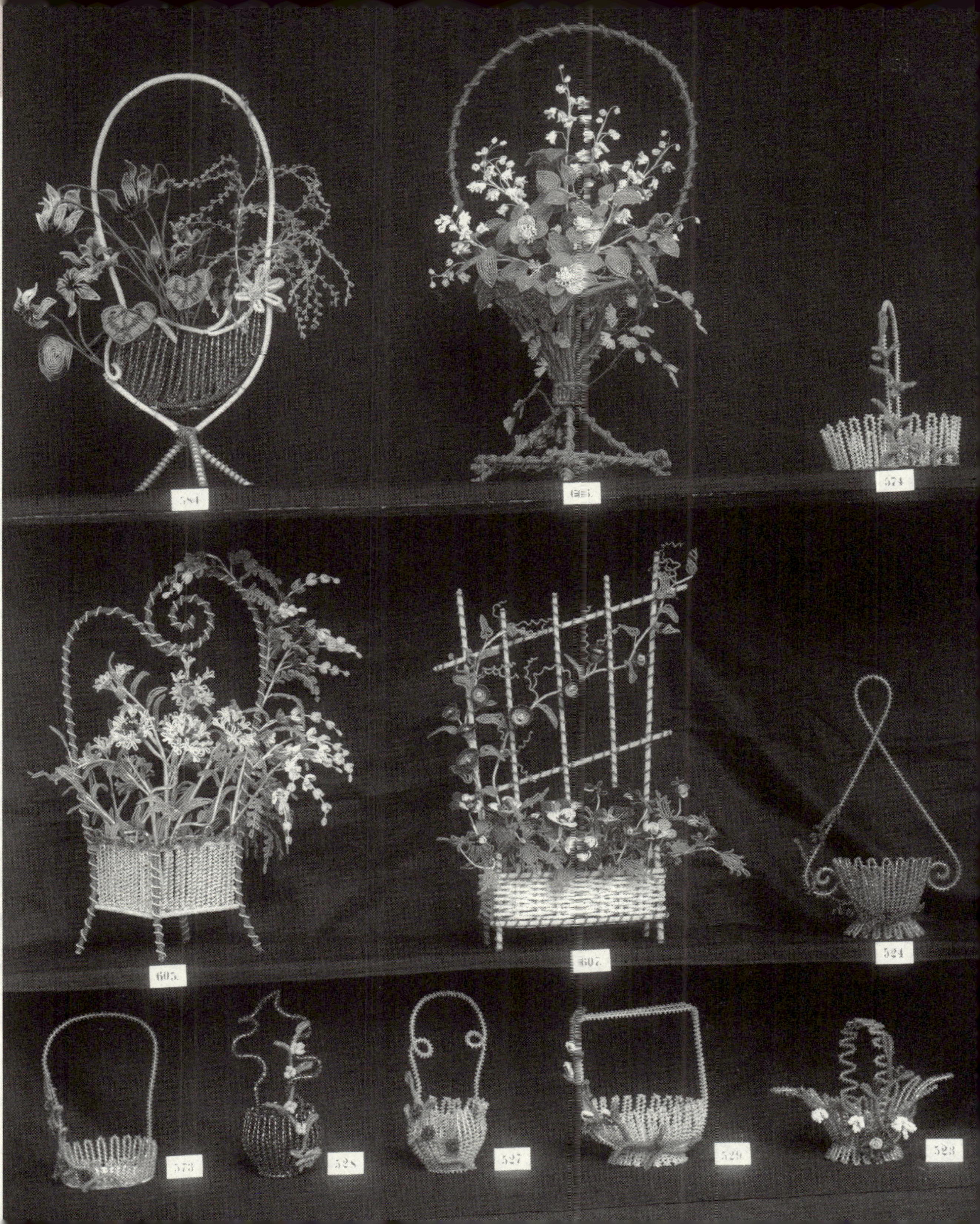

Do not wait; the time will never be "just right." Start where you stand, and work with whatever tools you may have at your command, and better tools will be found as you go along.

NAPOLEON HILL
American author
(1883-1970)

The Eye of the Needles

Aldo Bullo was born at home in a Venetian neighborhood of lower Castello in 1905. He was raised in a tiny house which consisted of two rooms, two kitchens, and two families. At that time, it was common for families of twelve or more to live together. Having such limited living space, the Venetians spent most of their time outside on the streets no matter what season. Living conditions were poor and food was scarce.

As the oldest son of the family, Aldo Bullo was forced to go to work at the age of nine. He found a meager job working on the cargo ships that came into port. Like most Venetian children, he had no shoes, so little Aldo reported to work wearing his mother's wedding shoes.

Aldo was blessed with incredible energy and with the mind of a genius. He attended a trading school on the island of San Giorgio where he excelled in naval engineering and machinery. By age nineteen, Aldo was teaching precision mechanics at the same school. Shortly thereafter, he was hired by the German company, Junghans, located on the island of Giudecca. Junghans was a large company that specialized in clocks and time pieces. They also fabricated detonators for bombs and for land mines. Bullo worked for this company for forty-five years and achieved great status as director, overseeing nearly one hundred employees. His affiliation and distinction with the company allowed him to enter the Venetian Naval Arsenal during WWII to do classified work for the navy. This was a period when the guards would cautiously monitor the gates, permitting only military personnel to enter.

Although Bullo earned an honorable position at the respected enterprise of Junghans, his job didn't provide enough income for his family. His wife had to sell her gold jewelry to pawn shops in order make ends meet. Bullo understood he needed to supplement his income. Recognizing the hundreds of impiraresse in his neighborhood, all struggling with poorly-designed needles for stringing the conterie beads, he devised better, hair-thin needles in the loft of his house. His artisan production of needles began around 1952.

According to his daughter Laura, "*the needles that were used at that time came from Germany and weren't properly tempered. They weren't flexible enough and would break easily.*"

Using old pieces of iron, wood, tools and whatever he found around the house, Bullo invented a makeshift operation to produce the needles. In fact, so rudimentary was the quality of his operation, Bullo would look at it almost apologetically, considering it as only a prototype. He promised his family that if the machines functioned properly, he would one day build better ones made of superior materials.

The material used for making the needles was fine steel musical wire, which he ordered from Milano. To produce the needles, Bullo would cut the wire according to length and hold them over a gas stove. Once heated, the needles were put into a kiln where Bullo would raise the temperature until they turned blue. Once the needles reached a high temperature, he would drop them into a basin of water. Producing the eye of the needle was a very delicate

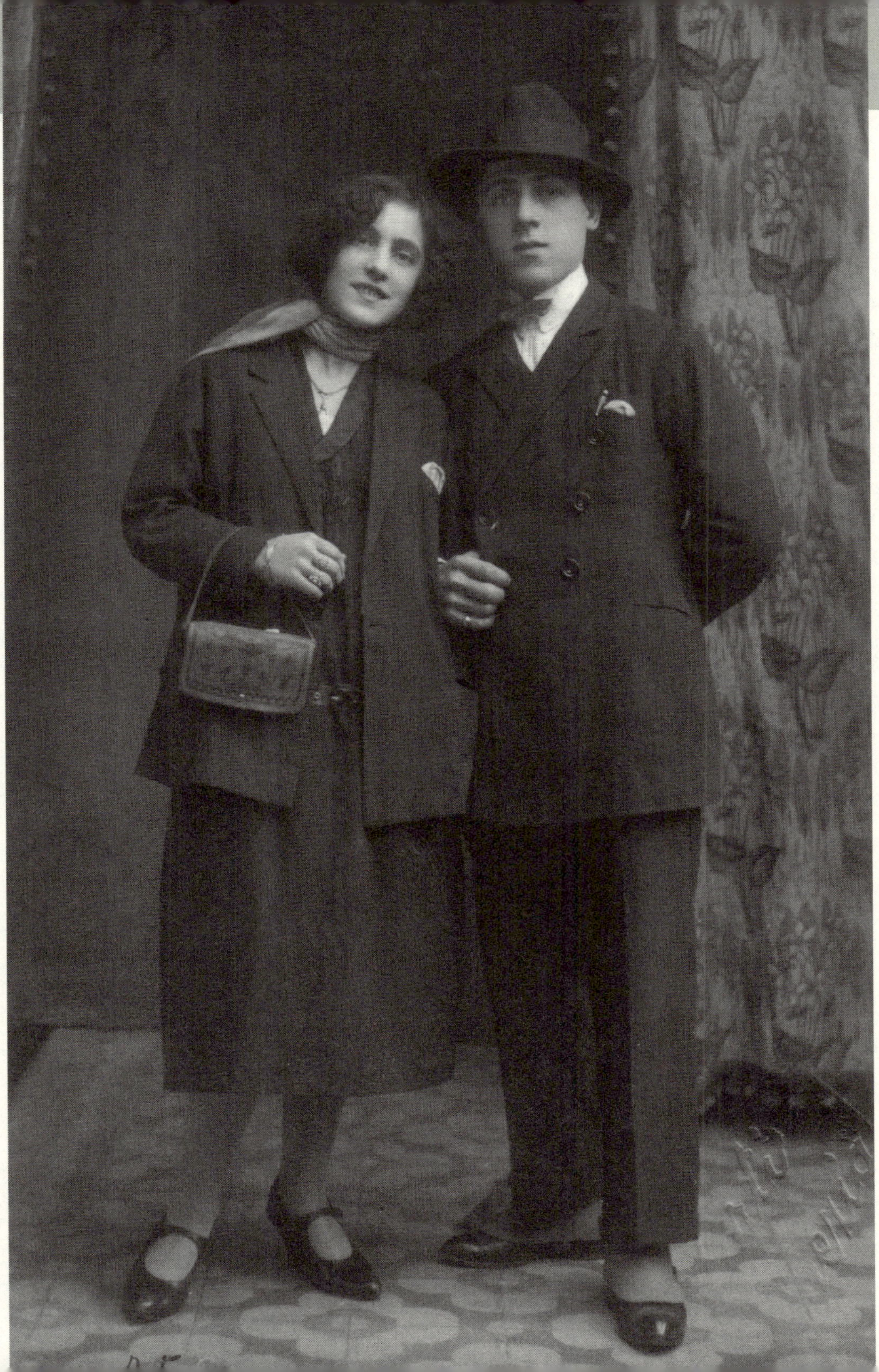

< ALDO BULLO and wife Elena.
(Circa 1930.)

operation, one that required precision and good vision. The needle would be placed on a table and positioned below a drill. The drill was not electric, but upon releasing a pedal, it would come down and strike the needle. The drill bits were all fabricated by Bullo himself. The thinner the needle, the more difficult and risky the operation. In fact, the thinner needles required the most time and the most material.

Laura Bullo remembers, *"in order to make a 'mua di aghi' [Venetian dialect for forty needles] we would have to make two hundred needles because only forty out of two hundred came out right...Because of this, the thinner needles were the most expensive."*

After the eye was made, both ends of the needle were filed using a wheel that operated on electricity. The tip of the eye was rounded off, smoothed and shaped. The tip of the point was sharpened.

The term 'hair-thin needles' has an actual mathematical basis. Using a caliper, one strand of hair measures approximately 0.7mm, and the thinnest known needle made by Bullo measured 0.5mm. In addition, Bullo produced larger gauge needles for stringing larger beads; the larger the gauge, the easier the needle was to produce.

Quality control was a family effort that involved lining up the needles on a tabletop and rolling them under the fingers. If a needle was found to be wavy or wobbly, it would be discarded.

The finished needles were polished individually with a soft cloth and then wrapped in tissue paper in quantities of forty.

"It was always a celebration for us when all the needles came out perfectly. We couldn't even work with the windows open because the breeze could alter the process of tempering the needles. My father was a genius. We could have owned Venice with our production of needles, but my father was too nice and too honest to take advantage of the situation. We had customers even in England."

Bullo's primitive invention was such a success that it consumed all of his leisure time. His artisan production couldn't meet the ever-increasing demands for his needles. Although he yearned to update his workshop with finer machinery and higher quality materials, he never had the time. Bullo worked endlessly, rising at five o'clock in the morning to report to the Junghans company, and then returned home to make needles in the evening. He would come down from the loft for dinner, eat, and then immediately returned to the loft where he worked continuously until one o'clock in the morning.

"My father slept four hours a day for fifty years," recounts his daughter. *"We come from a family of humble mechanics. We are very energetic, simple, hard-working and live a long time."*

Bullo's wife, Elena, took on the administrative tasks of this small business. Signora Bullo went out into the streets of Venice, took orders, and collected the money for the needles. The needles were sold in packets according to the size of diameter. The thinnest needles were the most precious and costly of Bullo's production.

Elena was born in 1905, the same year as Bullo. She was the daughter of a fisherman. She was a very petite woman, weighing only forty kilos, yet she was very healthy and had a strong character. Elena was instrumental in the success of Bullo's needles. She was the intermediary between her husband's product and the mistre, the impiraresse, and various bead factories such as the SVC and Mazzega. Her job was to sell the needles and keep a record of who paid and who didn't. Walking through the streets of lower Castello, she was often mocked and scorned by many impiraresse who disliked her for coming to collect payment for the needles; the impiraresse often lied or pretended to forget they hadn't paid.

In the 1950s, the cost of one packet of medium sized needles was 2,500 lire (approximately $1.25 today). Although this was a costly investment for the impiraresse, they really had no other choice but to buy their needles from Bullo. Having no competition, Bullo could have been easily consumed with greed. However, coming from a poor family himself, Bullo empathized with those less fortunate and was a charitable man. For the poorest impiraressa, the needles were given to her as a gift. But for those impiraresse who were actively working in the trade, the needles had to be purchased. The Bullos allowed the impiraresse to set up a payment plan. Bullo always considered the price of his needles to be fair. He took pride in his delicate production, paid careful attention to detail, and ensured a top-quality product.

Bullo's entire family was involved in the needle-making business. Each person was assigned a specific task and was compensated. The family got along well and Bullo lived a very long and harmonious life. In the early 1970s, as Bullo was running to catch a *vaporetto* (a public transport boat), he had a mild heart attack. It was then that he decided to retire. His vision worsened over the years—the consequence of using a monocle most of his life and performing intricate work. Sometime around 1976, he decided to sell his machinery to the Societa' Veneziana Conterie for 1,800,000 lire (approximately $900 today), but only under the condition that after he trained the workers, he would not have to return to Murano for further instruction or assistance; Bullo never had the time to construct better machinery and didn't want to be responsible for the maintenance of the machines. Plus, he was tired and had far more interesting ideas for his retirement. During the final years of his life, he studied astronomy, anatomy, photography, mathematics, and enjoyed classical music and the opera.

Even after Bullo trained the workers of the SVC, they still were not able to fully understand the functions of the needle-making machines. While it was understood at the time of the sale that the SVC would not disturb Bullo, they had no other choice but to call him for assistance. Bullo didn't have the heart to deny the SVC and willingly returned to Murano on three separate occasions. In 1992, the SVC closed its doors. That same year, Aldo Bullo died of natural causes at the age of eighty-seven. His wife followed him a few years later.

Although overlooked in the production of conterie beads, Bullo's contribution to the industry was outstanding. Had it not been for Aldo Bullo and his quality production of hair-thin needles, the impiraressse could not have been nearly as productive. Bullo's needles were essential for the impiraresse; the needles were their primary tool. The more rapid and efficient the beads were strung, the more quantity they produced. The more quantity they produced, the more money they made. And the more money they made, the more likely they could afford to send their sons to work wearing his own pair of shoes.

Bullo's descendants do not deny that he earned a good income from the sale of the needles. So successful was his production that he employed many family members, built three homes for his children, and increased the income potential for the poor impiraresse. Bullo's retirement created an obstacle for the impiraresse. Although some needles were still in circulation, they became increasingly scarce, especially the thinnest ones. When the SVC closed, five thousand packets of needles were found in the warehouse. It is uncertain what happened to them, but Bullo's daughter has an idea:

"Those needles that still exist are hidden away in the dresser drawers of women next to their gold jewelry because that is the value of my father's needles...they are like gold!"

Strive not to be a success, but rather to be of value.

ALBERT EINSTEIN

German-born theoretical physicist

(1879–1955)

The Gems of Giovanni Giacomuzzi

Giovanni Giacomuzzi was born in Murano in 1817 to a family of distinguished glass workers who specialized in the production of lampwork and conterie beads and the fabrication of glass enamels. Giovanni's brother, Giuseppe, specialized in manufacturing and mechanically cutting glass rods. Like many Muranese families of the era, work ethics and a passion for glass were passed down from father to son.

His father Angelo exhibited Giovanni's lampworked beads in New York in 1854, and *"delighted every elegant middle-class person who, for just a few dollars, was able to flaunt necklaces, bracelets, and crowns of the latest fashion, making all the elderly ladies jealous who still wore the same-old jewelry of the empire."*[i]

Giovanni Giacomuzzi set out to create an attractive conterie bead that could imitate the color of gold. He experimented with various chemical formulas, investing time and money into studies and experiments until one day, in 1866, he discovered a beautiful *margaritina*.

The yellow glass beads, resplendent with the color of gold, were *"greeted like a gem and the queen of all others."*[ii] Even the Institute of Veneto declared Giacomuzzi's discovery as the *"transformation of glass into gold"* adding *"it is a shame that the hue becomes pale when observed under the rays of artificial light."*[iii]

Giacomuzzi achieved the golden tonality by adding uranium oxides to the glass composition.[iv] In fact, Abbott Vincenzo Zanetti described Giacomuzzi's gold beads as *"always attractive and radiant, twice as much in the sun and even more bright at night."*[v]

Two years later, in 1868, Giacomuzzi was given the opportunity to participate in the Industrial Exhibition in the Palace of the Doges in Venice. This was the chance for Giacomuzzi to show the world his accomplishment. However, during this period, the French dominated the European fashion market as well as the exhibition with their glass-beaded trimmings used to embellish women's hats, handbags, shoes, necklaces, and garments.

Giacomuzzi's yellow-gold conterie beads were recognized and praised at the exhibition and Giacomuzzi was awarded a silver medal. Because the exhibition's focus was on fashion, he declined to accept the medal on the grounds that he did not want his beads to be associated with the fashion industry, which was always changing, unpredictable, and uncertain. Instead, Giacomuzzi had other plans for his beads; he wanted them to be substituted for the gold threads that were embroidered onto textiles, tapestries, and fabrics used by the Catholic church and royal dynasties. These gold-colored threads would tarnish and, in a short period of time, lose their shine and brilliance.[1] Giacomuzzi's beads, on the other hand, would remain unaffected through the ages, resist humidity and weathering, and would cost less than the gold-colored threads which would eventually degrade.[vi]

1| Gold, silver, and copper are considered noble metals and were commonly used to manufacture metal threads. Pure gold does not change under normal circumstances and was rarely used as thread due to its elevated cost. The gold thread, used almost exclusively until the 19th century, was made with other elements such as silver and copper that tarnish due to humidity, dust, fats, oils, and oxygen. Today, the main metal in thread is aluminum. (Agnes Timar-Balazsy and Dinah Eastop, *Chemical Principles of Textile Conservation*, Butterworth Heinemann, Oxford, UK, 2005, pp. 128-132; Salvatore Lorusso and Luciano Gallotti, *Caratterizzazione, Tecnologia e Conservazione dei Manufatti Tessili*, Pitagora Editrice, Bologna, 2007, pp. 144-145.)

"Venice, in the most fortunate times of the Republic, created many wonderful fabrics that were stitched with gold. At least now there is the power to apply [Giacomuzzi's] glass to these fabrics which truly imitate the precious metal with all realness."[vii]

When Giacomuzzi attempted to apply the translucent yellow-gold conterie beads onto velvet, he realized that the single tone lacked dimension. If he wanted to create beautiful works of art, the kind which could adorn altars for centuries, he needed to invent a second bead—one that had the same effect as the yellow-gold bead but with a different tonality. Having two different colors of beads, Giacomuzzi could alternate his beading to create patterns onto fabrics.

Giacomuzzi dedicated himself to new studies and sacrifices and, *"enriched the conterie industry with yet another novelty eminently important, which is the gold mother-of-pearl (madre perla d'oro), radiating in a special light, much richer than any other margaritina in the past."*[viii]

Giacomuzzi was commissioned by local churches, such as the Basilica of the Madonna della Salute, to create altar accessories and dressing covers for altar columns. Two column covers, made of a rich-crimson velvet, were commissioned by the parish priest, Giovanni Nichetti, and represented Giacomuzzi's first attempt at applying his beautiful, gold-like beads onto a fabric worthy of its grace. The bead work for the columns and altar accessories was executed by the company Napoleon Jesurum of Venice.[ix] The altar columns went on display during an exhibit in the store Ville de Paris, located in Saint Mark's Square. The newspaper, Gazzetta di Venezia, (December 1868) reported on the event: ... *"the effect of the yellow-gold, imitating gold, is truly stupendous. The glass on velvet created such an illusion to all who gathered at the Ville de Paris that they were unaware this was a new product, convinced the glass was real gold. [The crowd] was dazzled by the magnificence and elegance of this combined work. We announce with great pleasure this new discovery because it can be considered as an industrial event."*[x]

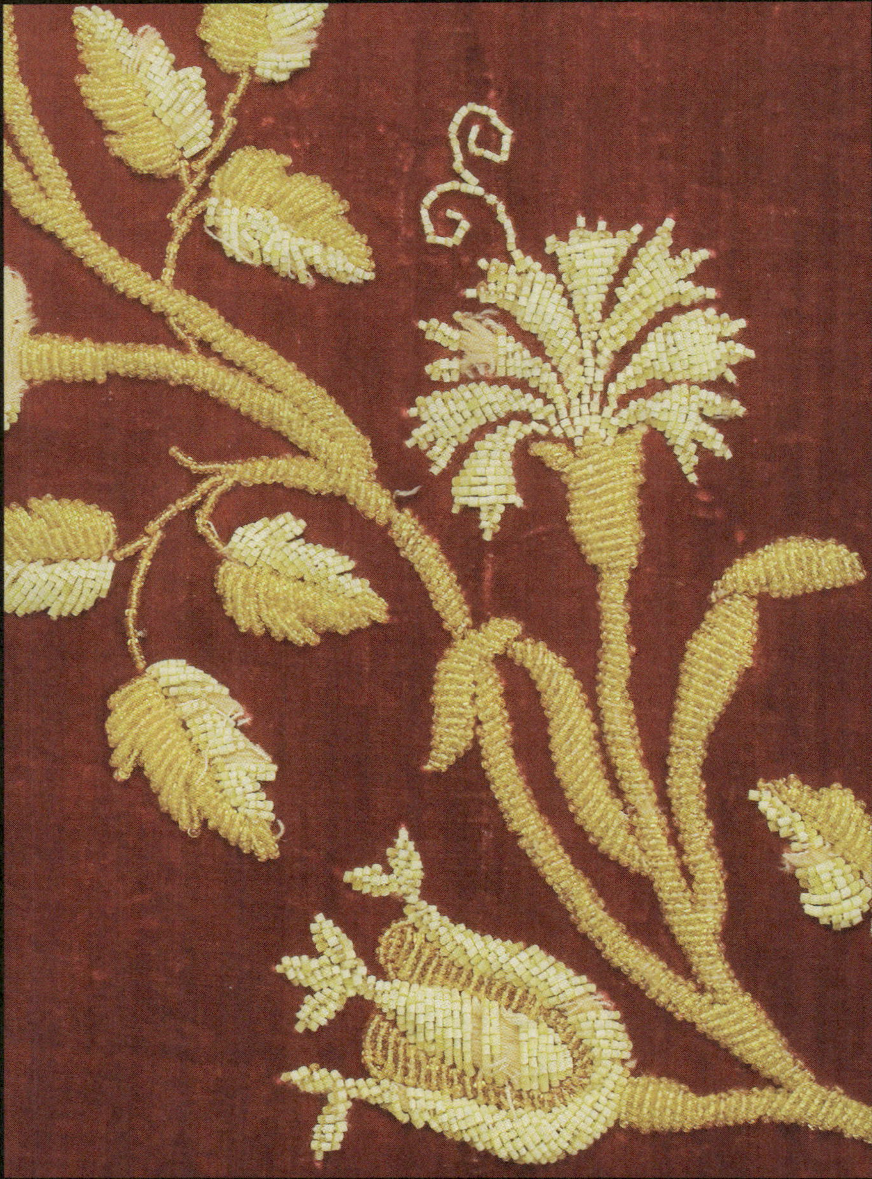

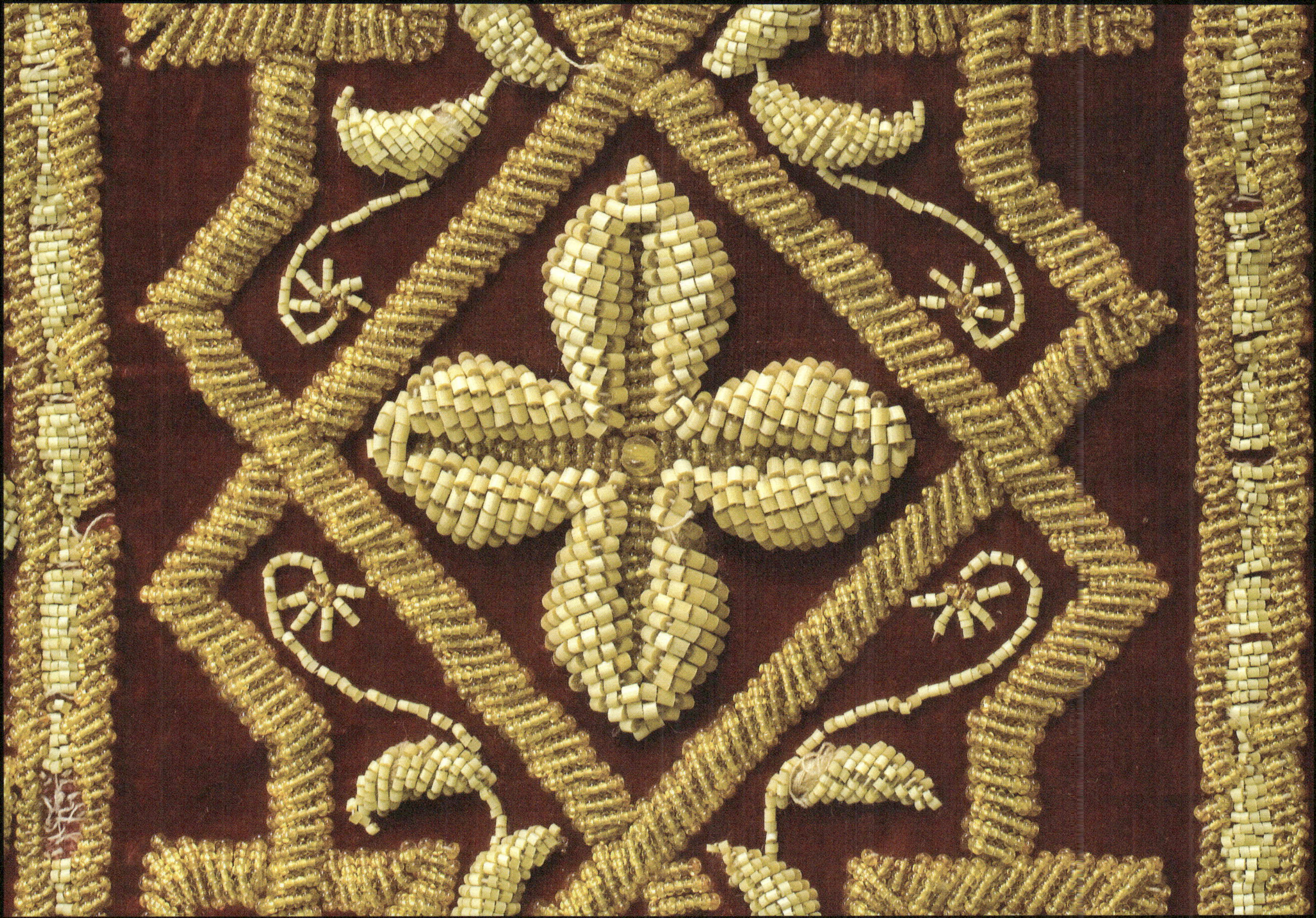

^ GIACOMUZZI'S COLUMN COVERS: Embroidered onto a deep red velvet, thousands of gold conterie beads create a striking and beautiful contrast.

Giacomuzzi participated in exhibits throughout Italy and went on to win many more honors and medals. In 1869, at the Glass Exhibition in Murano, Giacomuzzi was awarded the Medal of Honor—an award considered superior to the gold medal. This was a highly critical award given only to those who demonstrated great mastery in the art of glass.

Giacomuzzi's most grandiose and famous work was decorating the Theater of Treviso (a city on the mainland near Venice) using 500 libbre[2] of [gold] mother-of-pearl on seventy square meters of crimson velvet.[xi]

"Certainly the bead of Giacomuzzi deserves every attention: it is the perfect simulation of the most precious metal, and his applications present an indisputable glamour and brightness."[xii]

Although he could have become a wealthy man selling his gold conterie beads to notable tailors and dressmakers, Giacomuzzi was not motivated to commercialize his product for the fashion industry. He was selective in the projects he chose and remained true to his vision of using the golden beads on velvet. He aspired to have his beads gracing palaces, state rooms, ballrooms, theaters, and churches. He wanted his beads to trim the ceremonial vestments of dignitaries and religious clergymen, sacred books, and tapestries. One of his commissions was to create a velvet book cover for the visiting Empress Eugenia of France. He envisioned his creations to last for generations, to become heirlooms in a royal family, and to be admired by visitors in sacred places.

The museum chapel in the church of Saint Pietro di Martyr in Murano has Giacomuzzi's column dressings preserved under a clear acrylic frame. The choice of the color combination of this work—gold beads applied onto crimson velvet—suggest the two official colors of Venice, gold and *rosso Veneziano.* This art work is quite fascinating and reminds us that even the tiniest conterie can be considered a gem.

2| Libbra: An ancient unit of weight, of variable value according to the period and place, comprised of 330 grams to 550 grams. (*Moderna Enciclopedia Rizzoli,* Libane-Meris, Milano, 1977. Also, *Consiglio Superiore di Pubblica Istruzione of 1849:* In Veneto a libbra = 12 ounces or 0,476998 kg.)

CHAPTER TEN *Endnotes*

i Bartolomeo Cecchetti, Vincenzo Zanetti, *Esposizione Internazional Mariitima in Napoli,* pp.123-133, Napoli, DeAngelis, 1872, page 216.

ii Cavalier Abbott Vincenzo Zanetti, *La Perla di Vetro —Color Giallo Oro di Giovanni Giacomuzzi di Venezia All'Esposizione di Roma*, Venezia, Tip. Munic. di Gaetano Longo, 1870 cited in Voce di Murano—Giornale dell'Industria Vetraria, 28 February 1870, n. 4.

iii Atti del R. Istituto Veneto, Venezia, 1865-66, disp. V., page 584.

iv Giuseppe Morazzoni, *Le Conterie Veneziane,* Società Veneziana Conterie e Cristallerie,Venezia, 1953, page 58.

v Zanetti, page 17.

vi Ibid., page 25.

vii Ibid., page 29.

viii Ibid., page 14.

ix Ibid., page 16.

x Gazzetta di Venezia, December 21, 1868.

xi Zanetti, 1870, states "500 libbre" of beads, whereas Morazzoni, 1953, states "5000 libbre" of beads. Considering the date of these publications, the fact that uranium oxides were in the composition, and the given quantity of the glass, it could be surmised that Morazzoni's book erroneously added a zero onto the quantity of beads.

xii Zanetti, page 25.

The harder you work, the harder it is to surrender.

VINCENT LOMBARDI

NFL coach

(1913–1970)

The Rise and Fall of the Società Veneziana per l'Industria delle Conterie (1898–1992)

Glass beads were invented to imitate precious gemstones. The creators of the *conterie* (also known as seed beads) and the beads *a lume* or *alla lucerna* (beads made by using a lamp or torch, known today as lampwork beads) were the Paternostreri from the 14th century, who had originally been *Cristalleri* (crystal cutters). The Paternostreri were responsible for making beads for rosaries. This title was likely given because of the Paternostreri's connection with the "Our Father" prayer that is associated with rosaries.[i] The beads made by the Paternostreri were fashioned by melting and winding the glass onto a *speo/spiedo* (skewer/mandrel) using the flame of a torch.

During the third quarter of the 15th century, the work of the Paternostreri was simplified when Murano glassworkers invented the hollow cane. These canes were cut into small cylinders, then the cylinders were slipped onto a mandrel to maintain the hole, then the jagged edges of these cylinders were shaped and smoothed using the flame from the torch. In addition, in the early 16th century, the glass cylinders could be shaped and smoothed while cold with the grinding wheel. By the mid-16th century, the demand for ground and faceted beads made by the Paternostreri had declined in favor of the lampworked beads made on a mandrel.

Around 1575 A.D., a new technique was introduced in which large quantities of smaller beads (called by the antique Latin name *margaritine*) were made by the process of using a *ferrazza*.[ii] These beads were made by cutting slim, hollow glass cane into small cylindrical sections when cold. Then the cylinders were placed on a *ferrazza* (a round tray made of copper or iron), and then the ferrazza was inserted into a reverberating furnace where the cylinders were heated indirectly by means of a flame deflected downward from the roof. The process of using the ferrazza would result in smoothing the sharp edges of the cylinders, eventually making them into beautiful, uniformed rounded beads.[iii]

An early appearance of the word conterie was in the 1612 book *L'Arte Vetraria,* by Florence native and alchemist, Antonio Neri. This book was one of the first and most important publications in Italy regarding the technology of glass making.[iv] The word contaria/conterie continued to be used primarily when referring to the products of Paternostreri and margariteri.

In the 1800s, under the name of conterie, the beads were divided into three groups:

a) Beads made from hollow glass cane (*canna forata*) that were used for decorative stitching onto fabrics, purses, lampshades, gowns, religious vestments, and objects.

b) Beads called conterie, also made from hollow glass cane, for the sole purpose of exportation, especially overseas.

c) Beads made a lume or alla lucerna which were made by the *suppialume* or the *perleri* for the intention of making jewelry.[v] These beads were fashioned from solid glass cane (*canna massiccia*) made by artisans who specialized in blowing glass.[vi]

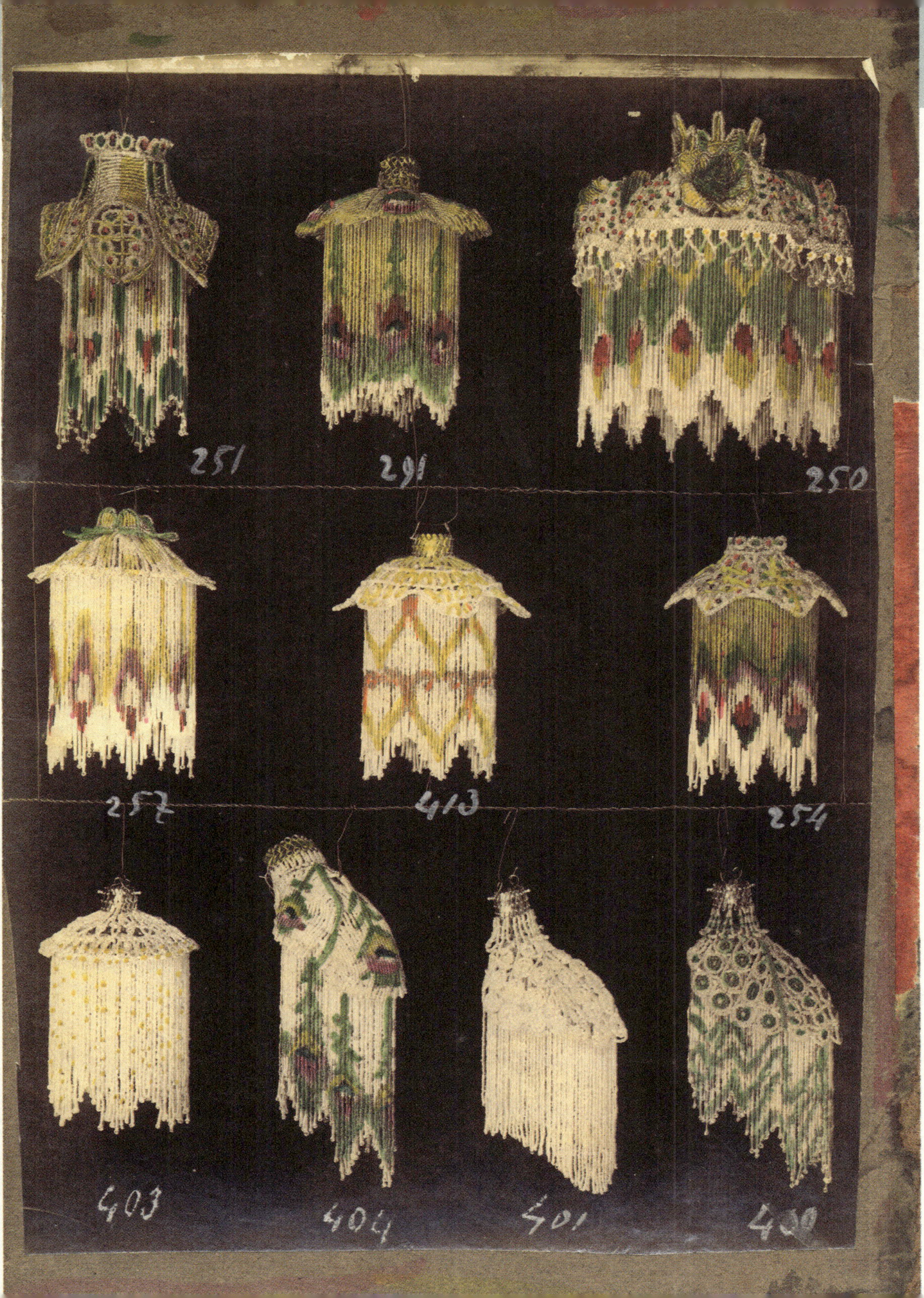

< IN THE EARLY 1900s, fringe lampshades were very popular and the SVC produced hundreds of them, such as these in 1909. The seed beads were weaved on a loom and could be designed in a variety of patterns and colors. This technique was also used to create handbags, tobacco pouches, waistbands, necklaces, and trimmings for dresses.

Trading conterie beads with natives from African countries

In the 17th century, conterie beads made in Venice were used for trading with natives of the African colonial countries. In fact, the name conterie[1] may be derived from the Italian word *contare* meaning "to count" since the beads were used as a monetary value in Africa, Asia, and the Americas until the mid-1800s.[vii] Testimony to this comes from Giovanni Beltrame, a missionary from Verona, Italy who, in 1858, evangelized a tribe along the coast of the White River in South Africa and confirmed that the conterie beads in Abyssinia (now known as Ethiopia) and Sudan were considered very valuable and used to exchange goods and favors. Beltrame himself distributed generous amounts of conterie beads to escape a challenging situation, as described and published in the newspaper *Gazzetta Ufficiale di Venezia* on August 19, 1858:

"On the night of January 28, our boat was pushed into a muddy canal by a strong wind. We were so stuck that it would have taken all the strength of our entire crew to pull it out and we would have had to wait until dawn. We called for help to some men from the Shilluk tribe who were near the left bank with their women. Our old and ruined boat, however elegant in its shape, soon found itself with about twelve people whom we promised a few glass beads. They used every force they could to dislodge the boat, but it was impossible to get us out of this difficulty so we had to make more promises [of beads] so that they would call their friends, who were observing from the bank, to come and help us.

Leaving their women and children, everyone came armed with spears. To tell the truth, we were all scared to be surrounded by these armed people who raised their voices when they saw how many, and what beads, we would give them for their trouble. They began to yell barbarically and pushed us out of the mud. Once our boat had moved just a little, they jumped into their canoes and went away without helping us any further.

We bought some of their merchandise with glass beads. I was thinking about these poor people, disheartened in such deplorable, miserable conditions and my heart ached just thinking that not one of us could stay with them and let them hear the gospel and teach them about their health.... We stopped to give our glass beads to the man who was sent by Mr. Lanz; he only had a few, and not very nice ones, with which to buy some grain. The women of Nuer rushed with their small baskets full of grain and within thirty minutes, more than two hundred people gathered to make a trade."[ix]

The torch, which was invented in 1528 by Andrea Viadore, was fueled by animal fat and by the forced air of a bellows.[viii] Viadore's invention enriched the art of the conterie, giving the beads an infinite number of shapes and polychrome decorations, gildings in silver and gold, and allowing the perleri to express their creative talents.

Like other industries, the level of production and commerce in the conterie industry has reflected the state of the global economy. During better times, numerous glass laboratories and small bead businesses were established in Venice and Murano and sales multiplied. An economic lull in 1898 ignited fierce competition amongst the conterie industries, but it eventually led to seventeen individual conterie bead manufacturers joining forces to strengthen and save their businesses. They consolidated their finances, expertise, equipment, and employees to form the Società Veneziana per I'Industria delle Conterie in Murano.

Many of these businesses were situated in the densely populated Venetian district of Cannaregio, an area located near the entrance of Venice which is easily accessible by sea, making it an ideal location to receive deliveries of raw materials from countries as far away as Syria. This area, with its long canals and embankments, allowed the construction of long corridors for the pulling of glass cane, as well as spacious sheds (*capannone*) to perform the function of smoothing and rounding the beads (*arrotondamento*). Cannaregio faced the island of Murano—the center of the conterie production—making deliveries and exchanges between the two locations convenient.

The consolidation of these companies was spearheaded by Cavalier Luciano Barbon, who served as the SVC's Director from 1898-1910. He was the company's largest shareholder and was regarded as an authoritative critic and expert in the production of conterie beads. Under Barbon's organizational savvy, all stages of bead production were united and transferred to the island of Murano to work under one administrative society (but not under

1 | The name can also derive from the antique Tuscan word *contigia* meaning "ornament" or the Latin word *comptus*, meaning "ornate" or "adorned." *Astone Gasparetto, Il Vetro di Murano dalle Origini ad Oggi,* Neri Pozza Editore, Venezia, *1958, page 177.*

one roof). By virtue of the careful planning and mass production of the conterie beads in Murano, countless quantities of these beads would reach the far corners of the world and forever contribute to the rich and complex history of the bead industry.[2]

The Barbon family was already well-known in the Murano glass industry. Luciano's paternal grandfather, Marco Barbon, worked in the glass factory of Giuseppe Bellandis (his brother-in-law) since 1820. Luciano's father, Isidoro Barbon, was the director of a very important conterie factory, the San Martino della Società Fabbriche Riunite. Luciano Barbon began working in the conterie industry at a very young age and then went on to successfully operate his own company, L. Barbon & Co. His brother, Apollo Barbon, was his technical assistant.[x]

Some of the companies that comprised the SVC included L. Barbon & Co., Fabbriche Conosociate Bigaglia-Flantini-Coen-Becher, F. Weverbeck & Co., Cavalier Salvatore Arbib, Giacomo & Pacifico Ceresa, Ceresa & Millin, V. Angeli & Co., A. Zecchin & Co., G & F. Fratelli Costantini, Emilio Brinis, Borini & Co., A. & L Bigaro, Augusto Casagrande, and Cavalier Federico Rechsteiner.[xi]

The headquarters and administrative offices of the SVC were in the Palazzo Trevisan, located on Fondamenta Navagero, which was situated across the San Donato canal opposite the main factory. The palace also stored the finished beads and artistic pieces that were transferred from the main factory by a transport boat (*the Peata*). A covered private dock located behind the palace served to receive and export goods.[3]

2 | The first to consolidate the different phases of the production of the conterie was the company Dalmistro-Errera & Co. around 1818. (*Vicenzo Zanetti, Guida di Murano e Delle Celebri Sue Fornaci Vetrarie,* Antonelli, 1866, pp.30-31.)

3 | Michelangelo Pasquato, Director of the SVC from 1935-1966, suggested the construction of a tunnel under the canal of San Donato from the Fondamenta Marco Giustinian to the Fondamenta Navagero to simplify the deliveries of finished products from the main factory to the main warehouse, saving time and the expense of the transport boat.

> THE DIRECTORS OF THE SVC were Luciano Barbon (1898–1910), Luigi Ceresa (1910–1918) Angelo Gino Toso (1918–1922), Maria Alverà (1923–1930), Vittorio Friedenberg (1930–1935), Michaelangelo Pasquato (1935–1966), Gino Cenedese (1966–1969), Telemaco Reali (1969–?), Mantovan (unknown), Cherzevani and Piovesan (unknown), and finally Dr. Chiapetta who was the director until the closing of the SVC.

This image depicts the SVC Director, Luciano Barbon, discussing currency with his accountant. Behind them is an open commercial safe, a portrait of Vittorio Emanuele III, King of Italy from 1900 to 1946, and a wooden wall telephone.

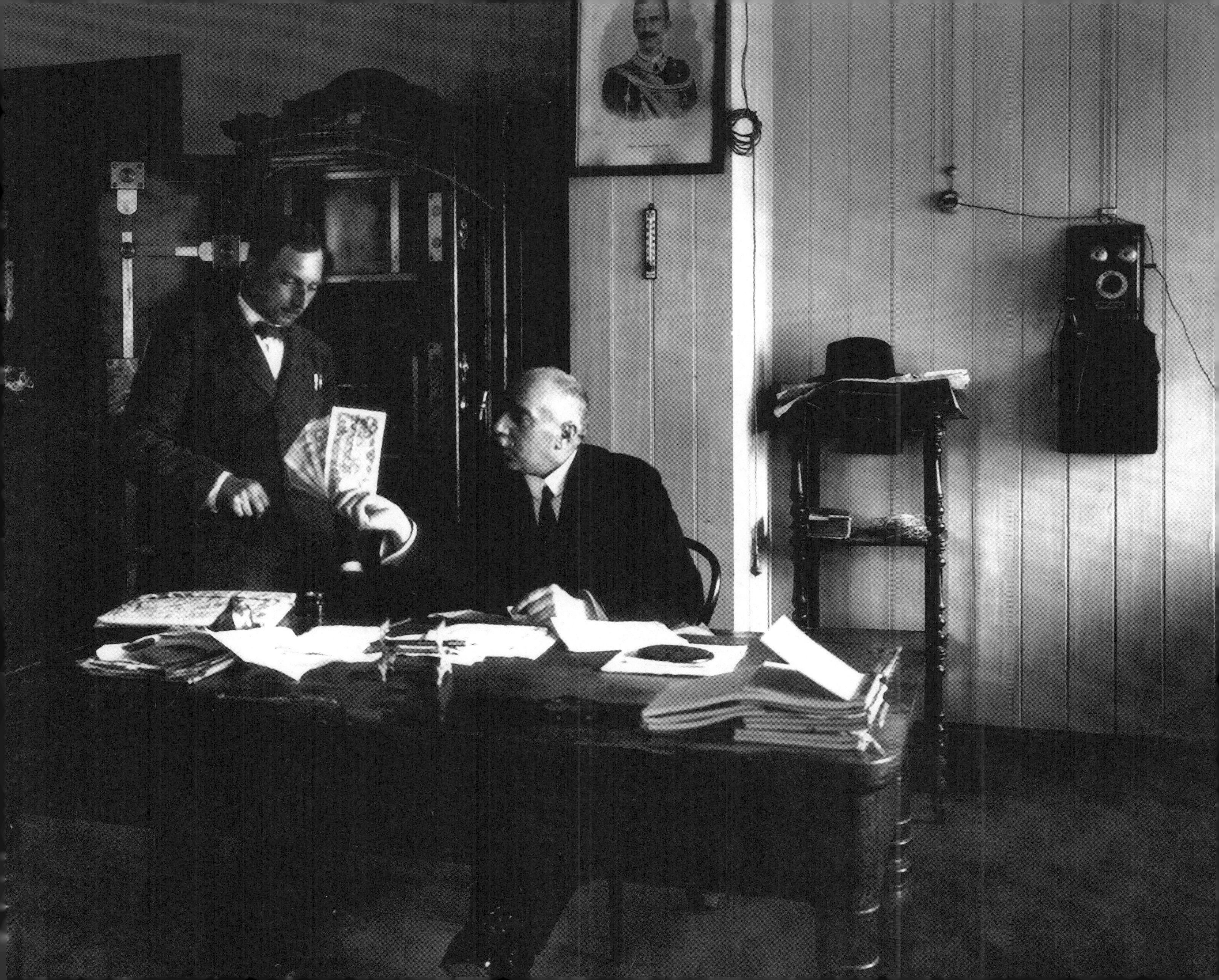

> FOR SMALLER LOADS, the Venetians used a transport boat as such as this to deliver and receive materials, food and supplies.

> (Opposite page): LOCATED IN THE BACK of the 16th century Palazzo Trevisan, the indoor dock ("*cavana*" in the Venetian dialect) of the SVC was convenient for receiving the raw materials necessary for the production of glass, such as coal, sand, and a variety of minerals. The dock was also used for loading/unloading bead assignments to/from the Venetian impiraresse, in addition to loading cargoes of beads for foreign shipments. Docked near the upper left is the Peata boat, specifically designed to carry heavy loads. Two small passenger boats flank both sides of the dock. These boats were used for transporting clients and/or the executives of the factory.

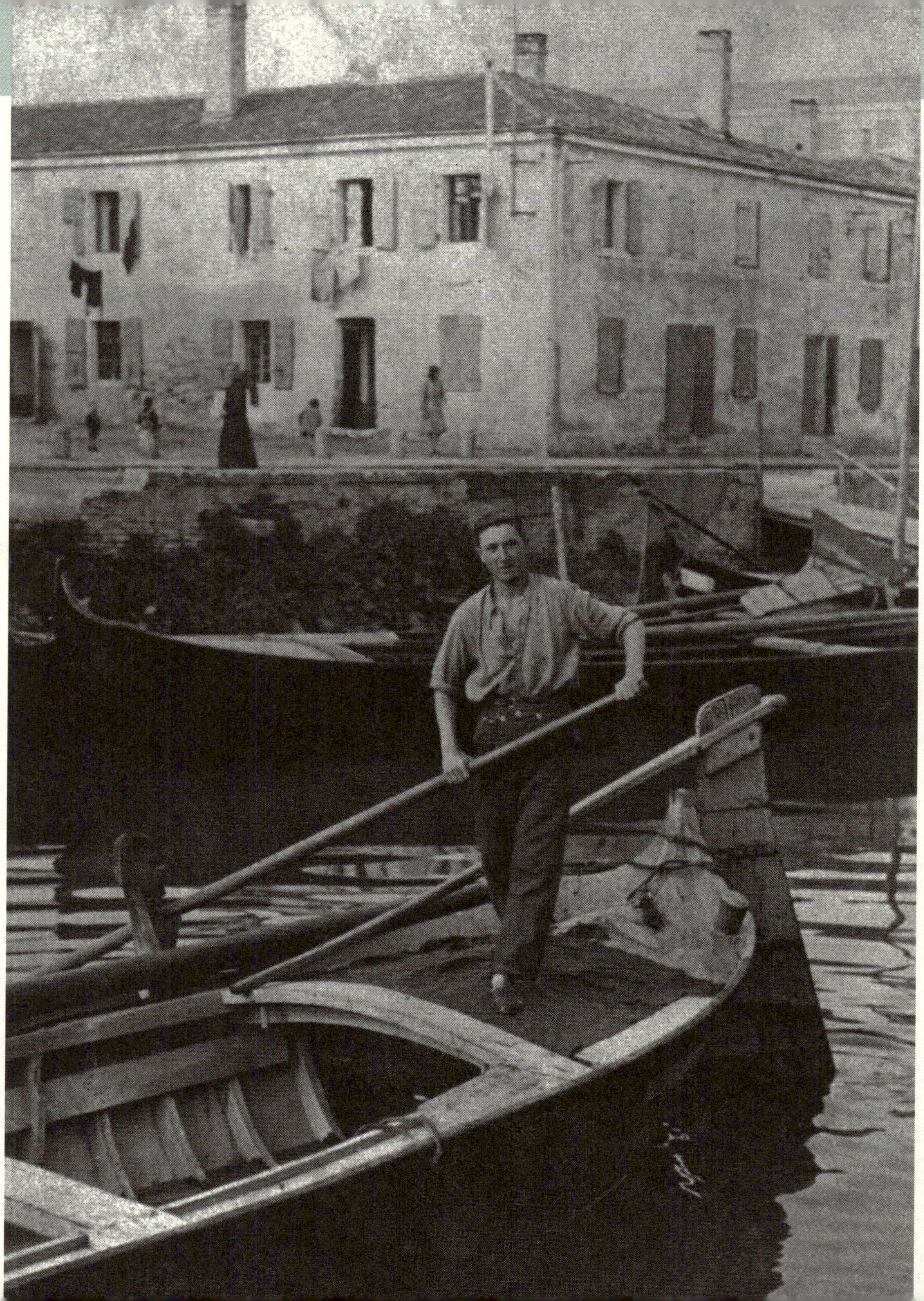

ARCHIVO FOTOGRAFICO FONDAZIONE MUSEI CIVICI DI VENEZIA

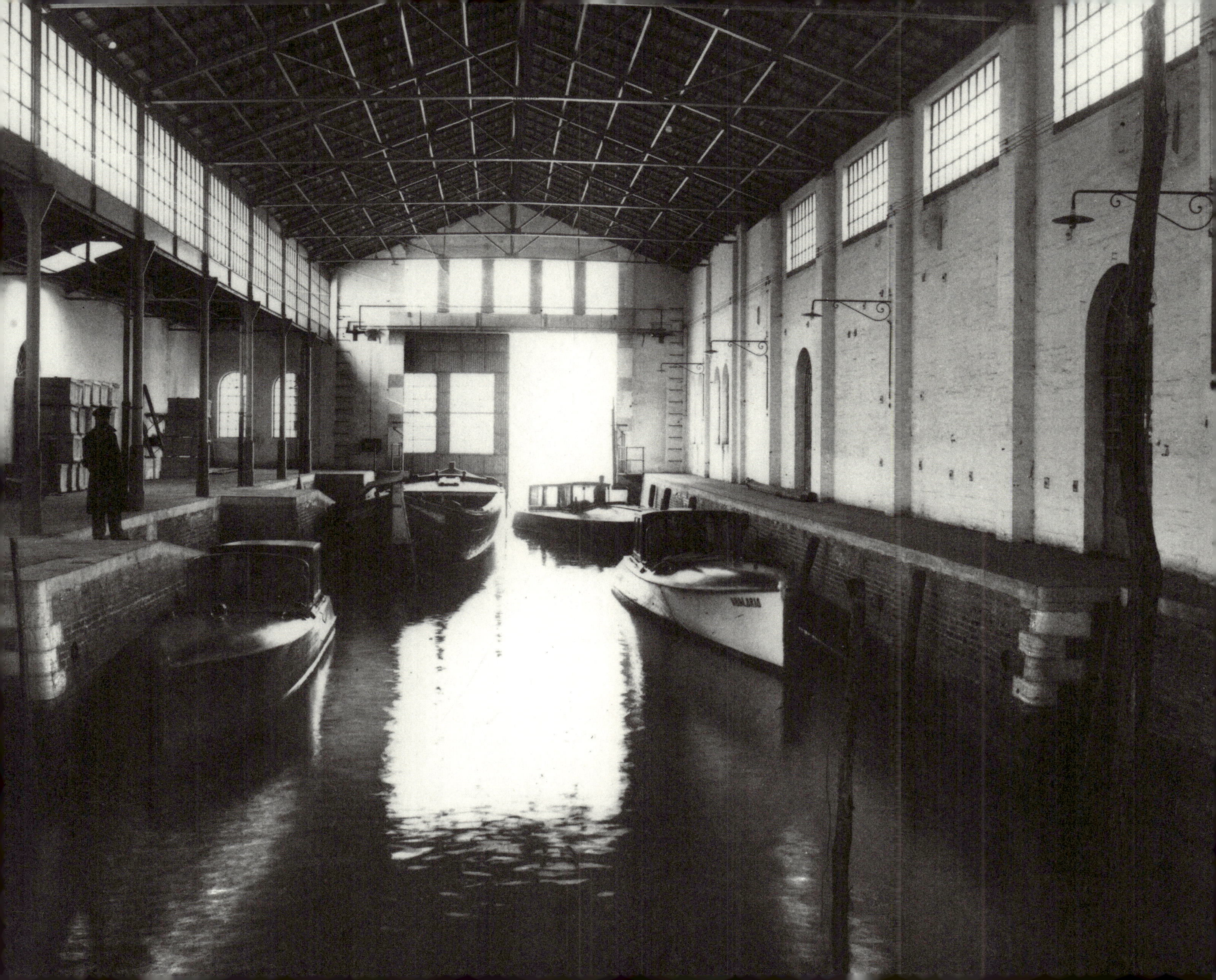

> NOTE THE TWO TEAMS of the porta massa carrying a heavy crate between them. The SVC was clever in designing a ramp (instead of stairs) to deliver the glass assignments from one floor to another. Together, the porta massa could carry up to 450 kilos.

> (Opposite page): THE SVC RECYCLED EVERYTHING. Made by the blacksmiths of the SVC, these large iron grinding wheels were in operation for nearly one hundred years. As they loudly rotated, the wheels crushed glass fragments (for later re-fusing) and refractory fragments (for later mixtures).

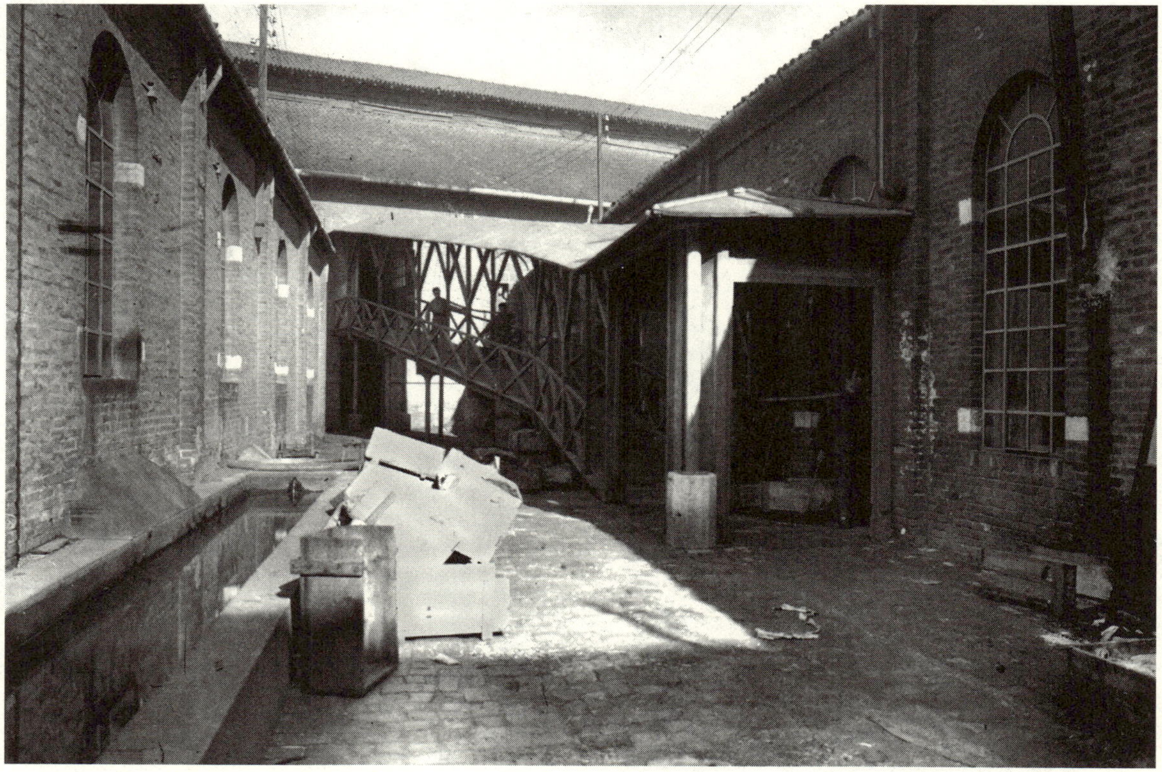

The new factory, built from the ground up, was truly grandiose. It was constructed of brick with one upper floor. Access to the upper floor was by means of a covered cement ramp with iron beams attached to cast-iron columns. The ramp was designed to transport the glass materials between the two floors. On the ground floor, consignments were received and raw materials (used for compositions of the glass) were weighed according to a specific recipe (*partia* or *ricetta*). There was also a utility room, similar to a hardware shop,

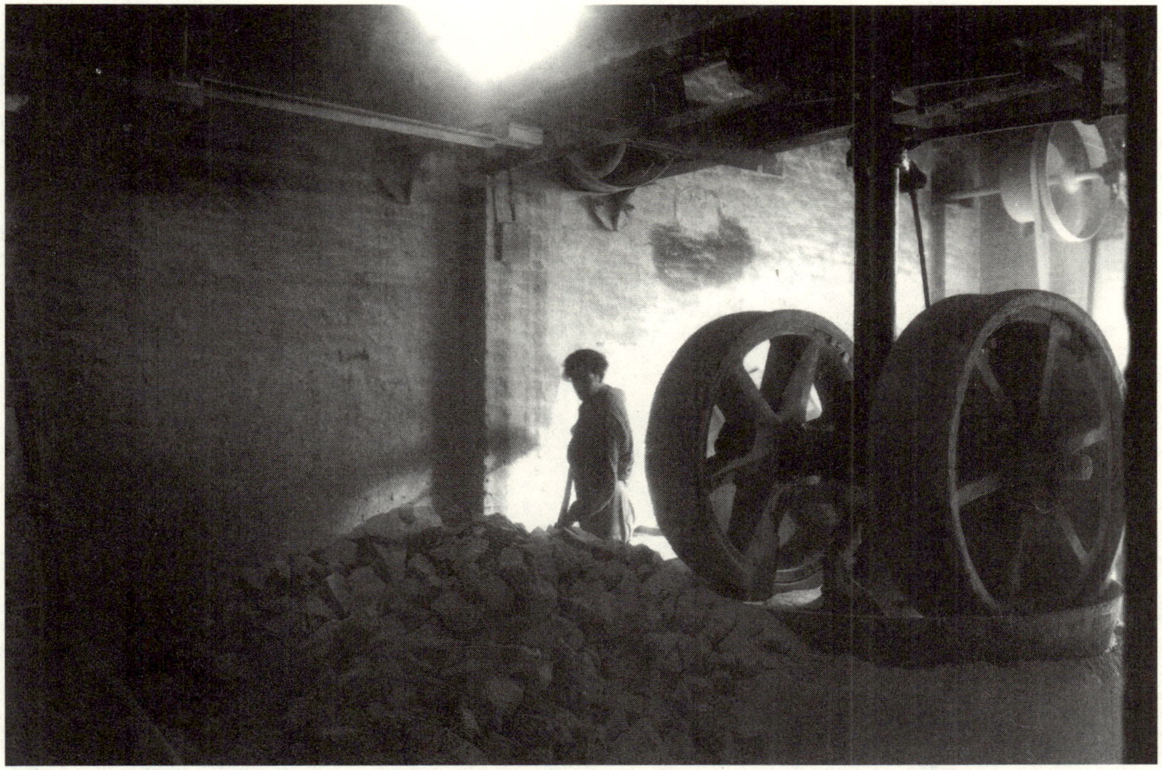

which stored all of the tools and accessories needed to maintain the factory and production of the beads. The departments for separating the cane according to diameter (*cernitrice*), cutting the glass cane (*tagliatrice*), and separating the beads according to diameter (*governa-dura*) were located on the ground floor, as well as the polishing of the beads (*lustradore*) and the Silver & Luster division. There was also an area for glass waste (*rottami*) which would later be recycled and re-fused.

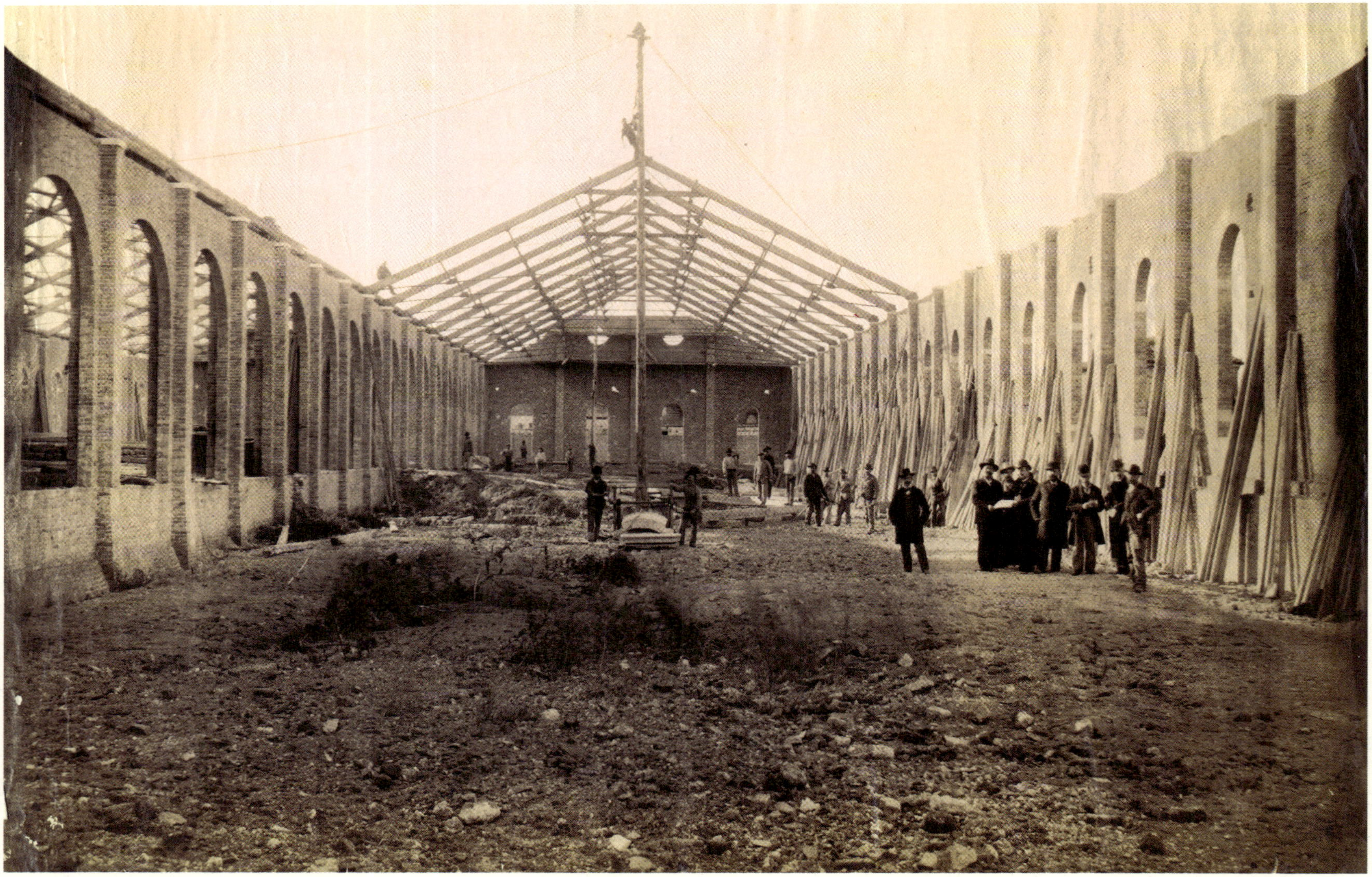

∧ CONSTRUCTION OF THE SVC BEGAN IN 1898: The gentlemen in the foreground of the photograph were probably the owners and executives of the SVC, whereas the laborers are seen in the background. Look closely, there are two men working on the roof.

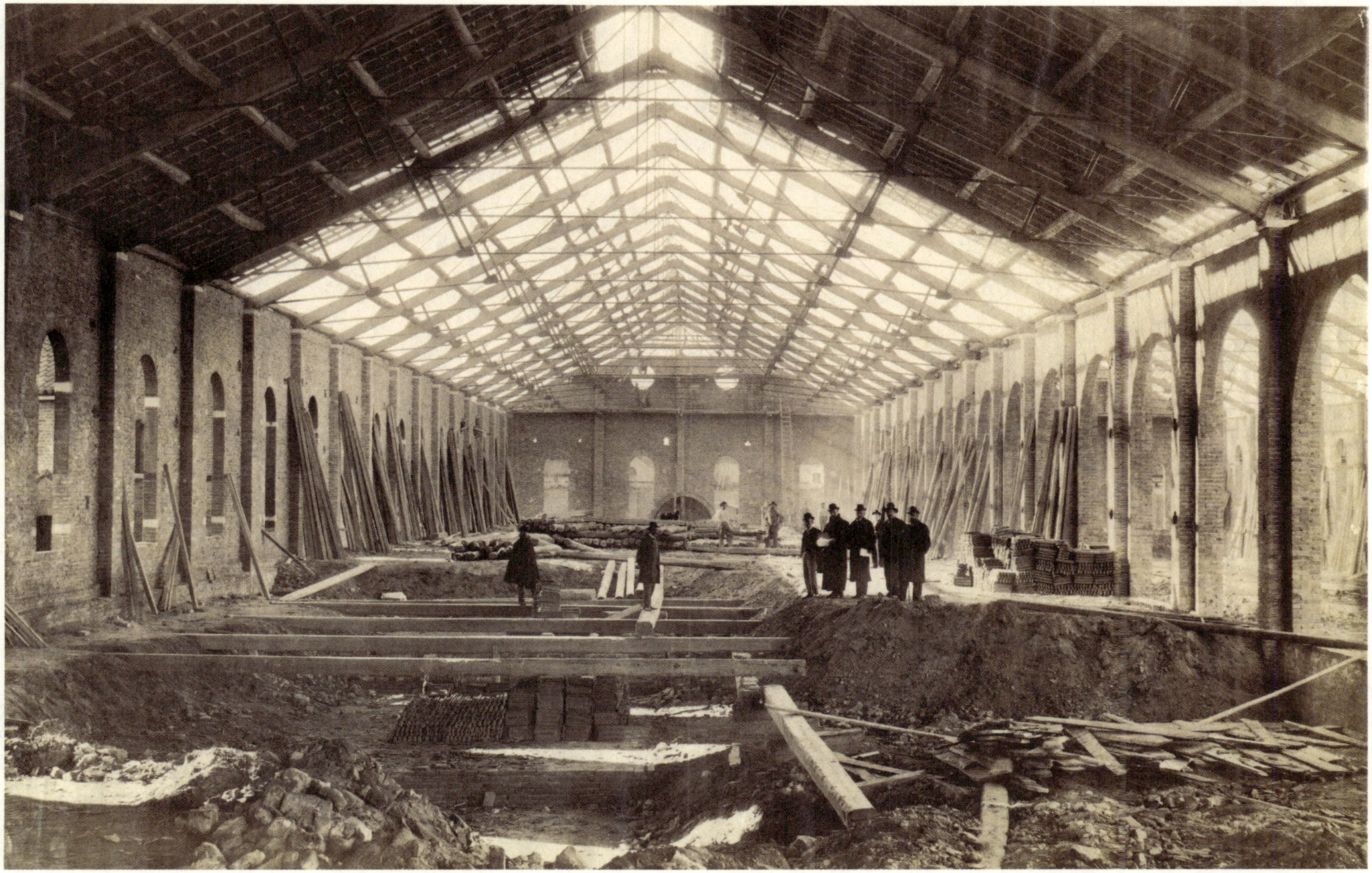

Λ THE ROOF OF THE SVC IS NEAR COMPLETION. High arched windows throughout the factory were specifically designed to allow light and air into the facility. The construction of the factory was an enormous endeavor with over 250,000 square feet of space, requiring hundreds of skilled laborers.

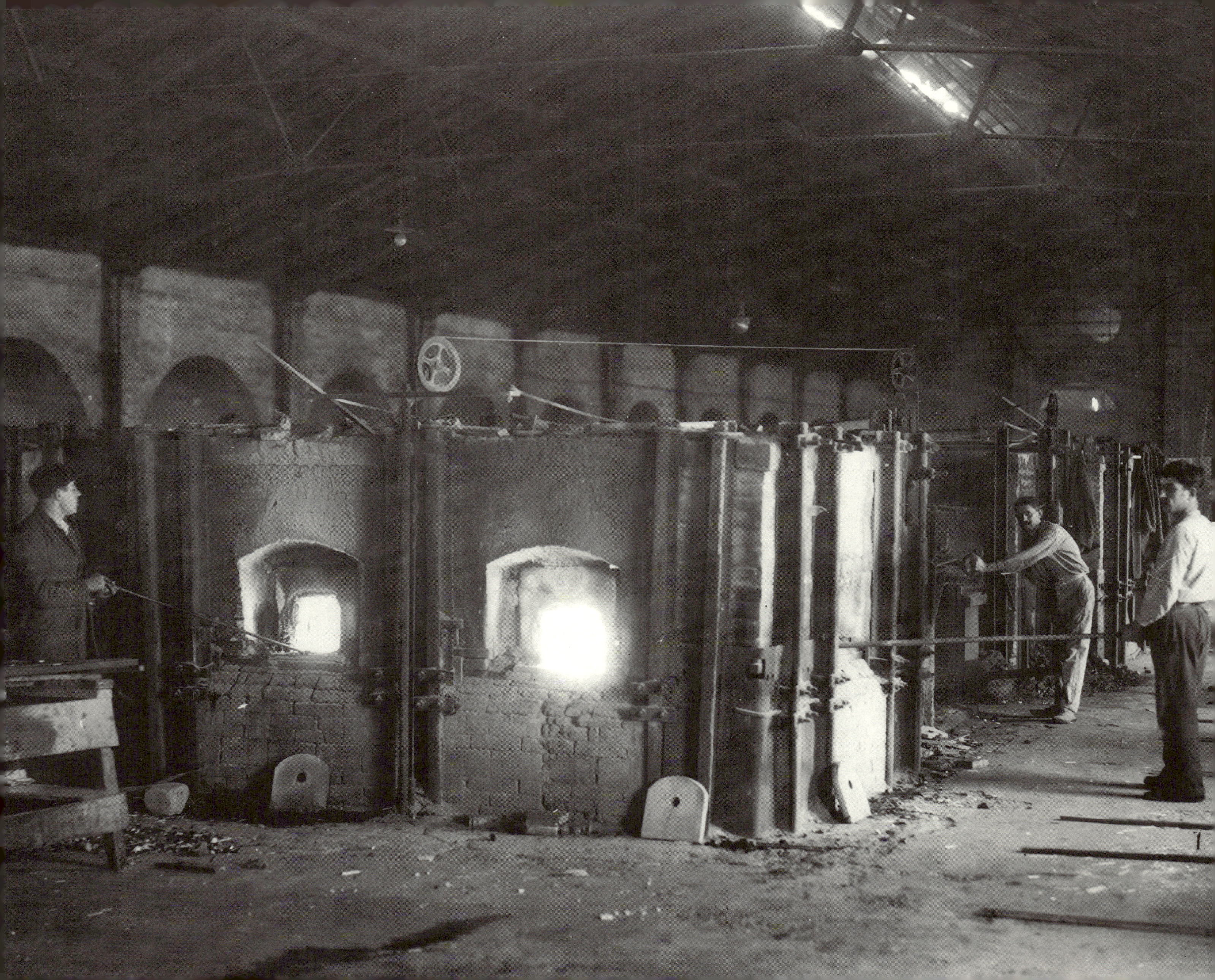

Ten oversized gas ovens were constructed by specialist engineer E. Spasciam. The foundation and combustible materials for these ovens were located on the ground floor; these ovens extended to the upper floor where the oven chambers and crucibles (for fusing the glass) were situated near the area for pulling the glass cane. Collectively, the ovens could hold more than 20,000 kilos of molten glass.[xii] Although the compositions of the glass were measured on the ground floor, the mixing of the raw materials (in an industrial-size dough mixer) took place on the upper floor in a separate room (*stanza di composizione* or in the Venetian dialect, *ogo dee partie*). The department for pulling the glass cane was divided into two areas or two *capannone* (known in the Venetian dialect as the *cason canna*), both one hundred meters in length with an additional twenty meters to accommodate the mixing of the raw materials (the *stanza di composizione*). Both areas designated for pulling the cane were twenty meters wide. This spacious area gave the workers the freedom to move about easily, synchronize their production, and pull glass cane. Moreover, the open space improved ventilation from the heat and smoke that was generated from the ovens. Also on the upper floor, but away from the cane-pulling area, was the department for the *arrontondamento* or rounding of the beads. This area was also spacious and allowed noxious fumes from the furnaces to escape through the chimneys. The upper floor also housed the department for separating the whole cylinders from the chipped fragments (*schizzadore*), the department that filled the cylinders (*fregadori*) with a compound (*siribite*) to maintain the hole during the arrontondamento stage, and the department that unclogged the cylinders (the *cavaroba*) of the siribite after they had been rounded (the arrontondamento stage).

Next to the cane-pulling department was the department for neutral glass (*vetro neutro*), used to manufacture fluorescent light bulbs and radio valves. Because this type of glass was pulled vertically, the SVC used a separate (but nearby) tower with four floors known as the

> THE WOODEN PLANKS ON THE GROUND indicate that these glassworkers were in the process of pulling glass cane. The openings to the furnaces, known as the glory hole (*bocca del forno*) are open to extract the molten glass from the crucibles. The doors to the furnaces are placed on the ground. The small, center hole of the door is used as a window to keep an eye on the fusion, to allow some air to pass, in addition to serving as an orifice for an iron poker to grasp onto when removing or replacing the door.

> THE SVC BUILT A FOUR-STORY TOWER, *il Torre*, to vertically pull glass tubes (for fluorescent light bulbs and radio valves). In the early 1920s, the Torre was also used to string beads vertically. The girls on each floor oversaw the vertical operation, making sure there was a continual flow of beads and, if needed, pushed the beads downwards.

> (Opposite page): THE SVC PRODUCED ITS OWN REFRACTORY (fireproof) bricks used to construct the furnaces. The brick department also produced the doors to the furnaces and the crucibles, all made with refractory materials.

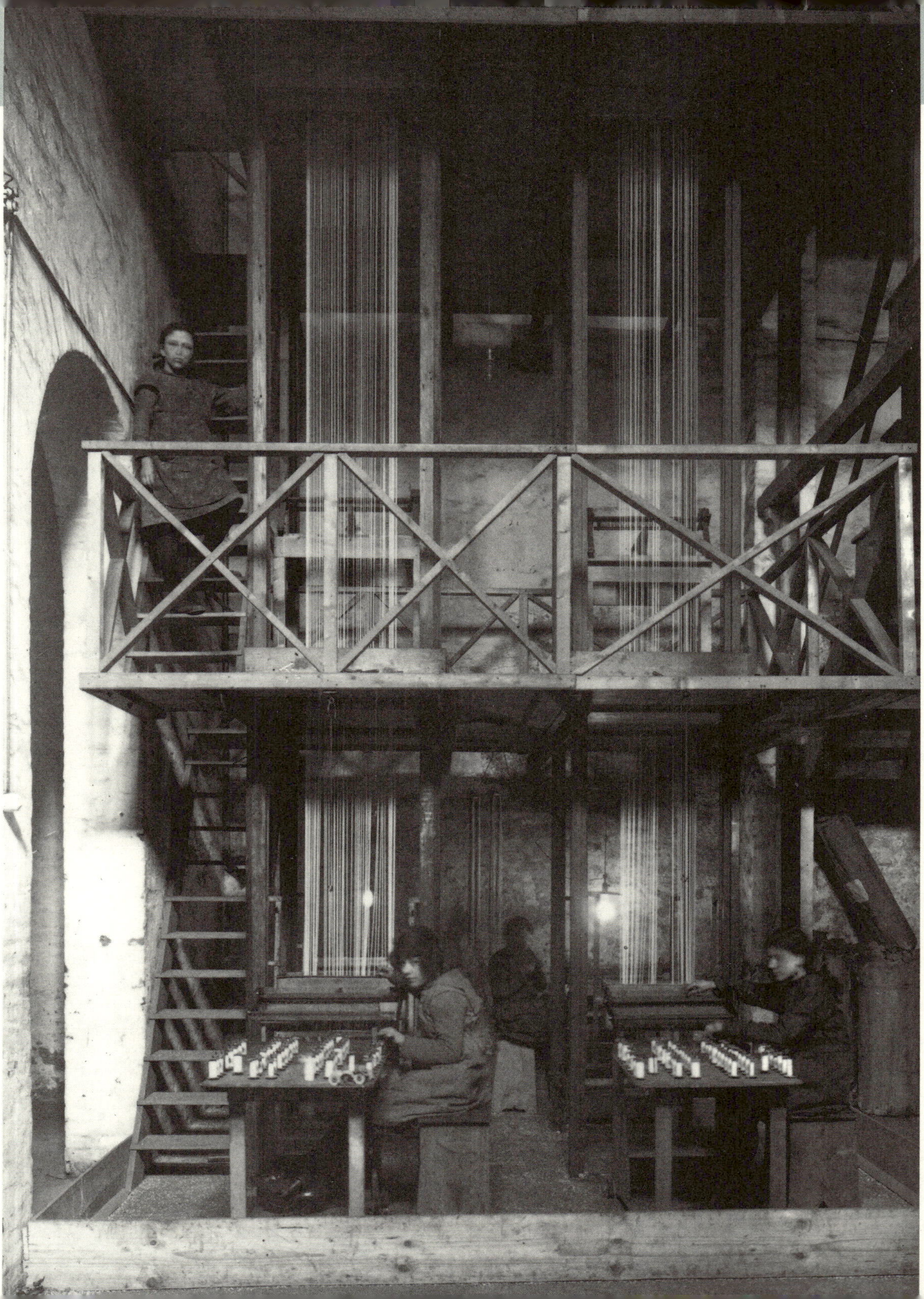

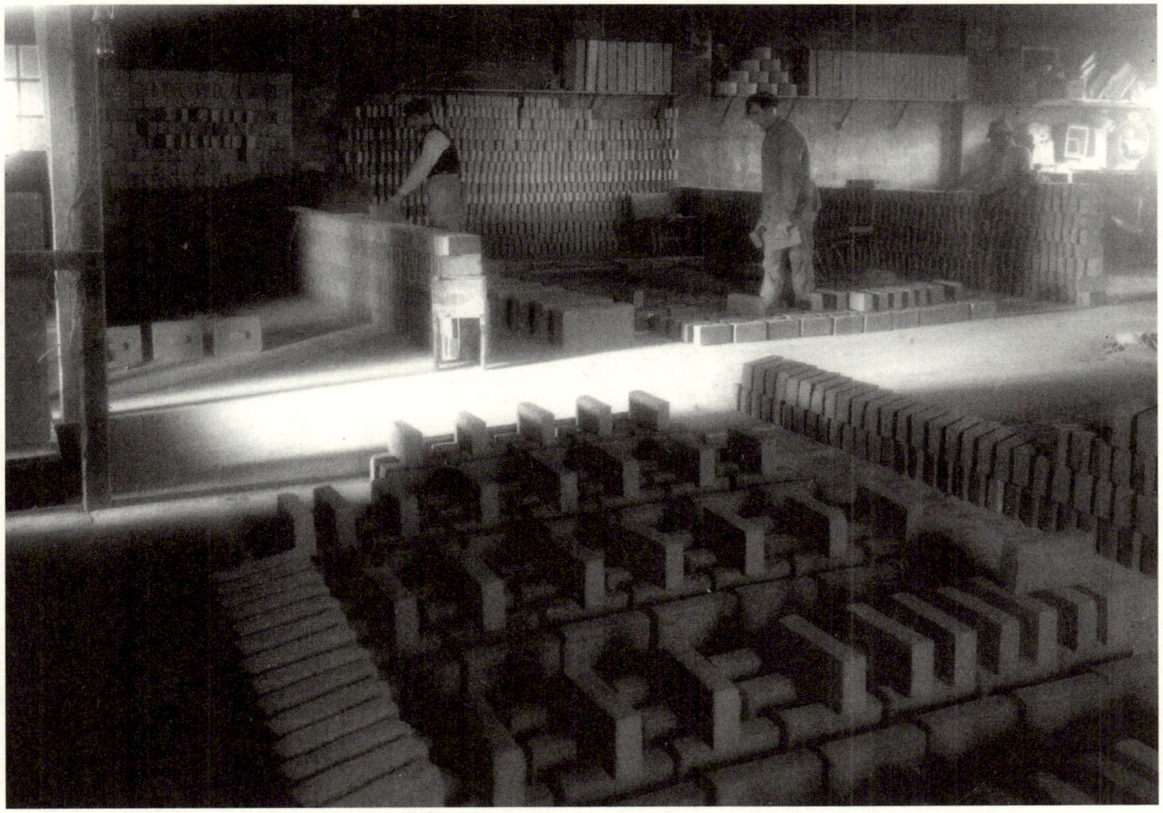

Torre to pull the glass tubes vertically from the fourth floor to the ground floor. In the early 1920s, the Torre was used to string beads in the same fashion.[xiii]

In the early 1900s, the SVC installed an area for a large, powerful steam engine which was made by the company Franco Tosi of Legnano. The steam engine provided power to one hundred twenty cutting machines, in addition to other machines that were engaged in

> THE MECHANICAL DEPARTMENT was dedicated to inventing, manufacturing, and repairing the machinery, tools, and equipment for the factory. The SVC was very independent and controlled every aspect of operations within the factory.

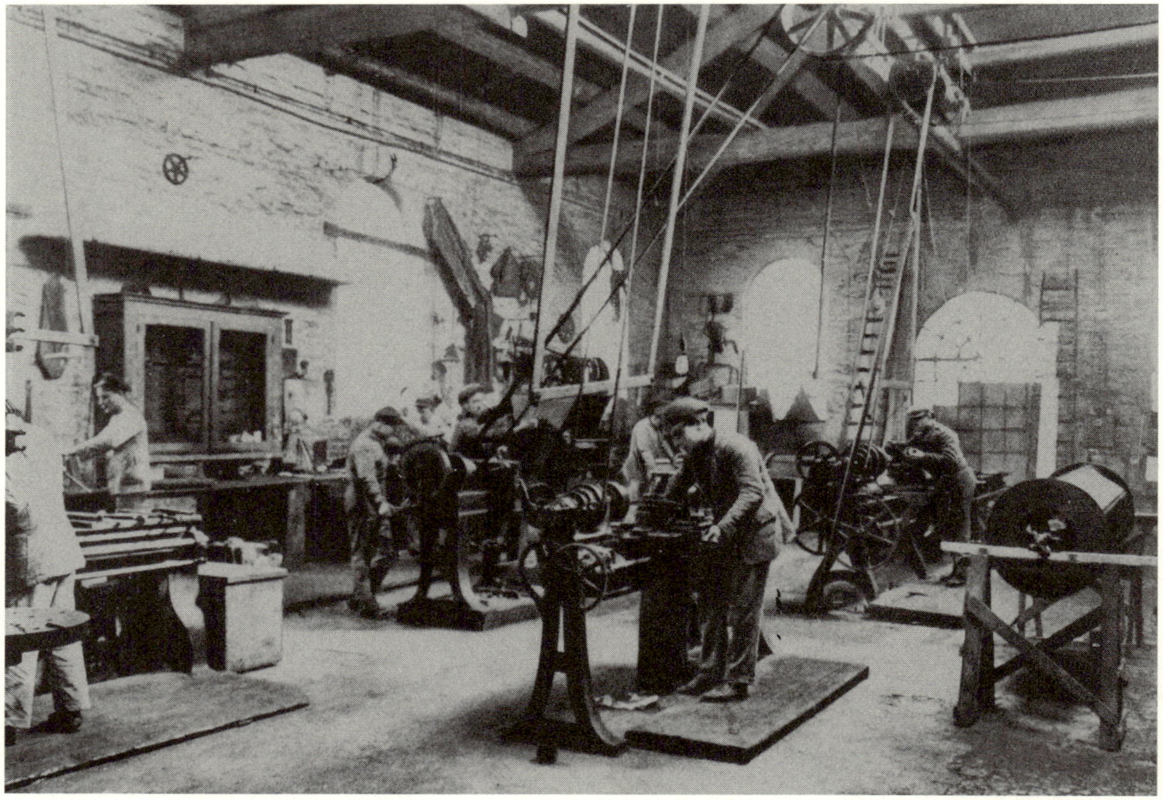

the functions of the bead production. The steam engine also recharged the generator of the factory, supplying light to all of the departments at night. Large arched windows allowed natural light to illuminate the SVC during the day which provided clean air and gentle breezes. The flooring was smooth, like a ballroom dance floor. The new establishment was refined with every modern convenience.[xiv]

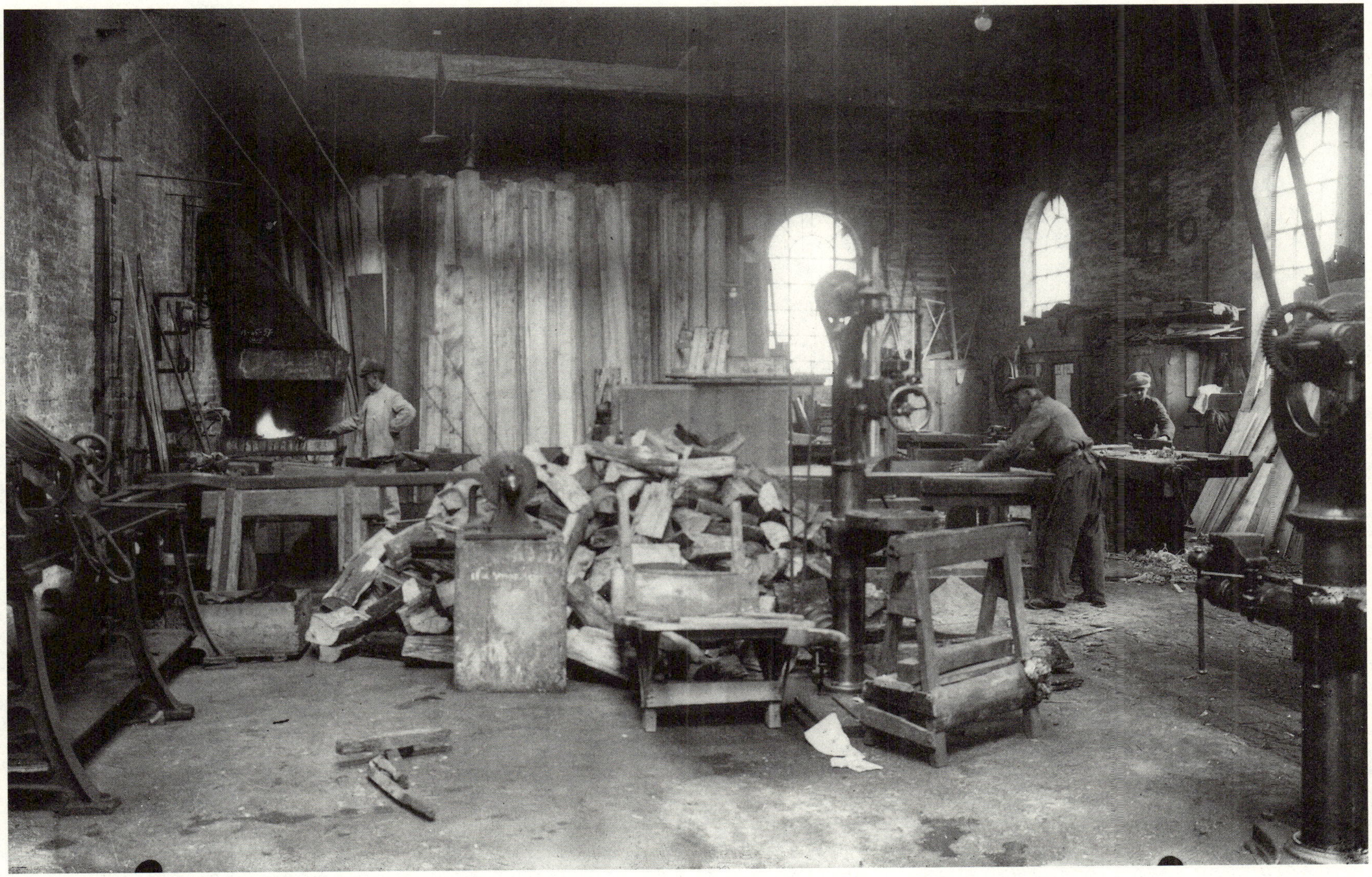

∧ THE SVC HAD ITS OWN TEAM of skilled carpenters. The carpentry department was kept very busy designing and producing an array of wooden articles such as benches, stools, ladders, pallets, molds, cabinets, tables, handles for tools, trunks, doors, window frames, stairs, boxes for shipments, in addition to repairing the transport boats, docks, and anything else made of wood in the factory.

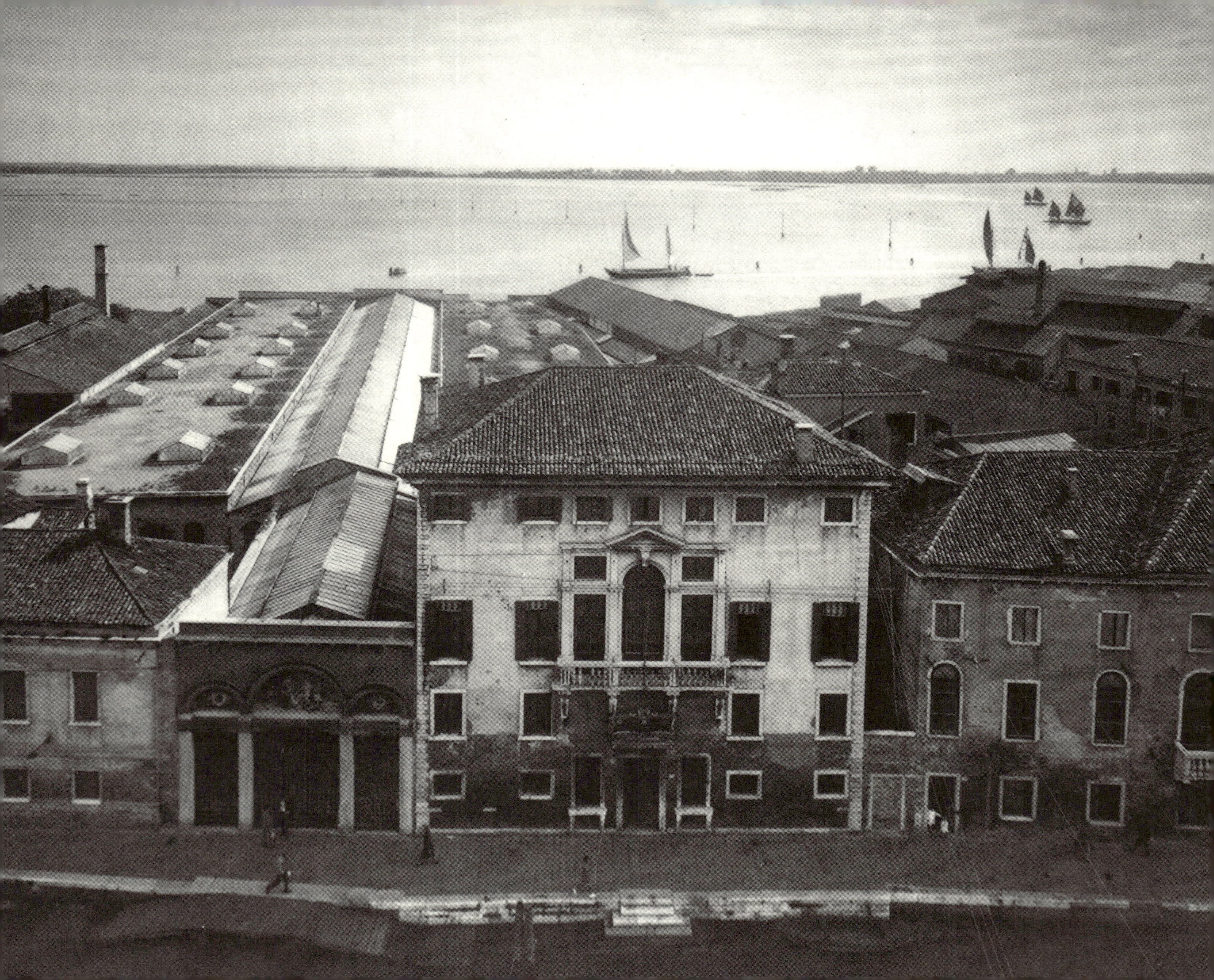

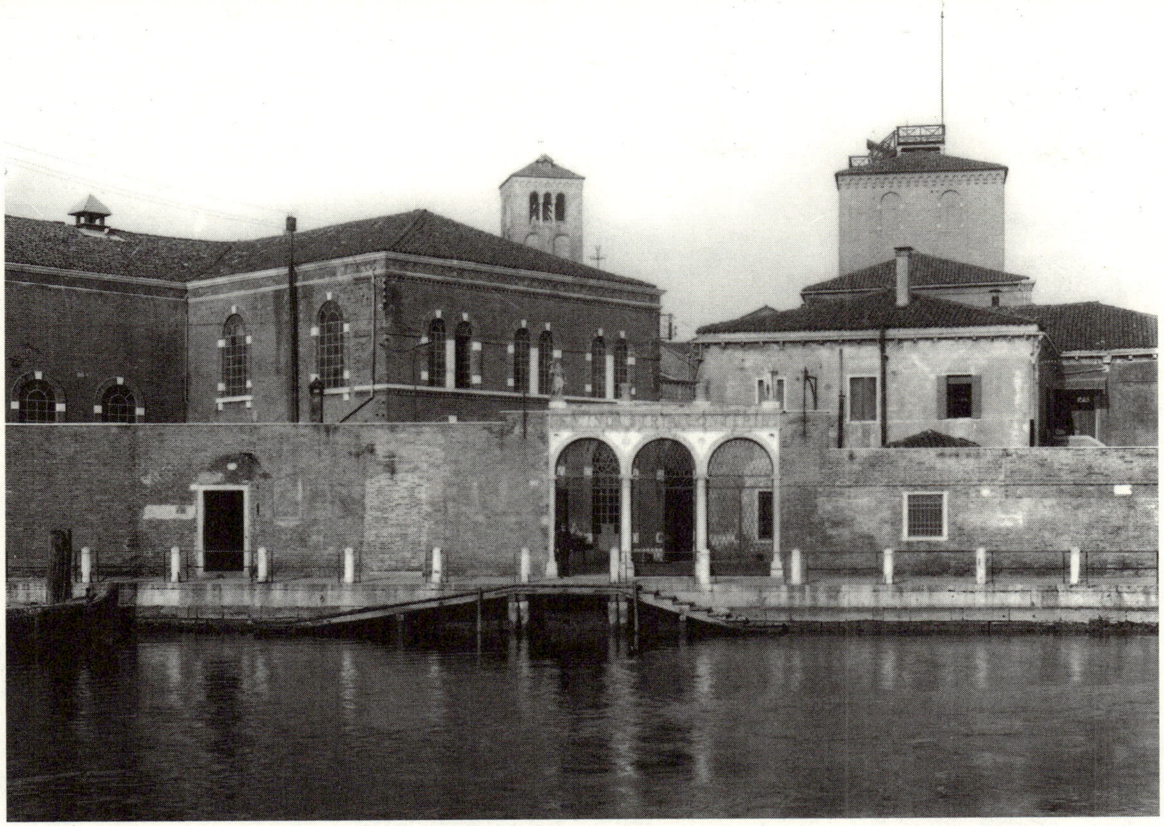

FONDAMENTA MARCO GIUSTINIAN

< (Opposite page): THE 16TH CENTURY PALAZZO TREVISAN was constructed in 1577 by Venetian architect Daniele Barbaro (or in collaboration with Andrea Palladio). The palazzo was built as a holiday residence for the aristocrat Camillo Trevisan. The façade of the palace was once decorated with frescoes. The interior walls and ceiling frescoes, now worn and faded, were painted by Venetian master, Paolo Veronese.

< THE THREE ARCHWAYS to the main factory of the SVC could have been an employee entrance, and/or a passageway for incoming and outgoing merchandise and raw materials. The large tower on the far right (now demolished) was once used for vertically stringing beads and glass cane.

The SVC was spread over three zones:

a) MURANO: Fondamenta Navagero accommodated the administrative offices in the 16th century, Palazzo Trevisan. Near the offices was an old factory, San Martino, that was used as a warehouse and occupied a total area of 23,000 square meters (247,572 square feet).

b) MURANO: Fondamenta Marco Giustinian was located directly across the canal from the administrative offices. This was the principal factory of the SVC, constructed to accommodate modern machinery and all forms of glass production, including the conterie beads. This facility occupied a total area of 23,800 square meters (256,183 square feet).[xv]

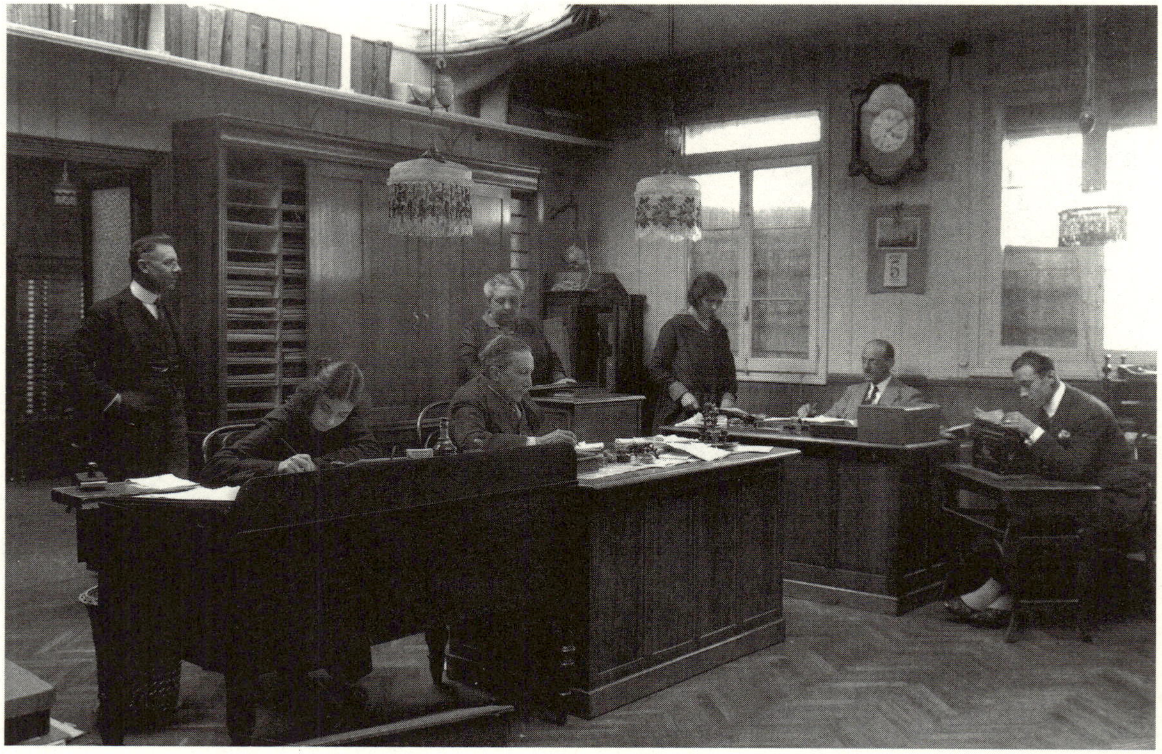

> THE ADMINISTRATIVE OFFICES were decorated with four fringed lampshades made with conterie beads. The male typist on the far right is wearing spatter guards (aka "spats"), which were protective shoe garments (from rain and mud) made of a heavy cloth and considered stylish in the early 1900s.

> (Opposite page): THE SVC HAD HUNDREDS of employees, dozens of departments, and many office workers. While the function of this office/department is uncertain, the bead sample cards on the desk may indicate that it was responsible for documenting foreign orders and cataloging jewelry samples and Bohemian-style crystal.

c) VENICE: Fondamenta della Sensa, located in the Cannaregio district, accommodated the warehouse and facility for the departments that created beaded flowers and beaded jewelry, bead strands and fringes, and lampwork beads.[4] This space occupied a total area of 3,250 square meters (34,982 square feet).[xvi]

In total, the three SVC establishments occupied a total area of 50,050 square meters or 538,738 square feet. It was the largest glass factory in the history of Murano.[5]

4 | In the early 1920s, the Venetians began using copper mandrels to create lampwork beads. All the beads (with the exception of those that had exterior gold gildings) were soaked in acid to release the copper mandrel, leaving the bead hole transparent. The SVC invented a machine to submerse the beads in the acid. This machine was located on the ground floor of the Palazzo Trevisan.

5 | Not included in this entirety were three locations in Murano that pulled glass cane—the San Martino factory, the Palazzo da Mula, and an establishment near Colonna.

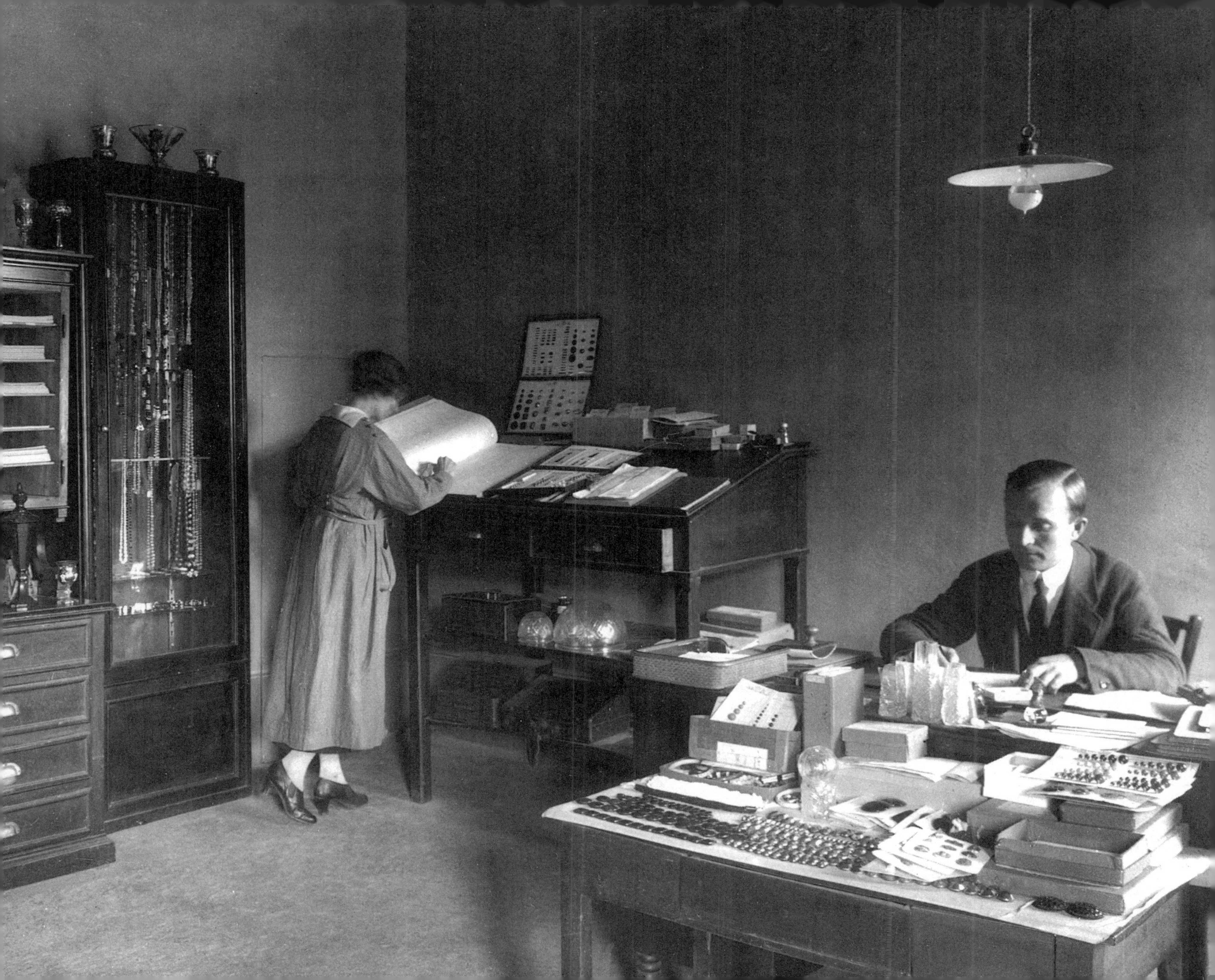

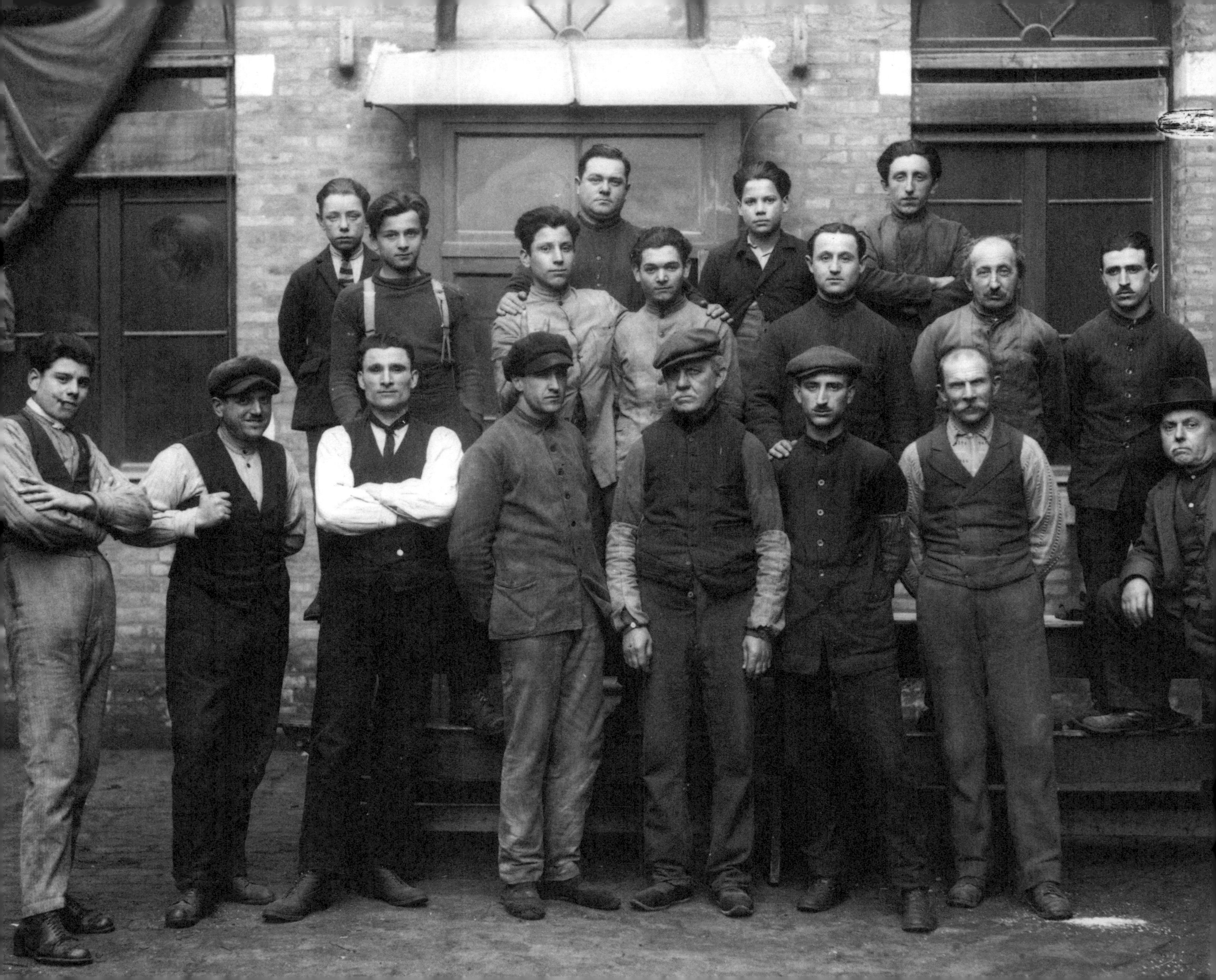

The SVC's workforce consisted of a consolidated force of talented glass masters, experienced production workers, skilled blacksmiths, carpenters, electricians, bricklayers, chemists, refractory specialists, salesmen, and administrative staff. The SVC was remarkably self-reliant and thrived for nearly a century. Under the leadership of Luciano Barbon, up to one thousand workers were employed, many of whom were women. By 1902, after only four years in business, the Chamber of Commerce of Venice affirmed that the beads produced by the SVC had reached the markets of France, Germany, England, Russia, Danube Regions, Turkey, Africa, East India, the Far East, and the two Americas.[xvii]

Over the course of its history, the SVC would export its beads to nearly every continent. Due to the close proximity, beads were most easily exported to neighboring countries such as Greece, France, Germany, Austria, Spain, Portugal, and England. The beads also arrived to customers in northern Europe such as in Belgium, Holland, Finland, Denmark, as well as Eastern European countries such as the former Yugoslavia, Czechoslovakia, Hungary, Bulgaria, Poland, and Russia.

Conterie beads were sent to West Africa to the Ivory Coast, Cape Verde, the Gambia, Ghana, Liberia, Niger, Nigeria, Senegal, Congo, Angola, Sierra Leone, and Mauritania. In East Africa, beads were delivered to Egypt, Sudan, Eritrea, Ethiopia, Somalia, Kenya, Tanzania, Zanzibar, Mozambique, and Madagascar, and then further south to Rhodesia and South Africa. The SVC shipped beads to the Middle East to countries in Afghanistan, Iran, Iraq, Kuwait, Lebanon, Syria, Israel, Jordon, Turkey, Libya, Tunisia, Morocco, Algeria, and Cyprus. The SVC also exported beads to Asian markets in India, Pakistan, Sri Lanka (Ceylon), Hong Kong, China, and the Philippines. While South America wasn't a principal market for the SVC, some orders came from Venezuela, Peru, Brazil, in addition to Mexico, Cuba, Haiti, Curacao, the United States, Canada, and even Australia.[6] In fact, the only continent that did not receive shipments from the SVC was Antarctica.

< THE WORKERS OF THE SVC were both young and old. The extra material on the forearms of the older gentleman (center) indicates he was probably a principal glassworker or glass master. The added material protected his arms from the hot, molten glass as he worked. He is also wearing handmade shoes called *Papusse*, which were commonly worn in Murano in the early 1900s. The upper for these shoes was made of a heavy-duty fabric and sometimes the soles were made of recycled bicycle tires which protected the feet of the factory worker from the sharp and hot shards of the glass. By the mid-1900s, a stronger and newer shoe came to Venice called the *Furlane* (named after Friuli—a northeast region of Italy, where the shoes originated). The upper for these shoes was made of velvet, while the sole was made of recycled bicycle tires The Furlane shoes became very popular in the Murano glass factories as well as with the Venetian gondoliers, preventing them from slipping or chipping the paint off their gondolas. Today, the Furlane shoes are created with a variety of colorful patterns and soft fabrics, such as silk, velvet, and cotton. The soles continue to be made from the same rubber as bicycle tires.

6 | All of the countries listed were found on original bead samples cards of the Società Veneziana Conterie.

Unquestionably, the SVC was ambitious in its quest to sell its beads to the entire world. The Venetians, masters of shipbuilding and commanding a naval port conveniently situated between the Far East and Africa, have always been merchants of the sea, exporting and importing goods.

This industry has traveled all over the entire world and has arrived in countries unknown to us ... it was [Christopher] Columbus who used [the conterie beads] to negotiate with the natives of America.[xviii]

While still under the direction of Cavalier Luciano Barbon, in 1900 the SVC purchased a conterie factory in Rhone, France. The *Societe Generale pour l'Industrie du Verroterie* was established exclusively to manufacture beaded flowers and beaded mortuary wreaths.[xix] Due to the embargoes placed on Germany and Austria-Hungary during WWI (1914-1918), glass exported from these countries was nearly eliminated from the international market, inadvertently providing an opportunity for other European glass manufactures, such as the SVC, to fill the niche left in their absence. The SVC's Department of Flowers, along with the Venetian women known as the *impiraresse,* created and strung (on a metal wire) thousands of glass flowers and leaves made of conterie beads which were then shipped to the branch in Rhone, France. In 1916, Luciano Barbon planned the construction of a machine that could thread the conterie beads onto metal wires.[xx] In France, the flowers were assembled onto a metal frame to create mortuary wreaths. Considering these wreaths were both heavy and fragile, some as grandiose as 125 centimeters x 105 centimeters (4 feet x 3.4 feet), the task of the final assemblage in France was convenient and profitable. The exquisite handmade wreaths were sold extensively to families who lost loved ones in the war. With grace and dignity, thousands of these delicate mortuary wreaths adorned the tombstones of the brave, fallen soldiers in military cemeteries throughout France.[7]

7 | It has been said that French policy allowed these wreaths to be displayed for one year; then the wreath had to be replaced with a new one or taken down permanently. This policy gave more business to the SVC.

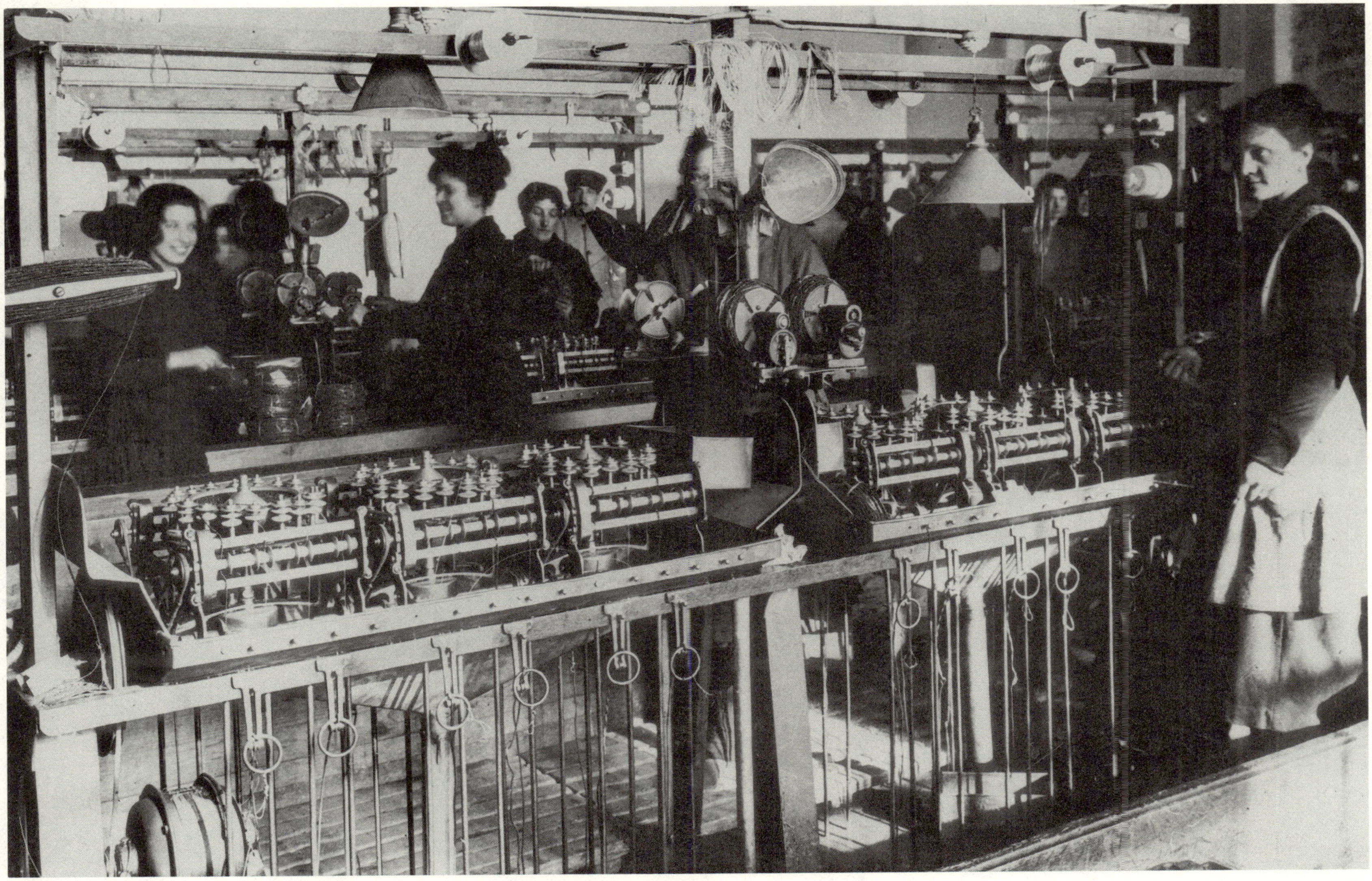

Λ IT IS UNCERTAIN IF THIS WIRE STRINGING MACHINE was semi-automatic or manual. It was invented and fabricated by the engineers and blacksmiths of the SVC around 1916. Its purpose was to string conterie beads onto a metal wire. The machine produced spools of wire-bound conterie beads which were later used for creating flowers and leaves to be assembled onto the metal frames of military mortuary wreaths destined for France.

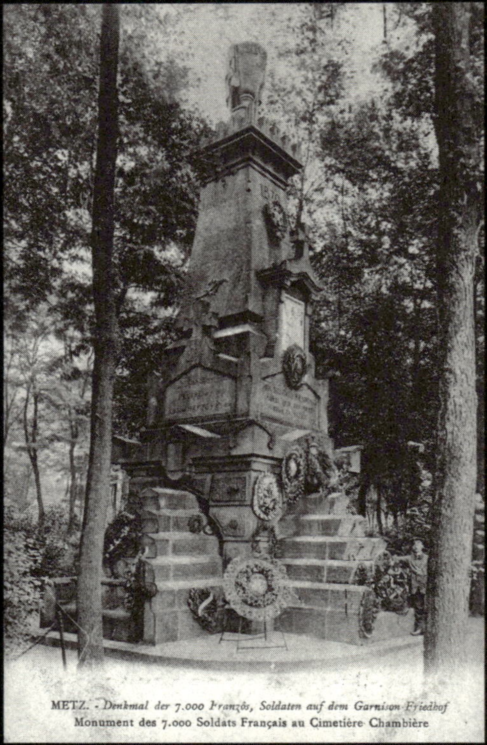
METZ. - Denkmal der 7.000 Franzôs, Soldaten auf dem Garnison Friedhof
Monument des 7.000 Soldats Français au Cimetière Chambière

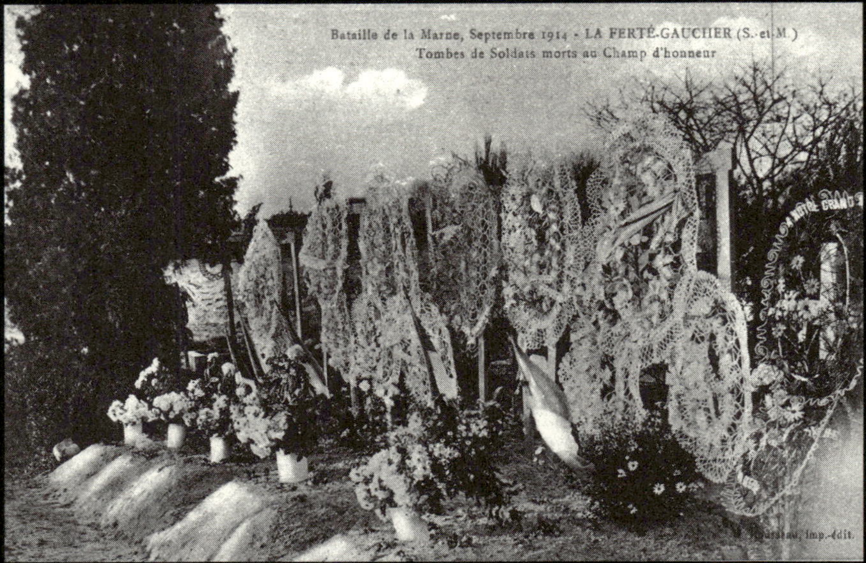
Bataille de la Marne, Septembre 1914 - LA FERTÉ-GAUCHER (S.-et-M.)
Tombes de Soldats morts au Champ d'honneur

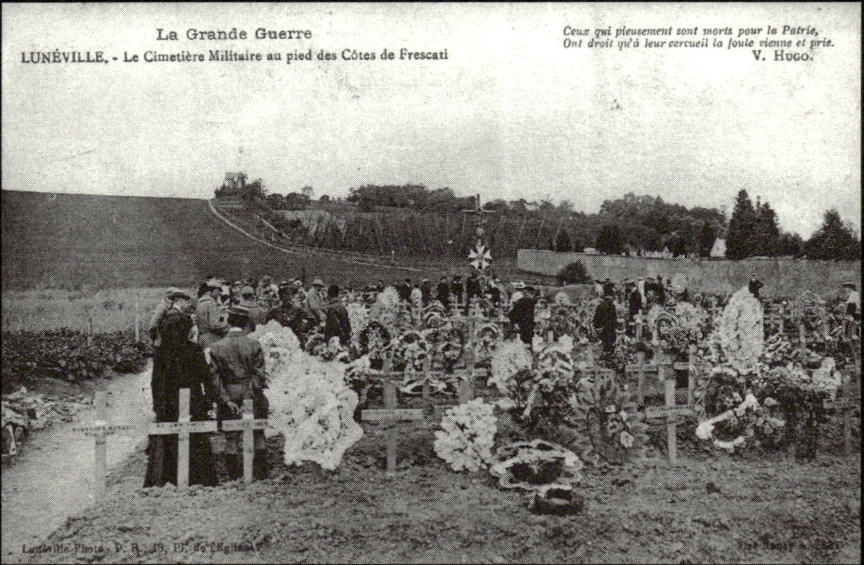
La Grande Guerre
LUNÉVILLE. - Le Cimetière Militaire au pied des Côtes de Frescati
Ceux qui pieusement sont morts pour la Patrie,
Ont droit qu'à leur cercueil la foule vienne et prie.
V. HUGO.

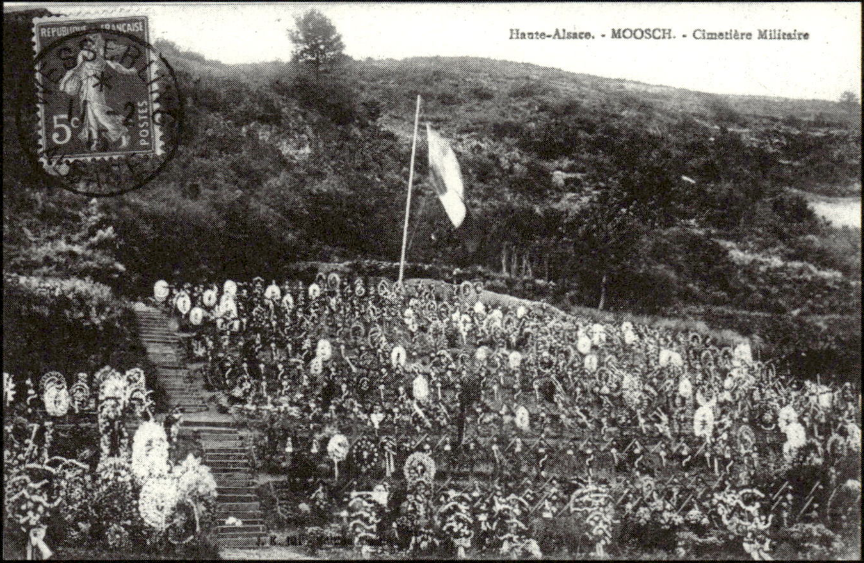
Haute-Alsace. - MOOSCH. - Cimetière Militaire
RÉPUBLIQUE FRANÇAISE
5c
POSTES

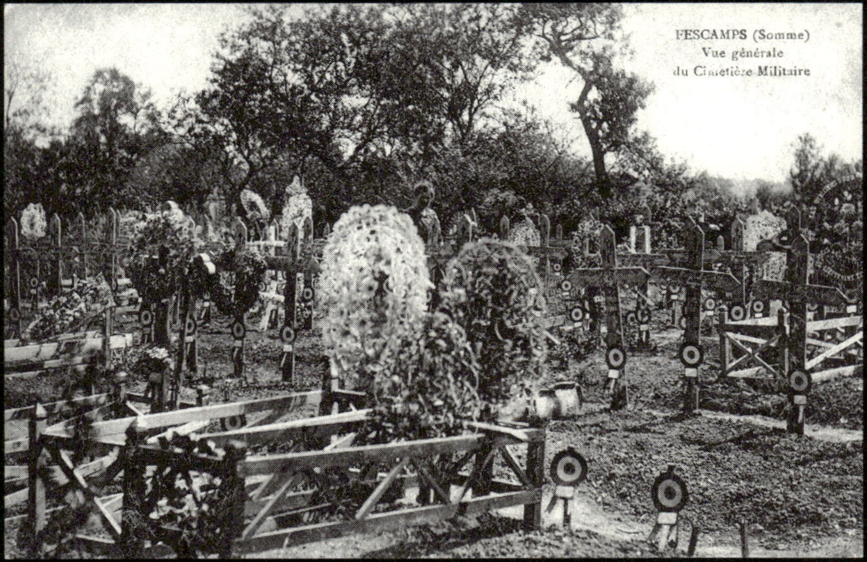

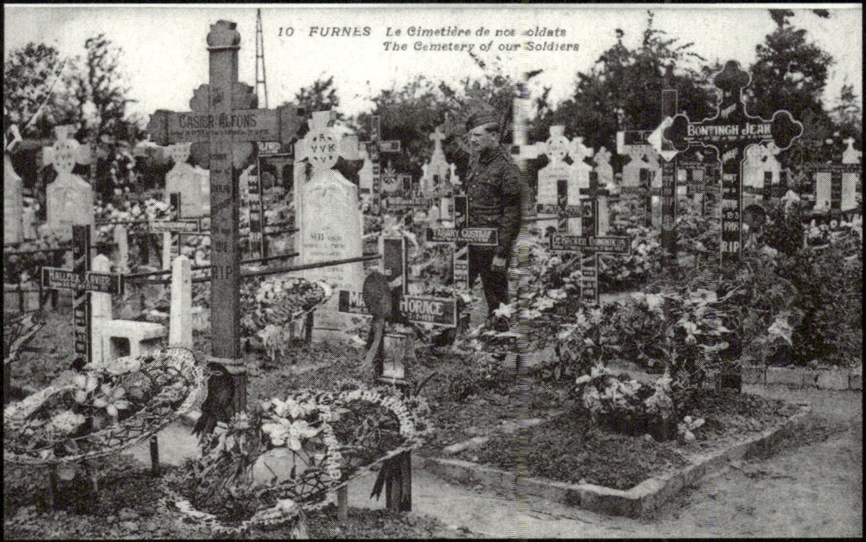

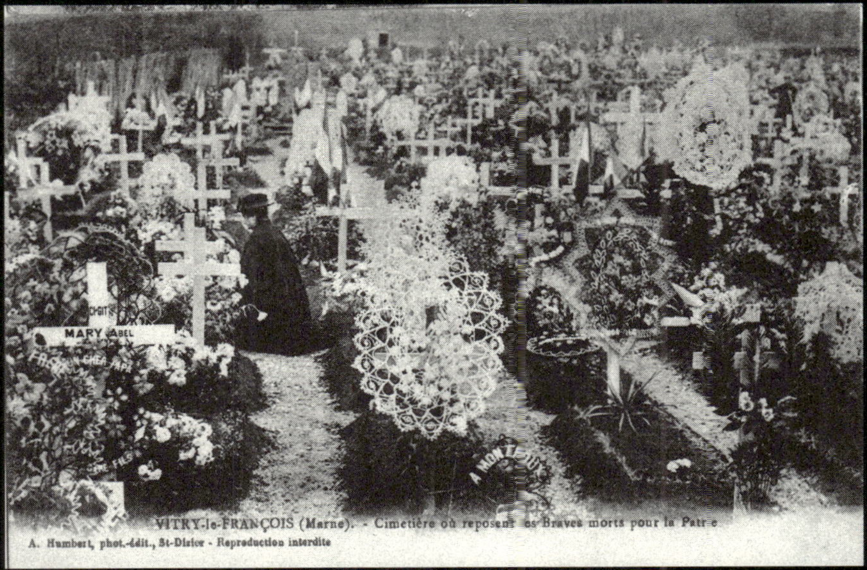

> HUNDREDS OF SEED BEADED MORTUARY WREATHS solemnly painted the landscape of military cemeteries in France during WWI. The Venetian women created the components of these wreaths using colorful conterie beads strung on a fine metal wire, but the final floral arrangement and assemblage were completed by the French women working for the SVC in its branch in Rhone, France. The metal wires gave the flowers greater resistance to the elements. It has been said that these wreaths were allowed to remain on a tombstone for one year, after which the wreath must be replaced or discarded.

> IN 1932, THE INDUSTRIAL GLASS DEPARTMENT was established to produce lead glass to manufacture pistil-shaped glass tubes for light bulbs, fluorescent tubes for neon lights, radio valves, reflectors for bicycles and cars, and traffic lights. The women here are bundling and packaging the glass tubes.

By 1917, with the war approaching Italy, the Veneto region was partially invaded by the Austrians, resulting in the evacuation of the Veneto population and the suspension of many industries, including the SVC. The Adriatic Sea and the ports of Venice and Trieste were also occupied by the Austrians. Cleverly, the SVC transported its offices and merchandise to a warehouse in Genoa where it could still export its beads utilizing the port of the Ligurian Sea.[xxi] During the remainder of the war, thanks to the abundant production of previous years, the SVC was able to realize enormous profits selling its bead inventory stockpiled in Genoa, while the German and Bohemian glass manufacturers encountered difficulty re-entering the international bead market.

In 1920, the SVC purchased A. Sachse & Company of Gablonz, Czechoslovakia, becoming the SVC's second foreign branch. Although this acquisition did not produce the profits it had anticipated, it allowed the SVC to examine the industrial and commercial organization of its greatest competitor. Soon the Muraneses understood how to reproduce the popular Bohemian-style crystal, some of which was unbreakable.[xxii] Over the following decade, the SVC maintained the branch in Gablonz. The operation at Gablonz was very similar to that of Murano, consisting of many small bead and glass companies that concentrated on just one phase of the conterie production.[xxiii] As such, the factories in Gablonz had a high degree of specialization.[8]

From 1921 to 1925, the Italian economy declined while taxes increased. The SVC faced both international and local competition and a post-war reduction in the sales of mortuary wreaths. The directors of the SVC took no immediate action to counter their losses as they considered the economic situation to be temporary. While sales continued to be modest, overall losses continued until after WWII.[xxiv]

By 1926, the SVC could no longer ignore their losses and developed a strategy that would result in a widespread reorganization of the company. In 1931 it sold the branch in Gablonz,

8 | The majority of the inhabitants in Gablonz were the Sudeten Germans. Sudeten Germans are a German-speaking ethnic group which belonged for centuries to the multi-ethnic Austrian-Hungarian Empire (as did the Czechs). After 1918, the Austrian empire was divided into several countries and the homeland of the Sudeten Germans (the former Bohemia and Moravia) became part of the newly-founded Czechoslovakia.

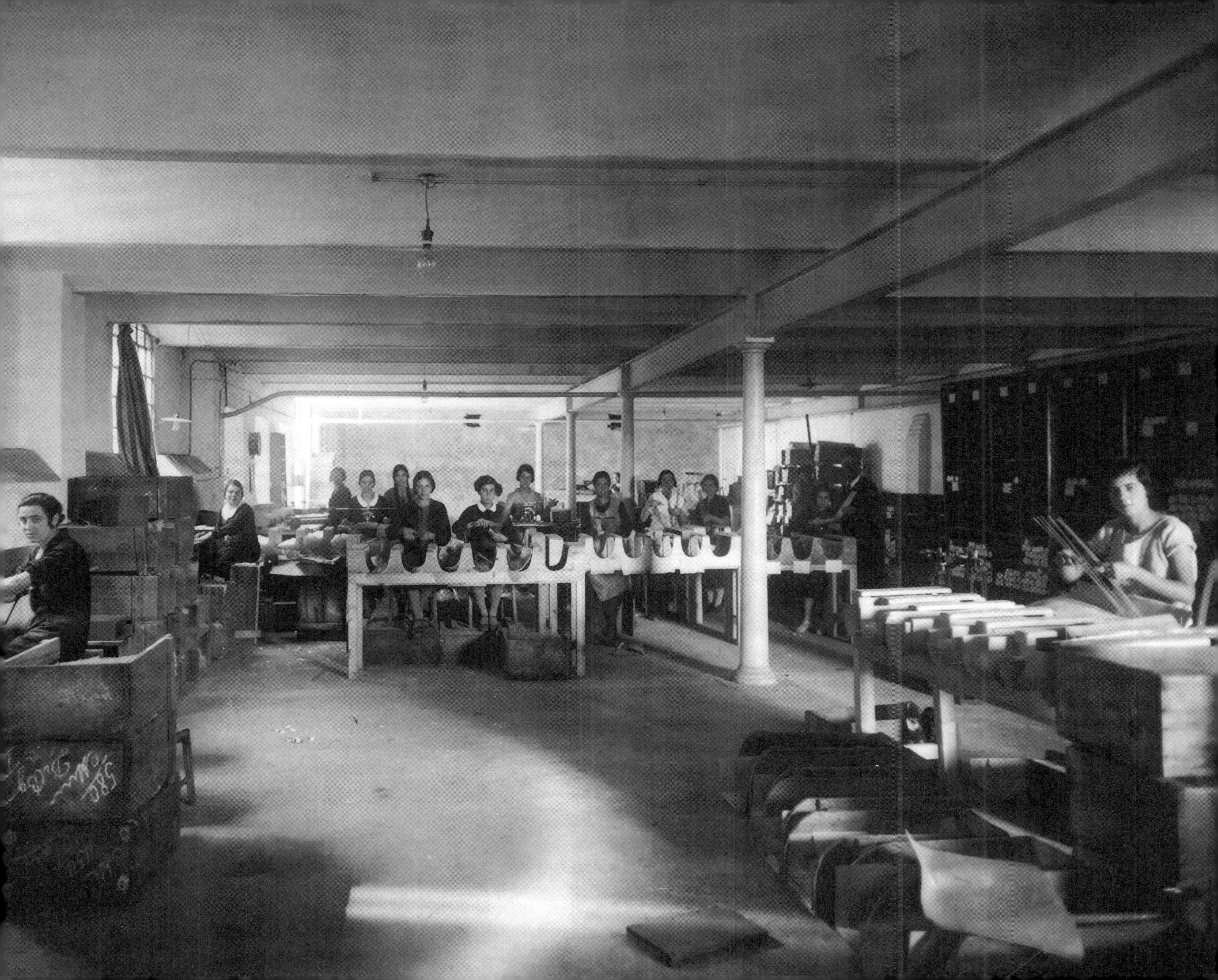

Czechoslovakia. The following year it formed the Industrial Department for the production of lead glass (*cristallo standard*) to manufacture *codete*, which were small, pistil-shaped glass tubes (used as an internal component in light bulbs), and black glass called *vitrite* (used as an insulation in the brass base of a light bulb), reflectors for bicycles and cars, traffic lights, fluorescent tubes, and radio valves. The formation of the Industrial Department was the SVC's first move away from conterie beads to diverse industrial applications for glass production.

In 1935, Italy invaded Ethiopia and, as a consequence, the League of Nations voted to impose economic sanctions on Italy. The sanctions included an embargo on arms, loans, and most foreign trade. Despite this hardship, the national demand for the glass lighting tubes increased and the SVC impressively satisfied most of Italy's requirements for light bulbs.[xxv]

The SVC continued its strategy of diversification and introduced a new line of crystal tableware in the 1930s. The SVC already owned shops in Venice, Milan, and Rome and supplied these shops with the new line of vases and crystal tableware (*cristallerie*). Thereafter, and for approximately sixteen years, the SVC became known as the Società Veneziana per l'Industria delle Conterie e Cristallerie. In effect, the SVC hired several specialized workers from Milan to work in the engraving and faceting division of the crystal department. Many of these workers spent the rest of their lives in Murano.[xxvi]

From 1935 until 1966, Michelangelo Pasquato was the President and delegated Director of the SVC and its main shareholder. Pasquato held many titles and positions during the post-war period, including the President of the Chamber of Commerce of Venice and a Senator of the Republic of Italy. Thanks to his numerous political, governmental and financial contacts, Pasquato, a gifted communicator, was able to gain financial assistance for the SVC. Senator Pasquato was known as a very generous man who improved the quality of work-

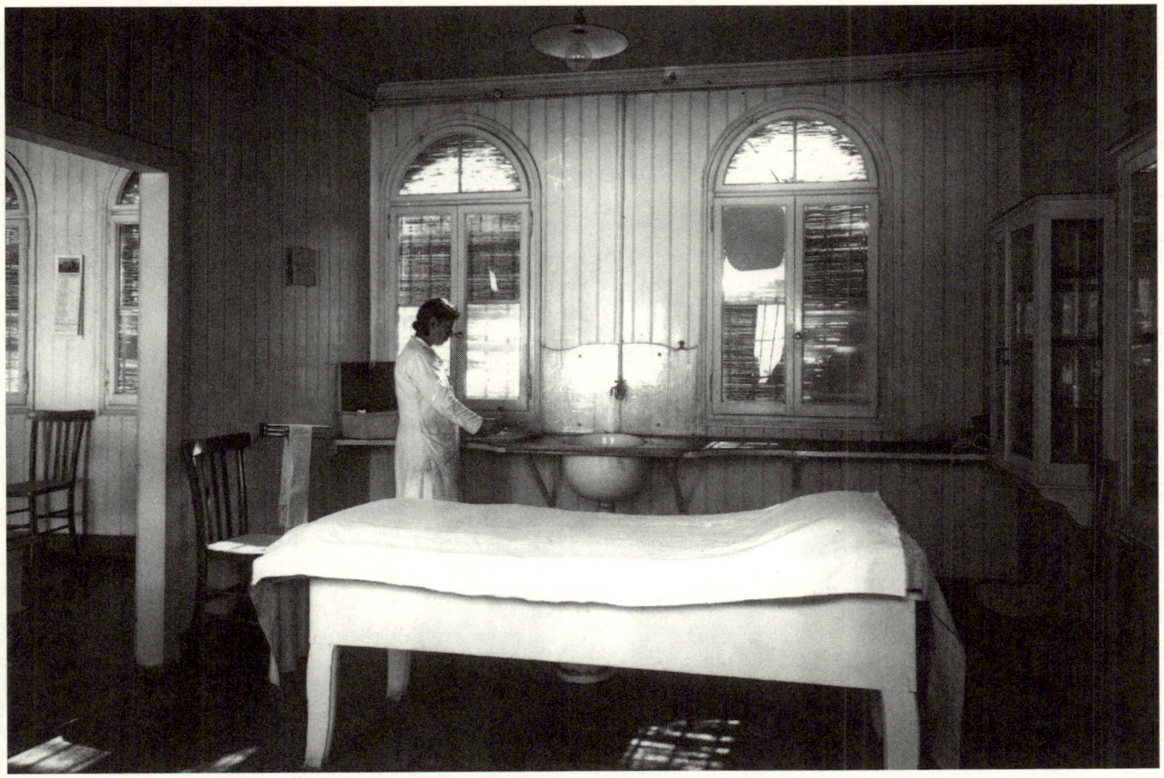

< AN INFIRMARY was established in the SVC to provide immediate first aid to employees who suffered from minor injuries and illnesses such as burns, cuts, blows, falls, dizziness, nausea, and fevers. If the injury or illness was serious, the employee could be transported by the SVC's private passenger boat to the hospital in Venice.

life by adding an after-work reception room, a lunch room, a dance hall, a choir, extended mountain or seaside vacations for the most needy children of the employees, gifts to all the employees' children on the Feast of the Epiphany, low-rental employee apartments, and annual excursions to nearby cities for all the employees. Pasquato even offered his employees an amusement airplane ride that departed from the island of the Lido and circled over the city of Venice. During his tenure, everyone enjoyed working for the SVC.[xxvii]

In 1940, diversification continued with the introduction of borosilicate glass for use in the fields of medicine, science, sanitation, and industry. Specifically, this glass was used for beakers, decanters, vials, cruets, bottles, syringes, and food preservation. One year later, the SVC began experimenting with fiberglass for thermal insulation and acoustic glass for sound insulation for military applications.[xxviii]

During WWII (1939-1945), Europe's infrastructure was severely damaged and many naval ports were closed. Due to the difficulty in transporting and locating raw materials and fuel to produce glass, the SVC was forced to suspend most of its operations. When operations continued, frequent power outages and electrical shortages interrupted and limited production. Despite these interruptions, the SVC was still able to produce its own electricity with a generator and four electricians on duty.[xxix] In 1943, the ovens that were used to produce conterie beads and crystal tableware were disconnected; however, for an additional year, the production of industrial glass continued to aid in the war effort. With the suspension of the conterie bead and decorative crystal operations, the SVC began to replace its manual laborers with machine-operated technology.

When Germany surrendered in 1945, the Czech troops forced the Sudeten Germans into exile from their homeland Sudetenland (border areas of Bohemia and Moravia). Thousands of Sudeten Germans were massacred or died en route to Germany. The Czechs overtook Gablonz and renamed it Jablonec. Thousands of conterie bead workers in the city of Gablonz left their homeland and resettled in war-torn Germany.[9]

Immediately following WWII, all Italian factories that relied on carbon fuel (including the SVC) found it difficult to resume their production due to a lack of combustible materials. While the SVC installations did not suffer structural damage during the war, they did suffer

9 | It is interesting to note that by 1952, Germany was operating with 951 small artisan businesses and employing about 12,000 people.

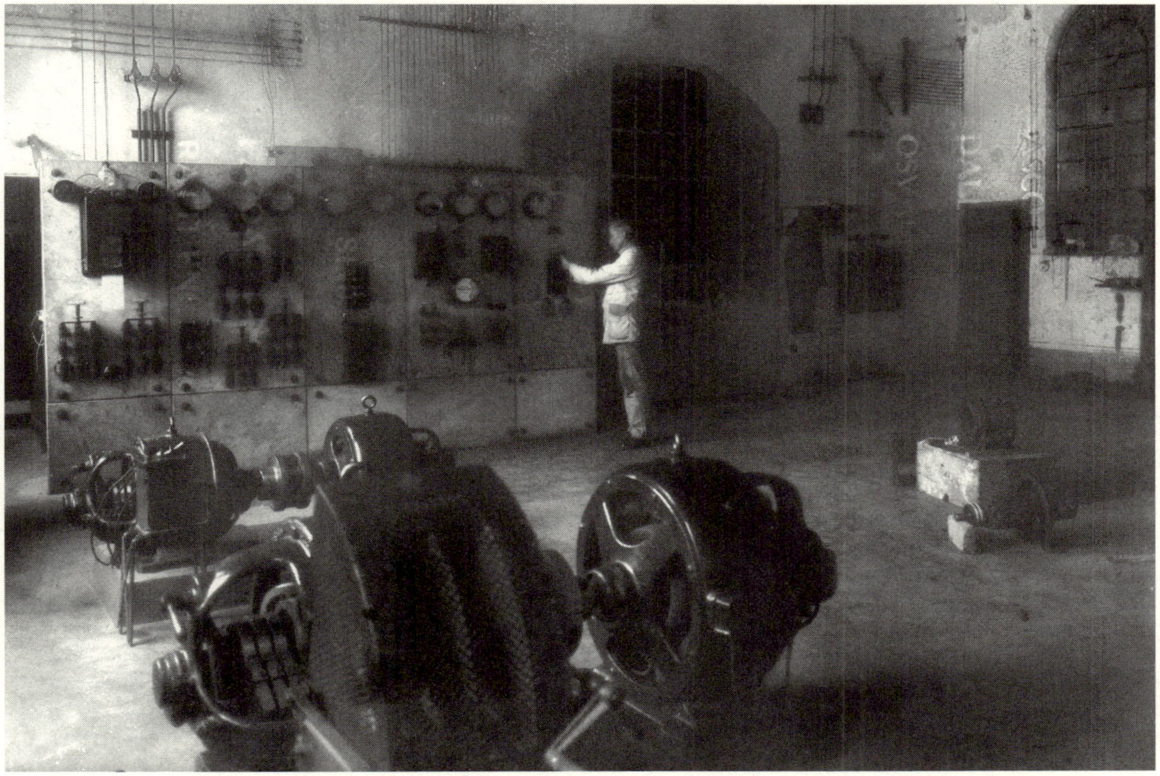

< DURING WWII, electrical power shortages were common, interrupting the steady operations of the SVC. As such, the SVC became energy independent and installed a generator, located within the factory, which provided electricity to various machines, allowing the SVC to maintain its momentum and yield a greater production.

from years of neglect due to the scarcity of parts and supplies. The SVC realized that in order to continue its industrial operations, it was necessary to update its ovens and machinery.[xxx] In July 1945, after repeated insistence, Director Pasquato obtained permission for delivery of carbon and naphtha (naphthalene-base oil or more commonly known as petroleum) from the Regional Economic Commission and the Commando Alleato (Allied Orders).[10] Although these combustible materials enabled the resumption of the cristallerie and industrial operations,

10 | Naphtha fuel was essential for the fusion of glass, whereas carbon and wood were used to maintain the temperature.

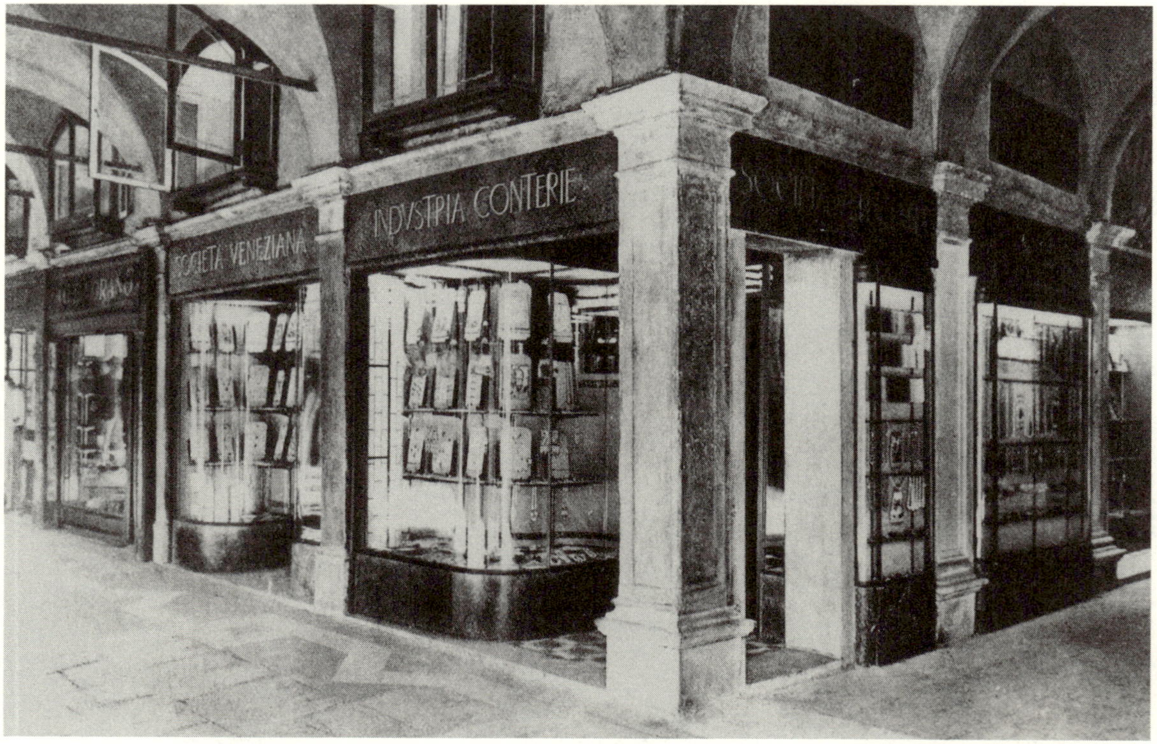

> THE SVC HAD A BEAUTIFUL STORE located in the heart of Venice's historical center, Saint Mark's Square. It sold lampwork beaded necklaces, conterie (seed-beaded) necklaces, bracelets, earrings, brooches, flowers and baskets made with seed beads, and crystal tableware and vases. The store closed in the mid-1950s.

problems persisted in obtaining these fuels.[xxxi] In the interim, Director Pasquato allowed the employees of the SVC to purchase carbon at a discounted price to heat their homes.

In 1946, the SVC resumed full operations in all of its departments (conterie, industrial, and cristallerie) with 747 workers—507 men and 240 women. The conterie department used ovens that were fueled by petroleum. The industrial department used ovens that were fueled by fifty percent carbon and fifty percent petroleum for the production of lead glass. The borosilicate glass operation used one oven that was fueled by seventy-five percent carbon and twenty-five percent petroleum. Since the conterie bead production still relied heavily on export sales, the SVC maintained its industrial line (light bulbs, radio valves, reflectors, and fiberglass) for a few more years. Following the war, the production of glass for medicinal purposes and food preservation did not resume.[xxxii]

In April 1946, the SVC made an agreement with the company Livellara of Trieste, Italy, whereby Livellara obtained the SVC's cristallerie department. Livellara was a wholesaler of crystal tableware and was already a client of the SVC. The agreement consisted of a five-year contract for the rental of the warehouse of San Martino (now-turned factory), including the engraving, grinding and decorative departments, tools, equipment, and client contact names. Livellara agreed to hire two hundred SVC workers who would have otherwise lost their jobs. Albeit the cristallerie department closed, the SVC's stores in Venice, Milan and Rome remained open for business, selling crystal tableware from other suppliers, including Livellara. In 1951, the stores in Milan and Rome were sold but the one in Venice that was located in Saint Mark's Square remained opened.[xxxiii]

In June 1947, India, Pakistan, Egypt, and Sudan established limited quotas of imports on non-essential goods. At the time, twelve percent of SVC's exports went to these countries. During this period, six other factories in Murano were producing conterie beads: Morassi, Costantini-Visdoni, Costantini-Moretti, Mazzega, Toso, Melloni & Moretti, and V.I.S.A.M. Despite the quotas, the SVC retained over fifty percent of all the Italian conterie bead export market with Morassi as its biggest national competitor. Foreign competitors were the Czechs, Germans and the Japanese. Of these, the Czechs were the Italian's biggest competitors in the conterie market.[xxxiv]

The Czechs had an advantage of producing their beads at much lower costs and sold them for lower prices than their Italian and German counterparts. As a communist state, the Czech government paid the companies and its workers poorly (and kept the profits).

Although technological advances were occurring in the marketplace, the SVC was reluctant to abandon its traditional and revered artisan production methods.[xxxv] Notwithstanding the Czechs were able to operate at lower costs, the SVC was more punctual and accurate in filling orders, had a better quality bead, offered a greater selection of colors, and proposed a variety of packaging options such as small packets, loose beads, or beads strung into hanks.[11]

In 1947, the SVC converted some carbon-fueled ovens to petroleum and installed generators to supply energy to ovens that could not be readily modified.[12] The generators would also supply electricity to other machinery that was used in the industrial glass and conterie production.[xxxvi] While efficiency improved, profitability was offset by increasing production and labor costs. In 1949, the SVC initiated a series of radical transformations to increase its productivity. For example, construction took place with an enormous oven with the capacity to hold 15,000-20,000 kilos of molten glass (33,000-44,000 pounds) and a machine that could pull and calibrate glass tubes (to manufacture fluorescent light bulbs) with precision. The new machine pulled the glass tubes horizontally (rather than vertically), reduced waste, and increased production. The design of this modern machine was accredited to the Schuler technology which calibrated the glass tubes in a larger diameter (such as those to produce fluorescent light bulbs) and had practical applications in scientific and sanitation laboratories. The Schuler technology provided the SVC with a high degree of efficiency, quality, and performance. Moreover, the technology was compatible across other departments, including the conterie department, where it was necessary to pull glass cane vertically instead of horizontally.[xxxvii]

11 | In the 1980s, the SVC packaged beads into sealed plastic bags, adopting the same technology that companies used for packaging hard candies.

12 | These same generators continued to supply electricity to the SVC up until its closure in 1992. The SVC had more than one electrician on-call in case of emergencies.

13 | The cornolia bead, with its white core and outer layer of a different color was always pulled by hand due to its two layers.

The 1950s were prosperous for the economy as a whole. The Italian economy was stimulated by the Marshall Plan (European Recovery Program) in which American relief was given to European countries to recover and reconstruct following the damages of WWII. With the reduction of tariffs on international trade, Italy increased its exports to the United States of America. The SVC continued to outsource work to hundreds of *impiraresse*, Venetian women who, working from home, strung the tiny beads onto threads. The impiraresse resided primarily in the Venetian districts of Castello and Cannaregio and also on the islands of Murano and Burano. Requesting strung beads, numerous orders from the overseas markets guaranteed these women endless hours of monotonous work.[xxxviii]

From 1953-1957, the number of SVC employees was gradually reduced, particularly in the department of industrial glass. Following the wars, beaded mortuary wreaths were no longer in demand so the branch in Rhone, France closed. During this period, sixty-two percent of the glass cane for the conterie beads was pulled by machine while thirty-eight percent was pulled by hand.[13] Pulling the cane mechanically was more cost-efficient (and yielded a perfect cane) than pulling it by hand.[xxxix] As a result, the SVC's Machine-Pulled Cane Department continued to thrive, as did the departments of Silver & Luster, and Flower & Fringe.[xl] During this time, the SVC sold its shop in Saint Mark's Square which had for years impressively represented its image in the heart of the city center. It also sold the factory/warehouse of San Martino, as well as some apartments that were used by former employees.[xli]

In late 1954, methane gas was introduced to the SVC furnaces. The new installations were constructed quickly and the results of the new combustible material were excellent. By 1958, the production of neutral glass (*vetro neutro*), a derivative of borosilicate glass, not only replaced the borosilicate glass, but it paved the way for the introduction of new products into

> THE GLASSWORKERS OF MURANO held many secrets of the trade. They guarded their inventions, studies and findings, practices, and formulas for developing colors. Murano soon became an island of intrigue and mystery. The worker on the far right has a rope around his shoulder, indicating that his job in the factory was that of a *porta massa,* the carrier of massive quantities of glass cane and beads. In conjunction with a second porta massa, the rope was used to wrap around one end of a wooden trunk and then tied onto a flexible, yet very strong tree branch. The tree branch would rest on the shoulders of the porta massa and together, they could carry up to 450 kilos.

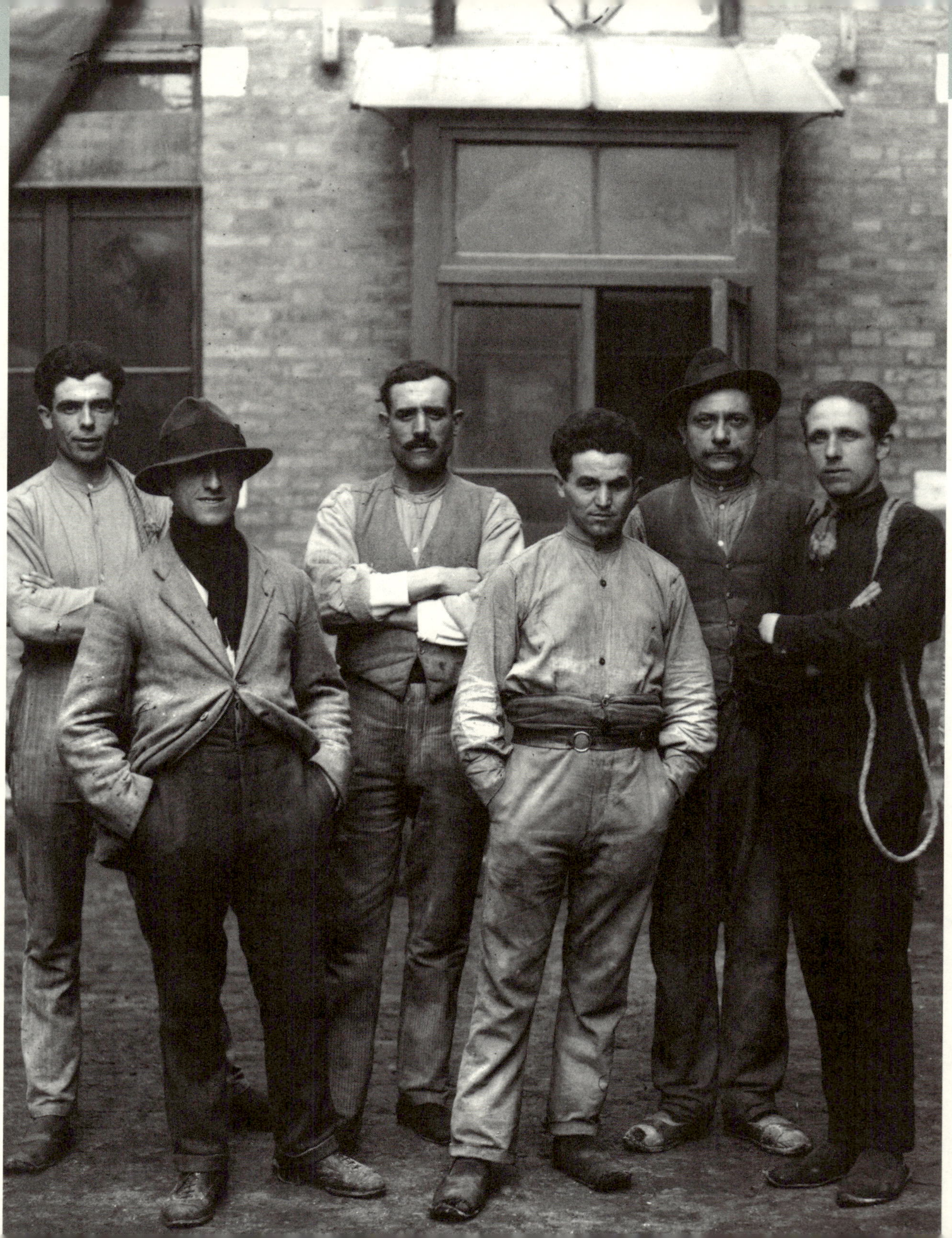

SVC Employee Numbers 1953-1957[xlii]

Department	**1953**	**1954**	**1955**	**1956**	**1957**
Hand-pulled cane	59	49	43	39	39
Machine-pulled cane	12	12	12	12	11
Cutting the cane	49	38	32	35	31
Separation of beads	37	36	32	34	33
Silver & Luster Dept.	11	11	11	11	11
Flower & Fringe Dept.	14	12	11	12	12
Warehouse	59	43	42	42	42
Industrial glass	80	76	62	63	62
Maintenance	67	59	52	49	50
Administration	46	39	35	35	36
Managers	4	4	4	4	4
Total Employees	**438**	**379**	**336**	**336**	**331**

the SVC's industrial line which was of particular interest to the pharmaceutical and scientific industries. Using neutral glass, the industrial department made clear tubes used to manufacture syringes and bottles and also amber tubes used to manufacture vials.[14] The amber-colored neutral glass prohibited ultraviolet rays from penetrating the glass, thus preserving the chemical contents for longer periods of time.[xliii]

The SVC accepted an exclusive contract with the glass company *Vetreria Scientifica Pisana* (an Edison company), to produce 25,000 kilos (55,000 pounds) per month of amber-colored neutral glass and 10,000 kilos (22,000 pounds) of clear, neutral glass. Thanks to the numerous sales and vast distribution of the neutral glass, the SVC became even more widely known and reputable. Seeing the potential in this market and the desire to work more independently, the SVC revoked its exclusive contract with the Vetreria Scientifica Pisana and opted instead for a lighter contract to supply them with just 15,000 kilos (33,000 pounds) of neutral glass per month. By 1960, the neutral glass was in such high demand that it became necessary for the SVC to build a second oven, increasing its production capacity to 40,000 kilos (88,000 pounds) a month. For the next four years, the sales of neutral glass more than doubled. To reduce delivery time to its customers, the SVC opened two additional warehouses, one in Milan and one in Naples (southern Italy). The SVC also became the Italian leader in syringe sales.[xliv]

It wasn't long, however, before the SVC met with competition from other producers of neutral glass. In mid-1964, a new and more powerful competitor came onto the scene—Kimble Italiana, a company that was given financial and technical support from the United States of America. Kimble's neutral glass was superior in quality to the SVC's neutral glass. Its canes did not present any aberrations; it was straight and the lengths of the canes had a consistent di-

14 | The neutral glass has a different chemical characteristic than the basic cristallo standard (lead glass); its pH is not altered when coming in contact with a chemical solution for long periods of time. The neutral glass possesses a greater chemical resistance in respect to the other types of borosilicate glass. Borosilicate glass can undergo alterations of its composition when coming in contact with a chemical substance and thus permit fluids to change or degrade over time.

ameter. The SVC's two other competitors, the Vetreria Scientifica Pisana and the Cristallerie Murano, suspended their production of neutral glass and began to collaborate with Kimble. To compete with the superior quality and workforce of Kimble, the SVC would have had to invest in new machinery and technology. Unfortunately, the SVC did not have the financial resources to do so and by 1965, the SVC suspended their production of neutral glass.[xlv]

In the period between 1954 and 1969, the use of conterie beads in the colonial markets (such as Sudan, Ethiopia, Somalia, Kenya, Tanzania, Mozambique, Madagascar, Senegal, Sierra Leone, Liberia, Ghana, Nigeria, Angola, Congo, Rhodesia, and South Africa) began to decline due to social and economic developments. With dwindling use in traditional tribal clothing and ceremonial vestments, beads began to lose their cultural value. It was during this period that the birth of a new market—costume jewelry—appeared in these African countries.

In 1955, the director of the sales office for the SVC, Fridolin Herzog, took a trip to Africa to survey the African bead market. To his dismay, Herzog discovered that the Czechs were selling their beads at considerably lower prices than the SVC. Herzog pointed out the disadvantages in dealing with the Czechs—their deliveries were slow and orders weren't always filled properly. Furthermore, he tried to convince the African customers that working with the Czechs could be risky with unexpected closings of their factories due to the Cold War. From Kenya, Herzog sent a telegram to the SVC describing the necessity to lower its prices or risk losing business in the African markets.[xlvi] To minimize its losses, the SVC was forced to reduced its prices.

As business declined in the colonial markets, the SVC concentrated on the growing demand for beads for the fashion industry.[xlvii] At the time, the United States of America was the SVC's largest customer for conterie beads, followed by China and Japan. Until this time,

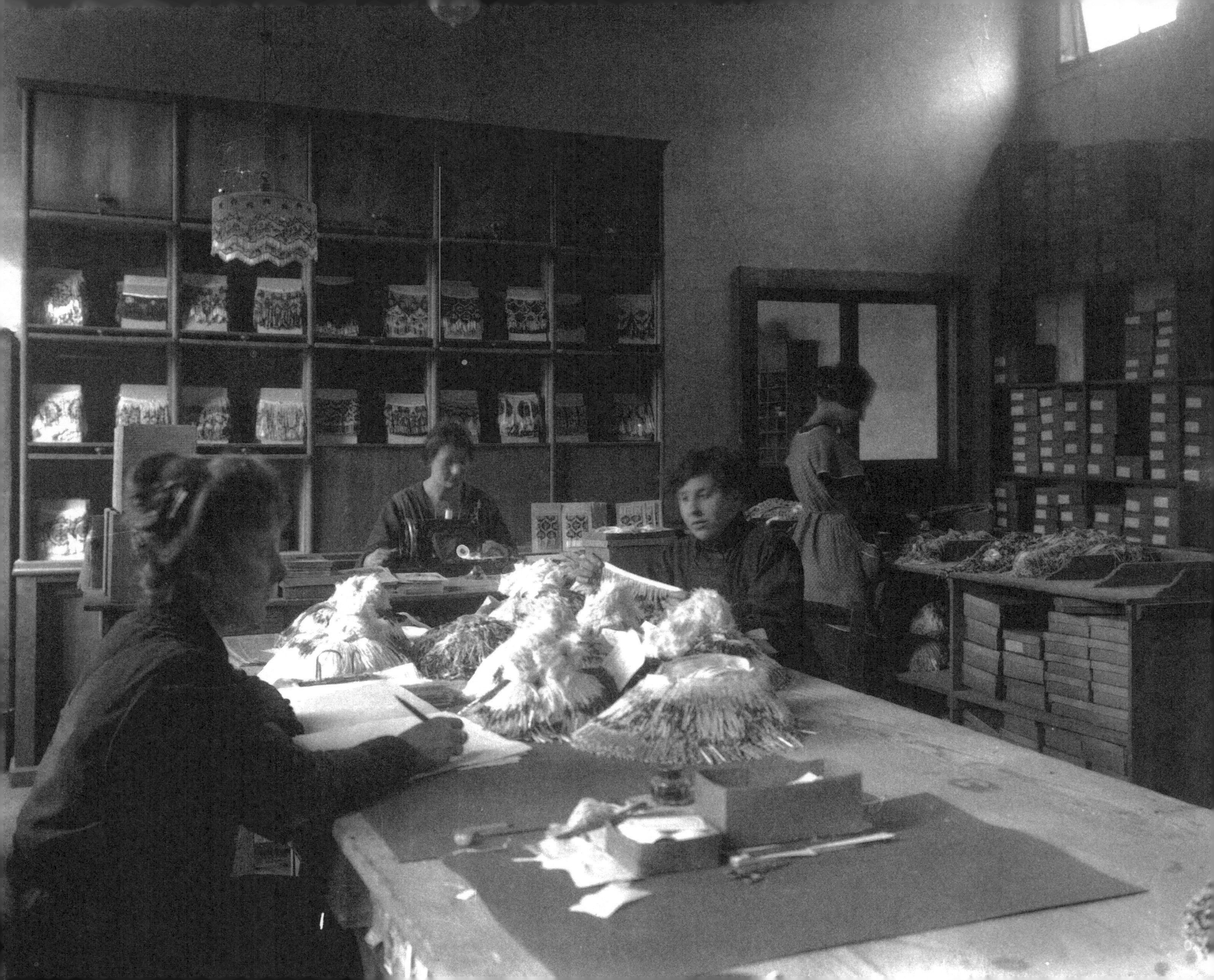

the SVC was known for its traditional artisan method of pulling glass cane by hand. This manual system produced irregular and inconsistent cane, bead diameters, and overall quality. Increasingly, customers were requesting beads with precise overall diameters, lengths, the size of holes, and colors. The demand for standardized beads of exact measurements and color prompted the SVC to make major production changes. The machine that had been used to mechanically pull glass cane was moved from the Industrial department to the Conterie department. Producing beads mechanically (rather than manually) yielded the desired consistent results and reduced SVC's labor and manufacturing costs. As an added benefit, the increased demand for these beads allowed the SVC to raise their prices.[15]

Despite dozens of layoffs and labor protests, the SVC was compelled to install two more mechanical cane-pulling machines.[xlviii] The glass cane, now pulled to perfection, allowed the SVC to create the finest conterie beads for the United States' fashion industry with new cuts, shapes, and dimensions. In addition, new colors and tonalities were conceived in the Silver & Luster Department, such as the scarab color, fuchsia, gun metal tonalities, Ceylon (pearl-like luster) and the *Tosca* bead with its painted core and transparent exterior. The Silver & Luster department was expanded to satisfy the growing number of requests for new varieties of conterie beads. The department for stringing beads and creating jewelry also expanded. New products such as earrings, necklaces, trimmings, purses, belt buckles, hair accessories, and buttons all contributed to the ever-increasing requests for conterie beads. The impiraresse's workload also increased during this period.

In 1958, the SVC introduced the production of the pressed bead and the faceted bead, a process that was dominated by the Czechs, Germans, and Austrians. The SVC invited Czech technicians to Murano to teach them how to make pressed beads. The SVC purchased automatic

> THE SVC PRODUCED SO MANY FRINGES that it was necessary to establish a specific area where the fringes could be cataloged. Additional employees were hired to oversee this division. Note the beautiful fringe lampshade hanging from the ceiling.

15 | The glass cane, pulled by machine, yielded 500 to 700 kilos per day, depending on the diameter of the cane. It is unknown how many kilos of manually-pulled glass cane the SVC produced each day, but certainly far less than 500 kilos.

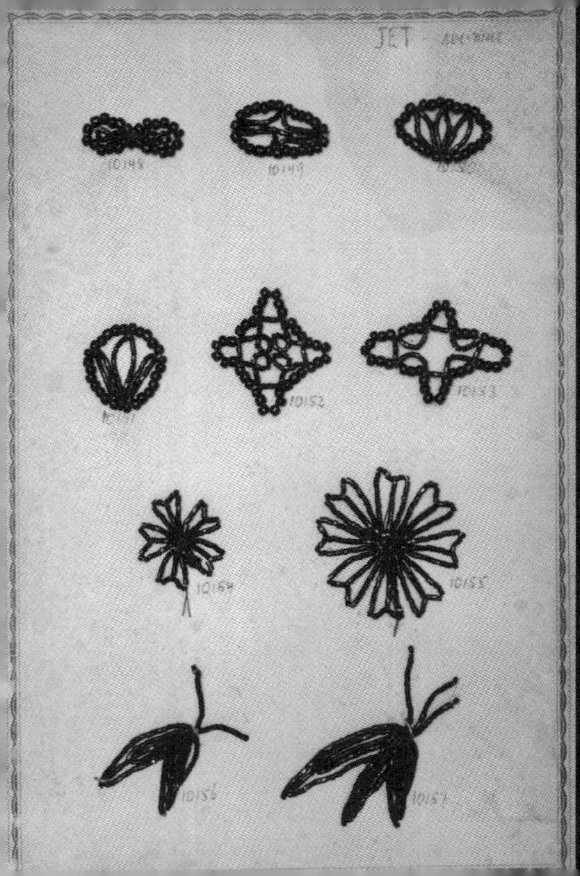
JET
10148
10149
10150
10151
10152
10153
10154
10155
10156
10157
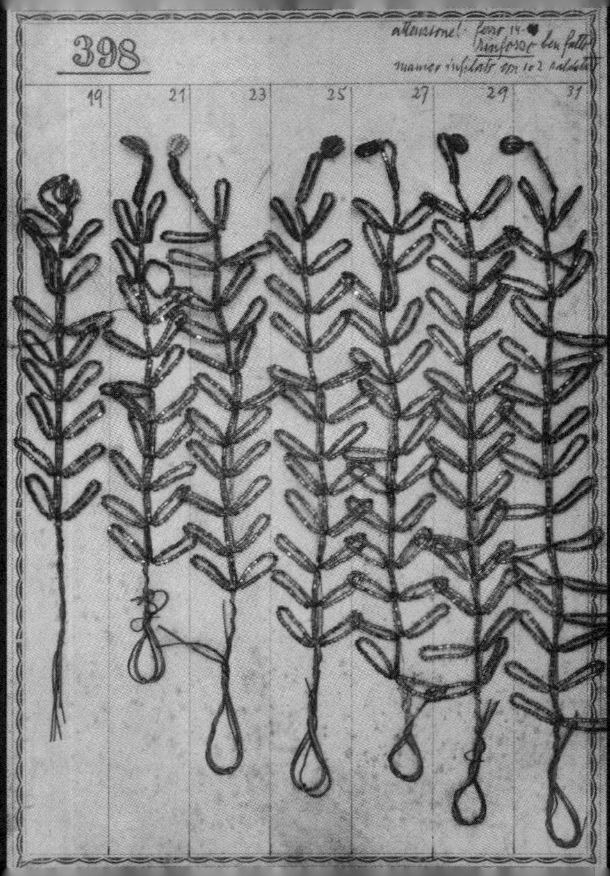
398
19
21
23
25
27
29
31
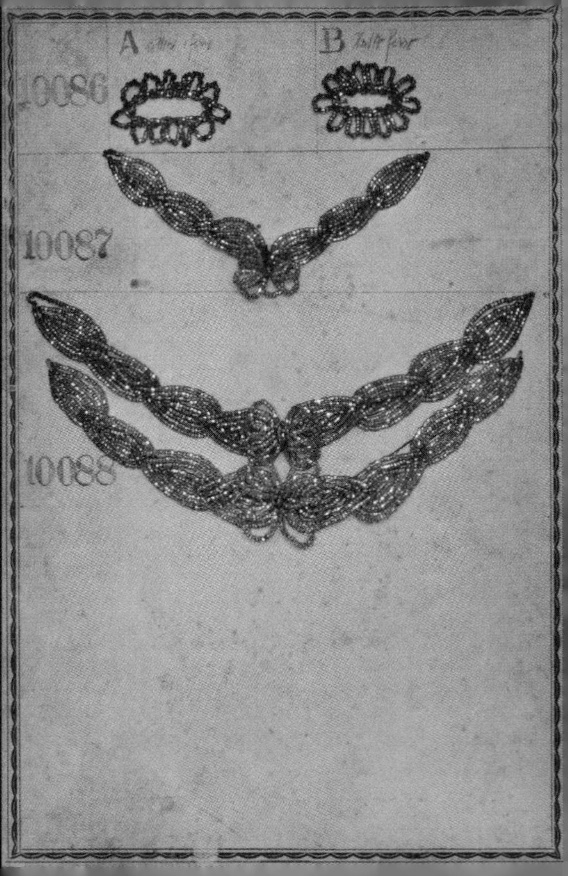
A
B
10086
10087
10088

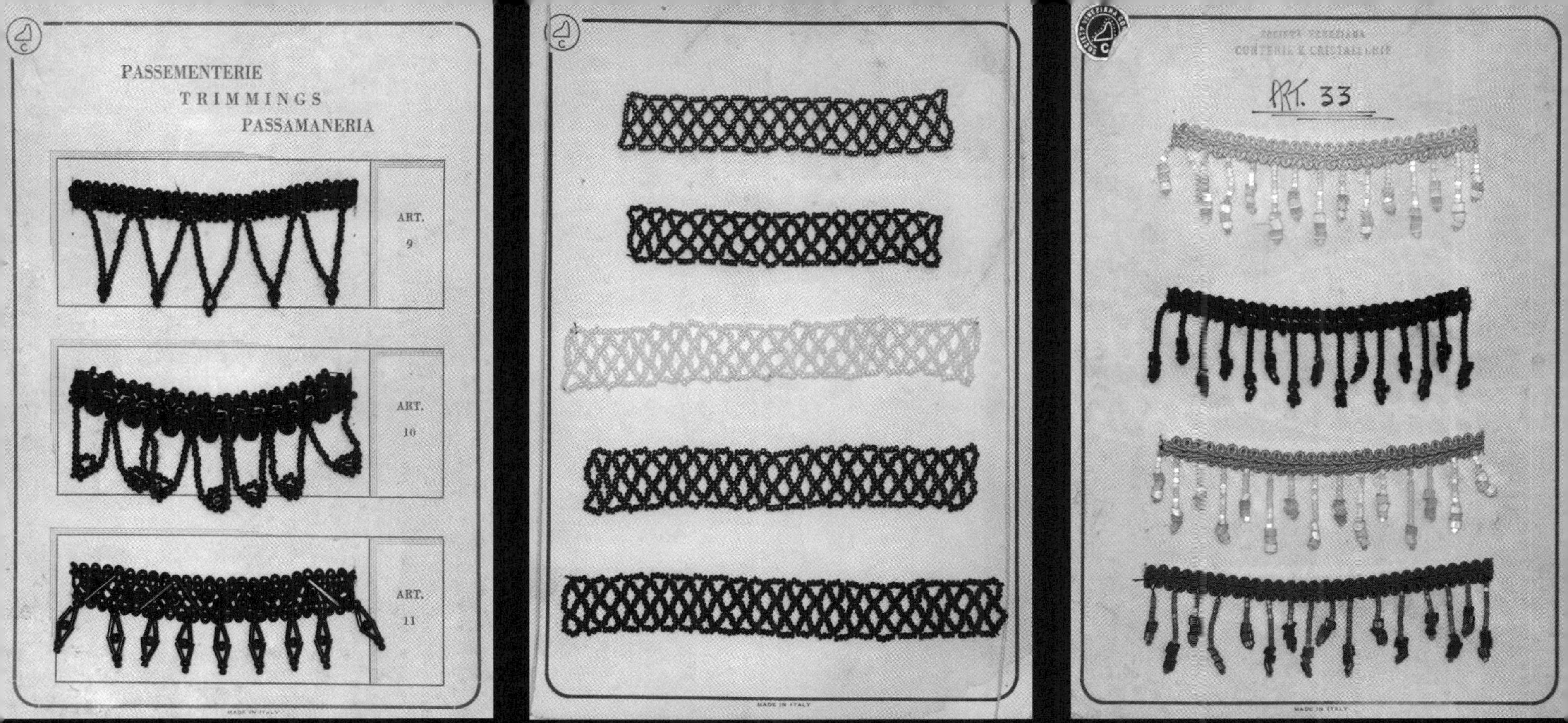

∧ EMBELLISHED WITH SEED BEADS, BRAIDED TRIMMINGS AND EDGINGS were applied to clothing, curtains, pillows, purses, and lampshades. The trimmings were popular with the French fashion designers and tailors. Note the logo of the SVC on the top of the card. Circa 1940–1950

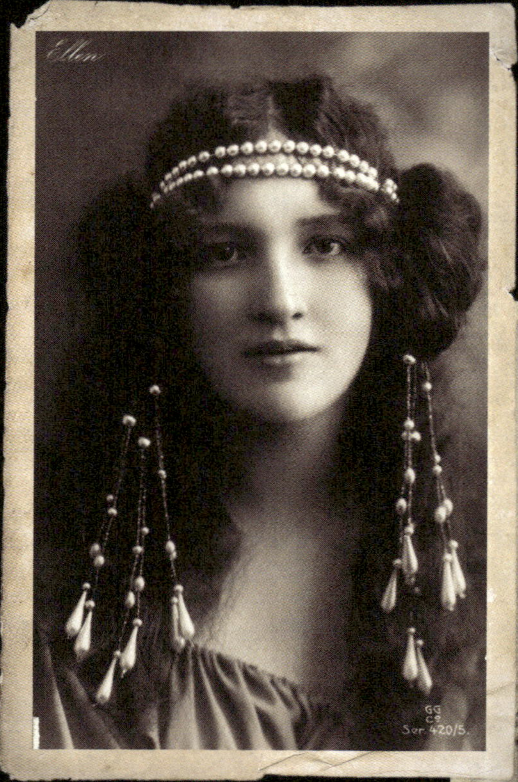
Ellen
GG
Co
Ser. 420/5.

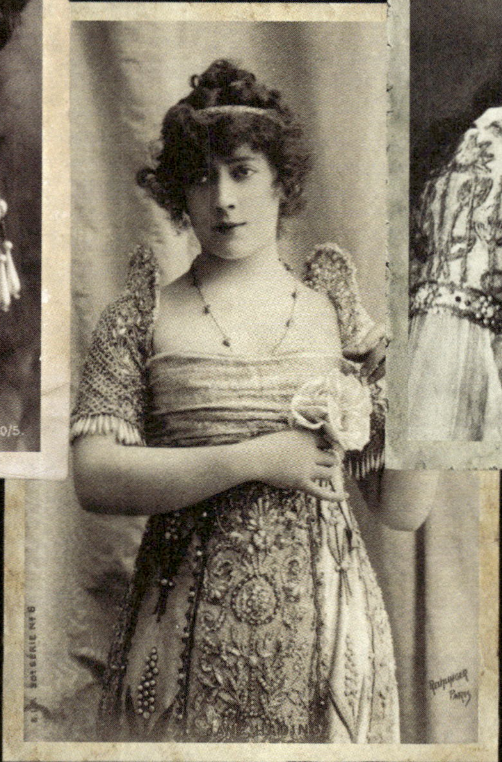

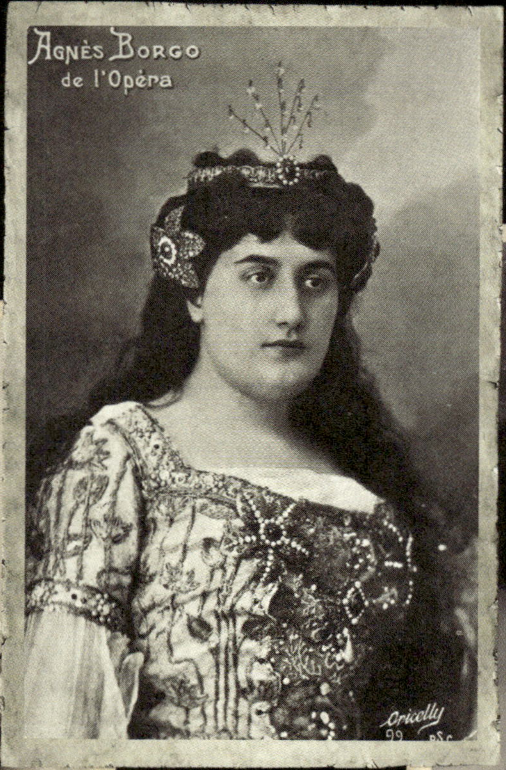
Agnès Borgo
de l'Opéra

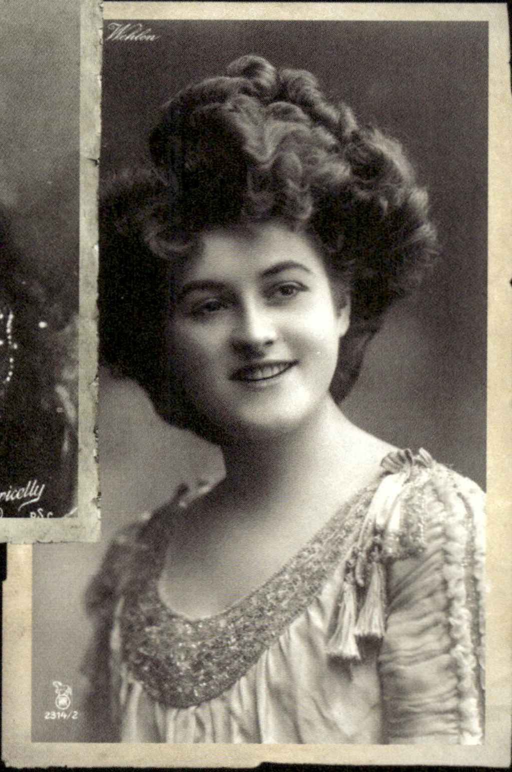
2314/2

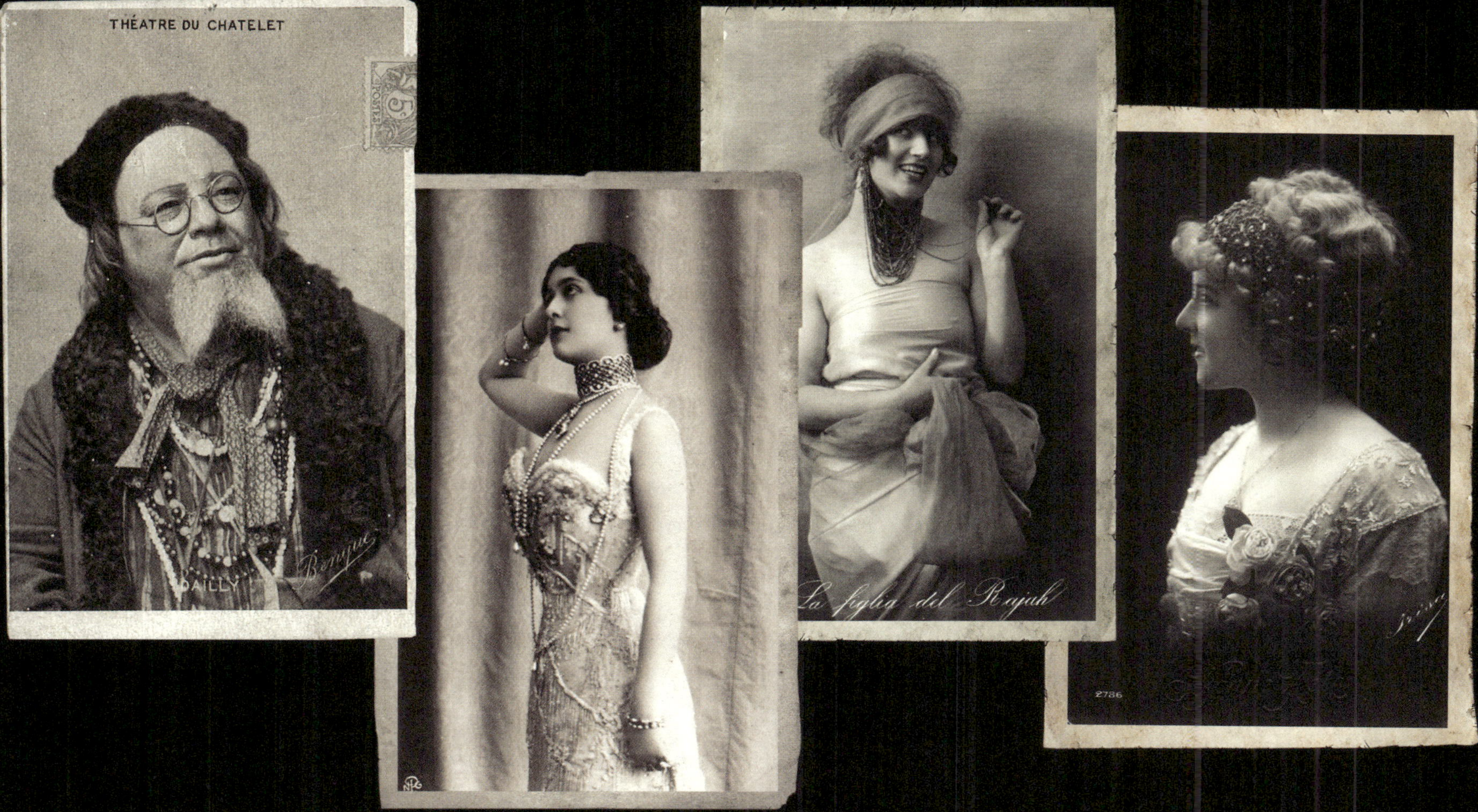

Λ SEED-BEADED GOWNS, HEAD-DRESSES, AND BLOUSES were popular amongst opera singers and theatre performers. It wasn't until the 1960s that plastic beads replaced the heavy, fragile (yet brilliant) glass beads.

press machines, manual presses (made of iron), and tools from the Czechs. Both the manual and automatic press machines included molds. By 1964, the SVC was ready to begin producing pressed beads. The beads that were created by the manual presses were made one at a time using a tool, similar to a pair of scissors, with a metal mold on its extremity. For both procedures, molten glass was poured into the molds and when pressed by the opposing matching mold, the shape and size of the bead would be produced. The molds for the pressed beads came in a variety of shapes and sizes, such as round, oval, square, pear, and triangular. In Italy, the pressed beads were used to make rosaries and decorate chandeliers. Some Florentine manufacturers used these beads for costume jewelry.[xlix] By 1968, the SVC's orders for pressed beads started to decline due to foreign competition. By 1978, the SVC's pressed bead production ceased.[l]

In 1962, the SVC introduced glass mosaics to its spectrum of products, destined for France and other European countries for use in murals. At this time, there were two other companies producing mosaics—Angelo Orsoni in Venice and Ugo Donà in Murano—both in the mosaic business for decades.[li] The SVC's earliest mosaics were produced using very little mechanization to press the tessellated chips, resulting in irregular cuts. The production began in an immense shed within the factory but by 1964 a second, more modern, installation was designed and developed by SVC technicians. The new system included an automatic press to ensure consistent chip cutting, in addition to a mechanism for gluing the mosaics onto sheets of paper. Like the conterie production, job losses resulted for many manual laborers when the glass mosaic production became automated. The glass mosaic production wasn't without drawbacks; the operation imposed frequent pauses, affecting productivity. In 1966, the mosaic glass line was dropped. The technical deficiencies and errors in strategy (such as entering the market too late), were a devastating loss to the SVC.[lii]

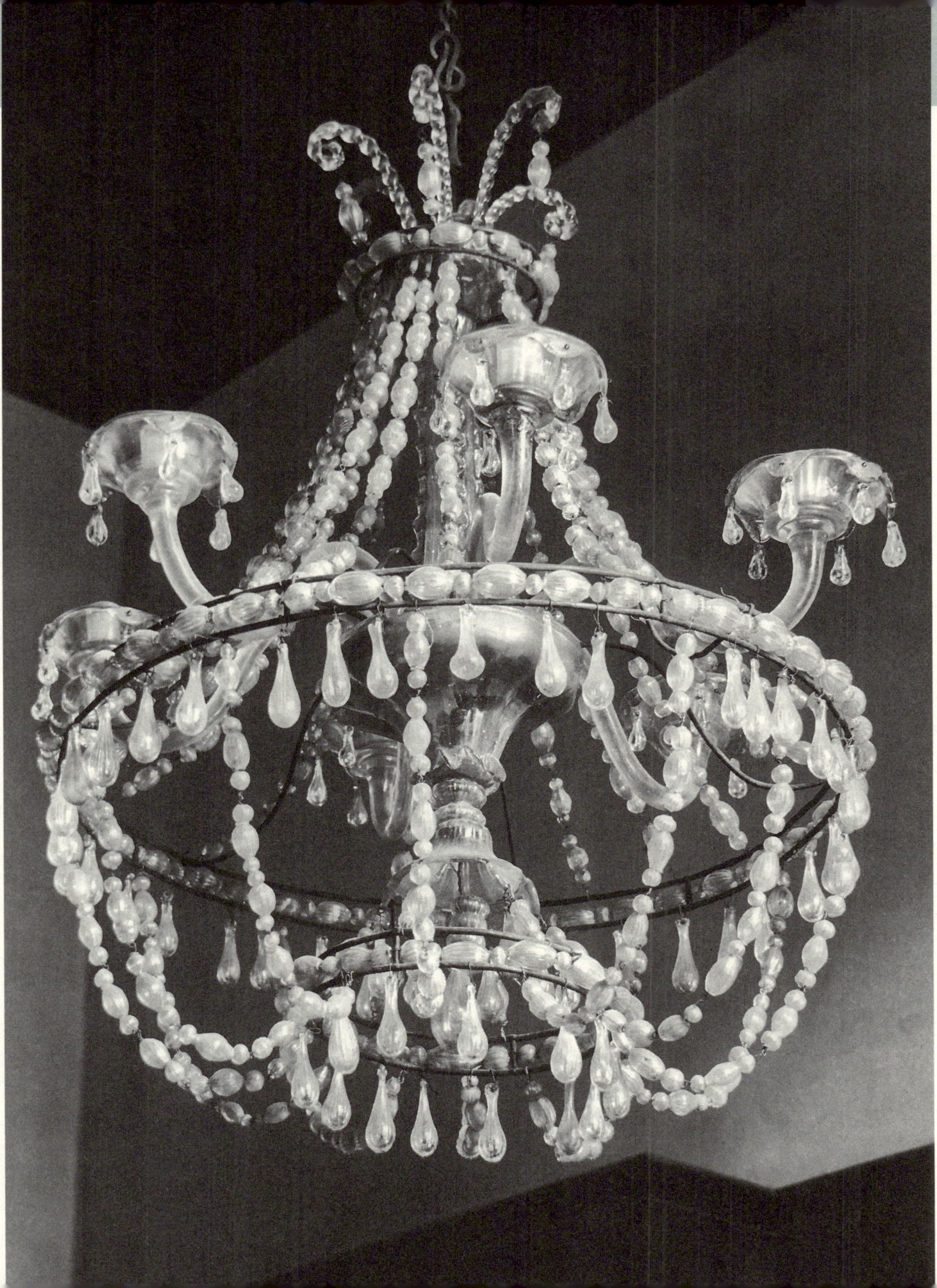

PHOTO COURTESY OF THE ARCHIVIO FOTOGRAFICO FONDAZIONE MUSEI CIVICI DI VENEZIA

< GLASS BEADS were also used to embellish and trim chandeliers. (Circa 1932)

> THE BEAD SURPLUS was enormous. When the SVC closed in 1992, the warehouse contained over 700 tons of beads, glass tubes, glass fragments, and cane. Note the high-arched windows allowing plenty of light to illuminate this area.

The 1960s saw the introduction of plastic beads. Germany led the way as the principal manufacturer and exporter of plastic beads, followed by Czechoslovakia and Austria. The Japanese succeeded in developing plastic beads with prices that were as low as the Czech beads. By 1964, the United States fashion industry shifted its interest from conterie beads to the lower cost, lightweight, unbreakable plastic beads and began placing their orders with the Chinese and German beadmakers.

China was one of the SVC's leading customer. But by 1967, labor dispute riots in Hong Kong, and hostility in Syria and Lebanon, halted orders from Asia and the Middle East.[liii] The other leading Muranese bead manufacturers—Costantini, Morassi, and Mazzega—also suffered from declining sales from competition and civil unrest in foreign lands.

In late 1964, the SVC reintroduced artistic/artisan glass to its production. Given its many talented glass workers, experienced technicians, and no shortage of ovens, tools, and raw materials, this was a natural transition. The Artistic Glass department was outfitted on the ground floor of the Palazzo Trevisan near the shipping and warehouse area. Additional workers, including four glass masters, were hired. The technical direction was entrusted to one of the greatest glass designers of that period, Professor Flavio Poli. After six months of intense experimentation with production and designs, the Artistic Glass department created a collection that was presented in national and international exhibits.[liv] Initial sales of artistic glass prompted the SVC to hire sale professionals in Europe and the United States to market the new items. Suddenly, and for unknown reasons, artistic glass sales dropped and the profits covered less than half of the department's excessive operating costs. Then in 1966, under a rental agreement with the *Vetri d'Arte Briati*[16] glass company, the Vetri d'Arte Briati took over the SVC's artistic department's warehouse (including the contents) and hired the SVC's artisan personnel. However, the artistic glass orders and sales remained under the SVC's control.

16 | The factory is named after Giuseppe Briati, described as "the prince of Murano glass workers," of the 18th century. (Giuseppe Morazzoni, *Le Conterie Venziane dal Secolo XIII al Secolo XIX,* Venezia, 1953, page 36.)

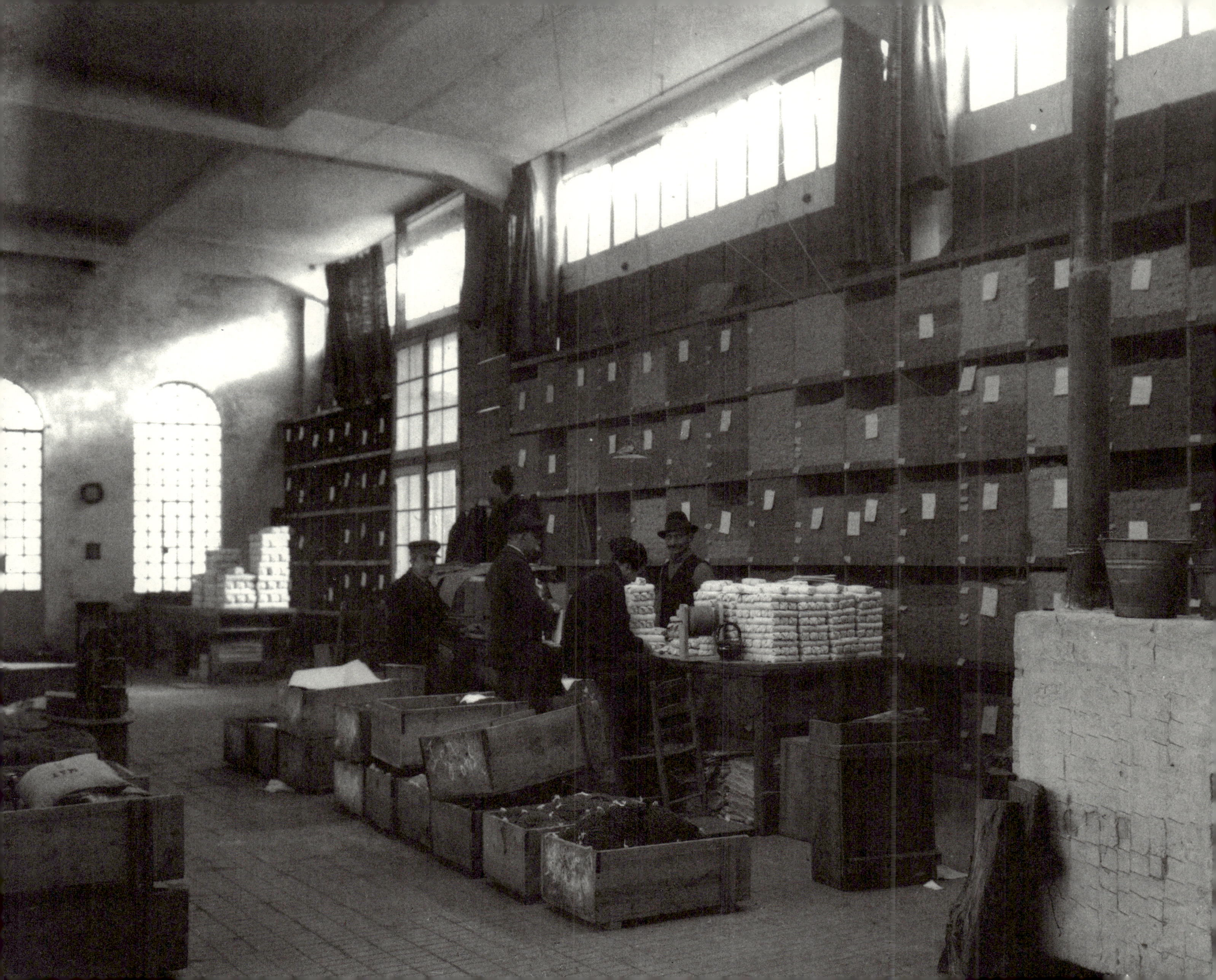

> FROM THE FLOOR TO THE CEILING, the SVC produced an abundance of conterie, lampwork, and mosaic glass beads to be shipped all over the world.

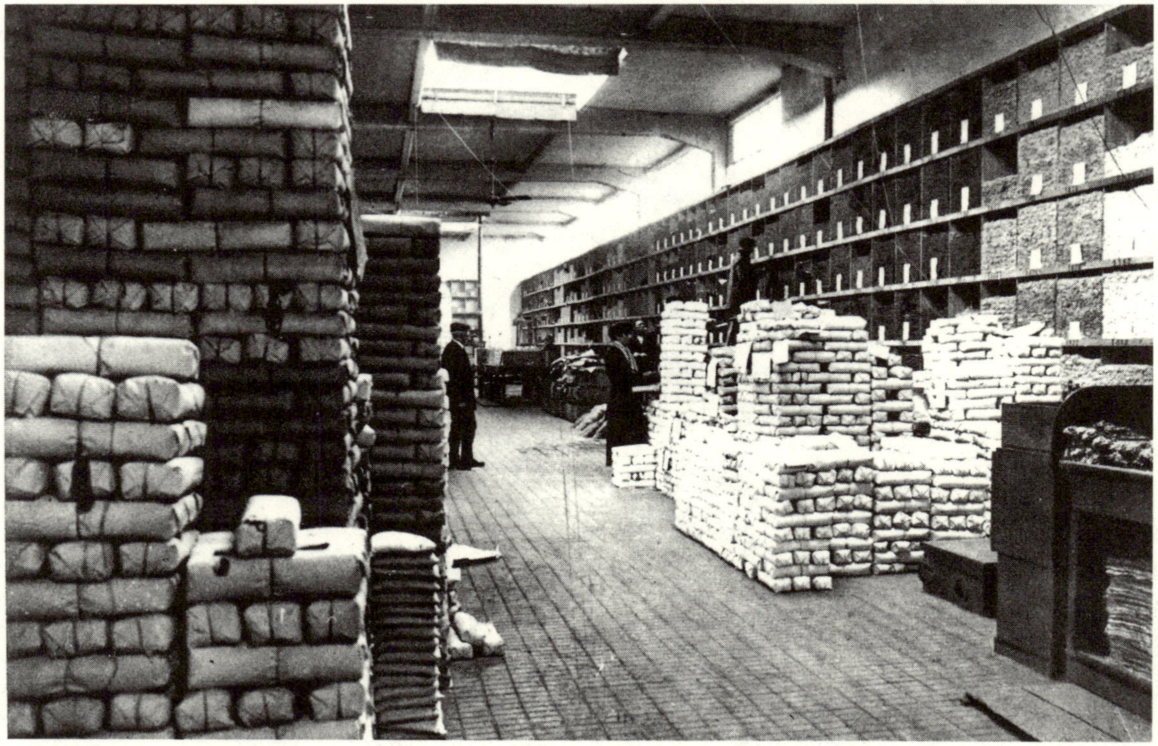

Between 1964 and 1969, operating expenses, raw materials, taxes, electricity, the cost of living, and salaries continued to increase. As a result, the SVC laid off more than half of its employees, reducing 405 employees to 166 and it closed the Artistic Glass department. This only magnified the SVC's financial woes, defining yet another failure in its history.[lv]

In December of 1966, the Senator of the Republic of Italy and Director of the SVC, Michaelangelo Pasquato, died. For nearly forty years, Pasquato influenced credit institutions

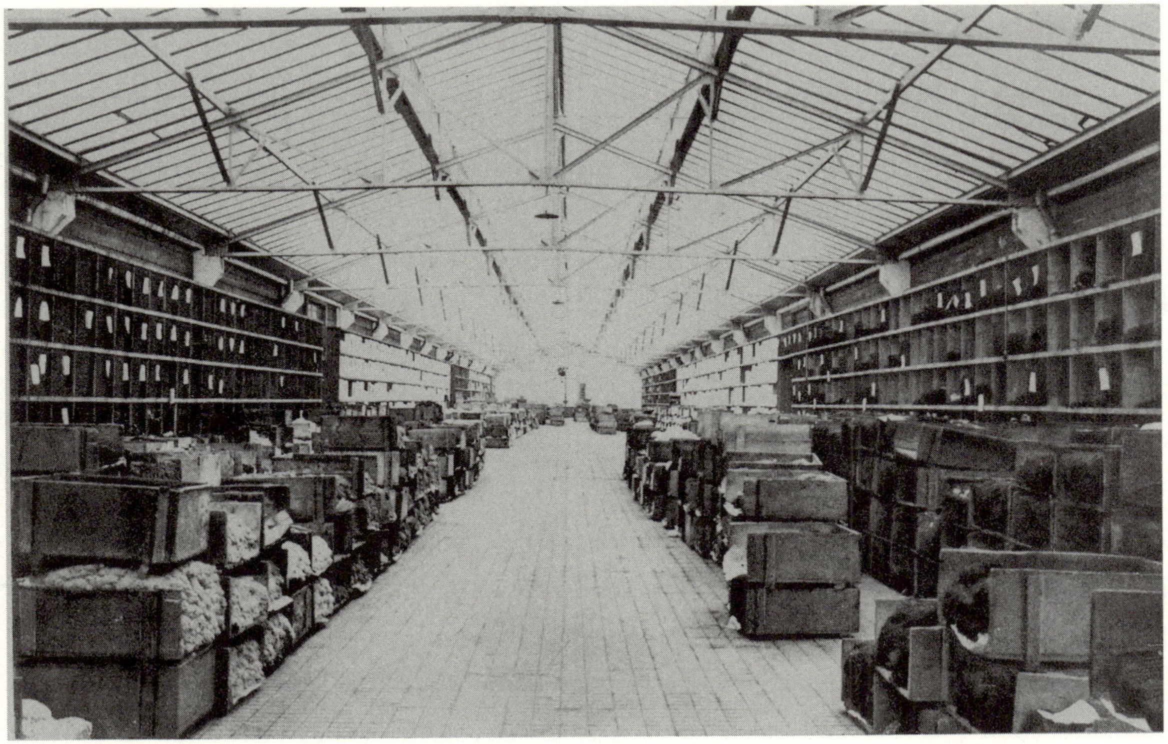

< THE SVC STOCKPILED ITS BEADS here in the central warehouse. The bead hanks were wrapped in white tissue paper and stored in labeled crates.

and ministry offices on behalf of the SVC. Had it not been for his leadership and political power, the SVC would not have survived its many financial crises. Following his death, the SVC struggled to regain its momentum and resolve its financial situation until an agreement was made with SVC shareholders to allow the factory to continue to operate debt-free for a period of time. The first months of 1968 were difficult for the SVC as the banks froze all payments from its customers. Deliveries from suppliers were also blocked. Moreover, many customers were led to believe that the SVC went out of business so they stopped placing orders.

This precarious situation began to change with the nomination of a new administrator, Dr. Telemaco Reali, who included the SVC in the program Salviamo Venezia (Let's Save Venice). With the support of this new initiative, banks and suppliers allowed the factory to continue its operation. By the end of 1969, the *Istituto Mobiliare Italiano* (a banking and loan institution), who initially helped finance the SVC, renounced a good part of its credit, clearing the way for the SVC to receive a mortgage on some property including the employee apartments. Thanks to this mortgage and the release of funds, the SVC was able to partially satisfy its creditors at least enough to maintain operations.[lvi]

By the 1980s, though, the SVC was again in financial dire straits. The SVC needed new machinery, ovens, and technology to be compliant with new environmental and safety standards. Surveyor inspections determined that the SVC's installations were inadequate and posed health risks. One citation was the cristallo standard glass installation that was used to produce the pistil-like filaments for light bulbs, which contained twenty-four percent lead.[17] Due to the lead emissions, the SVC was deemed the most polluted factory on the island of Murano. Already threatened by cheaper glass products, cheaper labor from Eastern European and Third World countries, and lower emission standards for those competitors, the SVC decided to abandon its Industrial department.[lvii]

During this period the SVC was no longer a private company but was operating with partial financial assistance from the government which opened contacts in fields unfamiliar to the SVC. Soon the SVC received a proposal from the *Comitato Nazionale per l'Energia Nucleare* (National Committee for Nuclear Energy, or CNEN) and *Agip-Nuclear* to produce *ballottini,* small (2.0mm) glass solid spheres that could be used to absorb nuclear waste. This

17 | The lead was removed from the composition of the glass and was replaced with the chemical element, barium.

collaboration was a perfect fit because the SVC had a wealth of knowledge and experience in manufacturing glass beads. After studying and accepting the proposal from CNEN, the SVC prepared to convert the machinery that was used for conterie bead production to ballottini production. The cane would be cut into small cylinders in the cutting department and the cylinders would then be tumbled and rounded by the *tubante* worker, transforming them into perfectly 2.0mm spheres.[lviii] It is noteworthy that during the production of the ballottini for nuclear use, the crucibles would corrode rapidly, becoming paper-thin, lasting no more than three days, and as a result, increased the expense of this production. (Most crucibles under normal glass fusing last a few months, even one year, before breaking).

Over time, radioactive waste corrodes and leaks and, thus, must be buried (or stored) in a proper environment. For this reason, testing of nuclear waste-absorbing ballottini was carried out in the central nuclear power plant located in Trisaia-Policoro, in southern Italy.[lix] Using the composition patented from the CNEN/Agip-Nuclear, the SVC produced a type of borosilicate glass that could absorb and encapsulate radioactive waste for long periods of time.[lx] In 1980, CNEN and the United Kingdom Atomic Energy Authority of Harwell performed the first experiments. Although the specifics of these tests are not known, the ballottini was apparently mixed with radioactive mud, put into a large metal drum, then placed in an oven and brought to the temperature of fusion, approximately 1050–1200 degrees Celsius. Presumably, the ballottini would augment the effect of the composition of the glass, allowing the absorption of the radioactive mud into the ballottini. When the glass spheres cooled, the radioactive material was encapsulated.

Other European nuclear power plants and research centers began to show interest in the ballottini. For two years, the SVC was not fully committed to a large-scale ballottini production as it still had to discern whether it could supply new clients with enough material to conduct their own tests. In 1983, the SVC took orders for ballottini from nuclear centers in Italy and Germany. By 1984, however, it was evident that the product could not provide the economic results that the SVC had desired. Ballottini production for nuclear practices required additional testing. Furthermore, it would take years for the SVC to establish a reputation as a supplier in the field of atomic energy, especially since the SVC was still known primarily as a producer of aesthetic beads.[lxi]

In 1987, following the nuclear disaster in Chernobyl, a referendum banned the use of nuclear power in Italy. Eighty percent of Italians voted against the construction and/or use of nuclear energy, sealing the fate of the ballottini production.[lxii] The SVC was the only factory to possess the special composition needed to produce ballottini and continued to do so for one more year for a customer in Belgium before stopping the production altogether.[lxiii]

During the 1980s, with the acquisition of Japanese technology, the Chinese were able to produce conterie beads at decisively lower prices than the competition. This allowed the Chinese to concentrate on poorer markets such as India and Pakistan, assuring themselves a place in the international market and thereby eliminating other producers from this market including the SVC. It became readily apparent to the SVC that ultimately it was the price that could make or break a sale, not the quality or design of the beads. If the SVC wanted to remain in business, it had no other choice but to adopt lower pricing that would attract consistent sales in volumes.[lxiv]

Despite centuries of glass tradition on the island of Murano, the romance of the Italian language and culture, the history of Venice, famous Venetian artists, and the notoriety for distinguished glass masters, the Società Veneziana per l'Industria delle Conterie came to the end of its legacy in 1992. It was a finale that no one wanted to accept. The SVC provided a livelihood for thousands of families for nearly one century. Almost all Muraneses are tied to the artisan workmanship of glass. At the time of its closing, the SVC's forty-three remaining employees, many who grew up in and around glass factories and descended from generations of glass masters, wanted to save their jobs and preserve the history of their beloved glass factory. The employees tried to keep the SVC open and operating, protesting at city hall, regional offices, and the state department, only to be greeted with indifference. Their discouragement intensified when they learned that the municipality of Venice was interested in the factory. As hard as they fought to save it, they were powerless. Gradually, employees were offered severance pay or early retirement packages. The final remaining twenty employees surrendered to large settlements but carried with them the burden of witnessing a painful event in Murano's history that would forever affect its glass production.[lxv]

When the Conterie closed, its warehouse contained 350 tons of beads, 300 tons of cristallo standard tubes, 50 tons of hollow glass cane, and 45 tons of rottami (broken glass pieces used for fusing). Part of the inventory was sold to wholesalers in Murano and in the United States of America. Some machinery was sold to factories in Murano and on the mainland. However, many tools, tumblers, benches, paddles and remaining equipment were discarded.[lxvi]

Since its closure, the 538,000 square-foot site has been remodeled into a supermarket and a working space for artisans. In addition, LaGare Hotel Venezia has recently reconstructed the Conterie into an elegant, beautiful four-star hotel.

From its beginning in 1898, the Conterie was autonomous and a pioneer in the bead production. It had its own blacksmiths, carpenters, handymen, mechanics, electricians, brick layers, chemists, and engineers who invented and designed its earliest machines and tools. It made its own bricks, ovens, and ceramic crucibles, in addition to producing its own electricity. Considering the Conterie existed in an era with limited means for communication, it was well organized and efficient in its administrative and shipping departments. The Conterie was innovative, creative, and employed hundreds of hard-working people, including many women and children. It was considered a company that had family values—a company with a heart. It prided itself on accuracy when it was time to pay the employees. The Conterie always sought to improve its productivity. During certain periods of growth, it was operating non-stop day and night. The Conterie withstood many challenges such as wars, embargoes, competition, price wars, government regulations, and inflation. Despite its battles and victories, however, it seemed that the Conterie was often operating on the defensive, continually struggling to overcome some form of adversity.

Many glass workers, in all of Murano, suffered and died of lung diseases caused by inhaling toxic fumes and powders. Due to the lack (and enforcement) of child labor laws and the necessity to work in order to survive, many children worked full time in the factory and were deprived of an education and playful childhood. Thousands of men, women, and children who were employed by the SVC contributed to the success and history of not only the Società Veneziana per l'Industria delle Conterie but to all glass factories in Murano.

The Venetians were masters in the art and trade of beadmaking. Executed to perfection, the Venetians not only made beautiful beads, but they also had the power and ambition to export these beads to every place in the world, leaving behind a tradition of travel, art, culture, history, and even love. Situated on the quiet, charming, island of Murano, the Conterie beads traveled to six continents and were embraced by nearly every nation on earth. Venetian beads touched every race, religion, culture, gender, age, and social class. They were worn by the poor women of Third World countries, as well as by the high fashion designers of western civilization. The conterie beads were used in African celebrations to embellish tribal costumes and yet were given a somber significance in the creation of exquisite mortuary wreaths.

From the high waters of the Laguna, to the salty air of the Adriatic Sea, from the dust of the coal yards, to the blazing fires of the furnaces, from the caravans of glass beads, to the hands of the people who praised them, the beads manufactured by the Società Veneziana per l'Industria delle Conterie were far-reaching and encompassed all elements on earth.

Today, Venetian glass beads are among the most collected and revered beads, steadily appreciating in value over time. Whether it is a seven-layer chevron, or a simple round bead decorated with colorful flowers and gilded with goldstone, Venetian glass beads appeal to everyone and are artifacts that can be found in museums throughout the world.

It has been said that should the world one day end in fire, the only remaining substance on this planet would be glass, born of fire. On that note, let us remember that although the Conterie is no longer with us, its glass will be with us until the end of time.

CHAPTER ELEVEN *Endnotes*

i Astone Gasparetto, *Il Vetro di Murano dalle Origini ad Oggi,* Neri Pozza Editore, Venezia, 1958, page 184.
ii Paolo Zecchin, *Storia del vetro di Murano-- la Nascita delle Conterie Veneziane,*
iii Astone Gasparetto, *Il Vetro di Murano dalle Origini ad Oggi,* Neri Pozza Editore, Venezia, 1958, pp.186-187.
iv Elena Bertagnolli, Maria Teresa Sega, Rossana Urbani De Gheltof, *Perle Veneziane,* Consorzio Venezia Perle, Venezia, 1990, page 35.
v Domenico Bussolin, *Guida alle Fabbriche Vetrarie di Murano,* Tip. Andrea Santini e Figlio, Venezia, 1842, page 30.
vi The art of *suppialume* existed up until the 16th century. (Cesare Moretti, *Glossario del Vetro Veneziano dal Trecento al Novecento,* Marsilio, Venezia, 2001, page 78.) The word "suppia" comes from the Venetian dialect meaning "to blow." (Giuseppe Boerio, *Dizionario del Dialetto Veneziano,* Tip. Giovanni Cecchini Edit, 1856, page 723.
vii Elena Bertagnolli, Maria Teresa Sega, Rossana Urbani De Gheltof, page 35; Giovanni Battista e Jacopo Franchini, Lavori alla Lucerna, Tip. P. Naratovich, Venezia, 1867.
viii Giuseppe Morazzoni, *Le Conterie Veneziane dal Secolo XIII al Secolo XIX.,* Venezia,1953, pp. 22-23.
ix *Gazzetta Ufficiale di Venezia,* August 19, 1858, N. 188.
x Michaelangelo Pasquato, *L'industria delle conterie nel Novecento,* Venezia, 1953, page 78.
xi Ibid., page 78.
xii Alessandro Zecchin, "La Società Veneziana per l'Industria delle Conterie", *La Voce di Murano,* February 11, 1902.
xiii This tower has been demolished due to recent construction of a hotel.
xiv Ibid.
xv In the early 1900s, the SVC had three subsidiary locations for pulling the glass cane—the Palazzo Mula, the San Martin warehouse/factory, and a location near Piazzale Colonna.
xvi Nicola Berlin, "Il Percorso Strategico della Società Veneziana Conterie nel Periodo Successivo alla Seconda Guerra Mondiale," thesis in economics, Università degli Studi di Venezia Ca'Foscari, Venezia, 1988-1989, page 15.
xvii Pasquato, page 78.
xviii Vicenzo Zanetti, *Guida di Murano e delle Celebri Sue Fornaci, Vetrarie,* Antonelli,1866, page 20.
xix Pasquato, page 79.
xx *Perle e Impiraperle—un lavoro di donne a Venezia tra '800 e '900,* Arsenale Editrice, Venezia, 1990, page 18.
xxi Berlin, page 24.
xxii Verbal interview with Iginio Costantini, *filatore* (blade sharpener) of the SVC from 1955 to 1990.

xxiii Berlin, pp. 40-41.
xxiv Ibid., page 4.
xxv Ibid., pp. 5-6.
xxvi Verbal interview with Iginio Costantini.
xxvii Iginio Costantini.
xxviii Berlin., page 6.
xxix Iginio Costantini.
xxx Berlin, page 52.
xxxi Ibid., page 19.
xxxii Ibid., pp. 14-16.
xxxiii Ibid., page 23.
xxxiv Ibid., pp. 39-40.
xxxv Ibid., pp. 41-42.
xxxvi Ibid., page 53.
xxxvii Berlin, pp. 56-58.The Schuler company was established in 1839. They manufacture tool and dies and coin presses. Http://www.schulergroup.com
xxxviii Ibid., page 46.
xxxix Ibid., page 124.
xl Ibid., page 70.
xli Ibid., page 71.
xlii Ibid., page 70.
xliii Ibid., page 141.
xliv Ibid., pp. 148-150.
xlv Ibid., pp. 150-152.
xlvi Ibid.
xlvii Ibid., page 127.
xlviii Ibid., page 48.
xlix Iginio Costantini
l Berlin, pp. 85-86.
li Gasparetto, pp. 218-219.
lii Berlin, pp. 87-90.
liii Http://wikipedia. Hong Kong 1967 Leftist Riots 4 November 2007.
liv Berlin, pp. 90-92
lv Ibid., page 102.
lvi Ibid., pp. 112-113.
lvii Ibid., pp. 231-232.
lviii Iginio Costantini.
lix Berlin, page 174.
lx Bonetti, G., "Caratterizzazione di materiali vetrosi utilizzati per lo smaltimento delle scorie radioattive," *Rivista della Stazione Sperimentale del Vetro.*, N. 3, 1986.
lxi Berlin, pp. 173-177.
lxii Http://www.zonanucleare.com
lxiii Iginio Costantini
lxiv Berlin, pp. 216-217.
lxv Iginio Costantini.
lxvi Verbal interview with L.Cattelan, Director of Production of the SVC from 1978-1998.

> SAMPLES OF SEED BEADS packaged in a lightweight burlap bag and closed with a metal fastener. They are labeled "*Campioni Senza Valore*" (samples of no value). Handwritten on each bag are the weight, a date, the port of entry, and the intended destination in the Democratic Republic of Congo such as Stanleyville (now known as Kisangani), Elisabethville (now known as Lubumbashi), and Leopoldville (now known as Kinshasa).

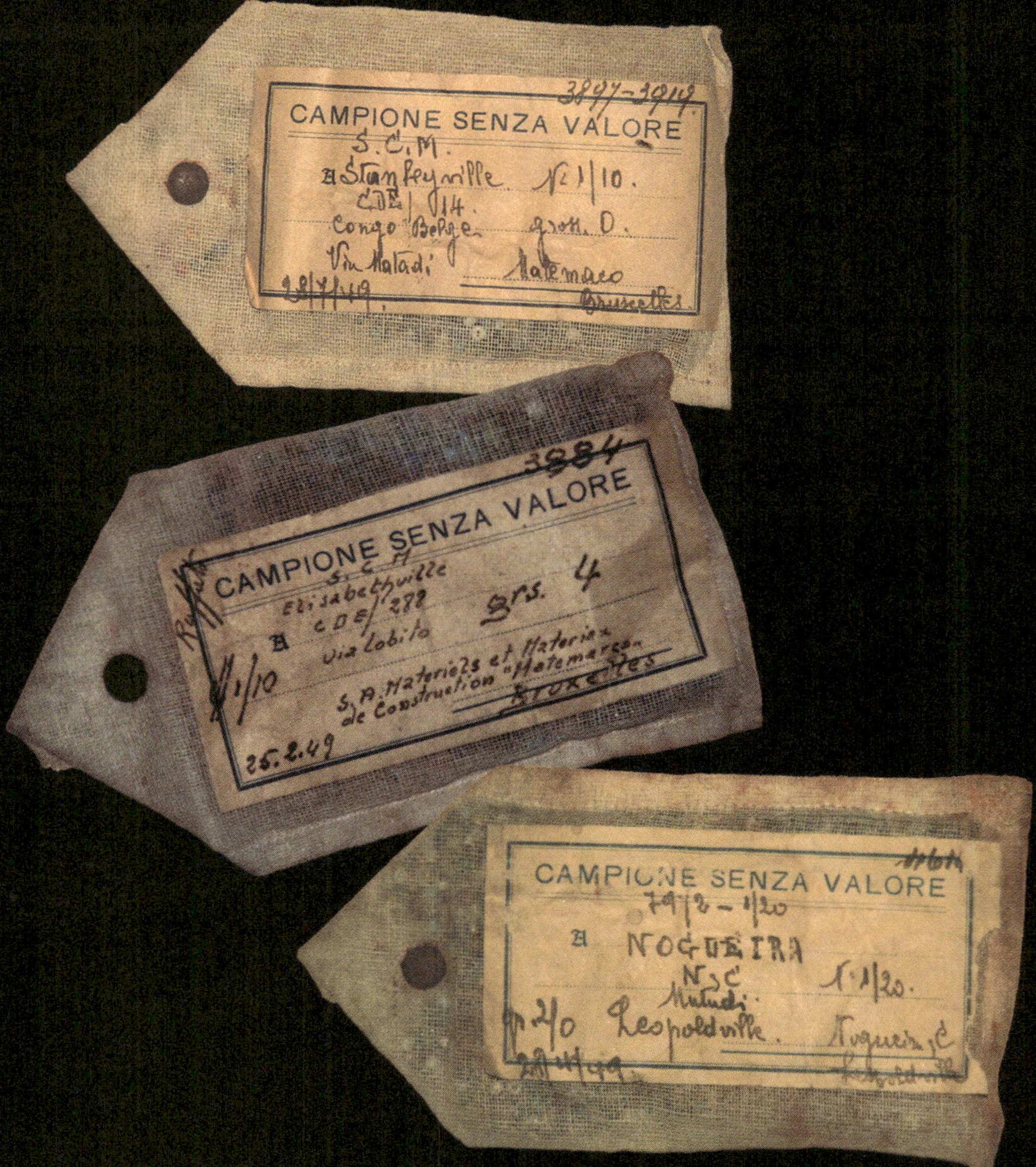

— Glossary —

AFFINAGGIO: The process by which the gaseous bubbles were eliminated from fused glass. In the early days of glass production, glass typically contained gaseous bubbles. The technology for fusing glass did not reach sufficient temperatures to facilitate the leakage of the remaining gaseous substances caused by the chemical reactions between silicate and alkaline carbonate. Later, it was discovered that by increasing the development of the gas, or decreasing the viscosity of the glass while fusing, gaseous bubbles would be released. The earliest attempts of *affinaggio* were achieved by combining sodium nitrate or potassium and arsenic dioxide. Later, sodium sulfate was mixed with coal to reduce the sulfate to sulfite, which decomposed during the development of sulfur dioxide gases. (Cesare Moretti, *Glossario del Vetro Veneziana,* Marsilio, Venezia, 2001.)

AGADA: A fan of needles (*aghi*) full of conterie beads which were threaded by the Venetian *impiraresse*. Two *agade* made one *marin,* which was the given quantity of threaded beads which was measured on the side of the wooden *sessola*. The sessola was engraved with the measurements of forty-two centimeters and thirty-two centimeters. (Irene Ninni, Impiraresse *L'impiarressa,* Venezia: Tip. Longhi e Montanari, 1873.)

AMURIANUM: Once the ancient name of Murano dating back to the 5th century.

ARROTONDAMENTO: An operation in the production of conterie beads where the jagged edges of the glass cylinders were rounded. The cylinder pieces were put in an iron drum together with the *siribite* mixture (see Siribite) and sand; the drum was inserted into an oven and rotated on an axis, smoothing the sharp edges to create homogeneous beads. *The arrondamento* process also enhanced the tonality of certain colors, such as amber and red.

ARTE DEI MARGARITERI: The production of glass beads with the intent to imitate gemstones.

ASSETE: Linen threads used by the *impiraresse* to string beads.

AVVENTURINA: A type of opaque glass in a reddish-brown color, known for its bright, shiny star-like appearance. The "stars" look like gold but are actually tiny pieces of copper which were crystallized during the cooling process. *Avventurina* was once known as *pasta stellaria* and *venturina.* In the recipe book of Giovanni Darduin (1644), he described the process of fabricating this enamel as more of an "adventure" than a science because of its inconsistent results.

BALLOTTINI: Small glass spheres of 2.0mm which were used to absorb nuclear waste.

BORSELLA: Long, iron pinchers used for various functions, such as shaping molten glass or for piercing a gather of glass to create a hole that runs the length of the gather. The *borsella,* the pipes (*canna di levar*), and the blowpipe (*canna da supiar*) are the fundamental tools for the glass master. (Moretti).

BRONZINO: A flat, cast iron plate that is polished on one side and used for rolling and shaping the molten glass on a pre-heated end of a blowpipe or iron staff to pre-shape (or marver) the molten glass into an evenly-rounded cylindrical shape. Its name comes from the cast iron plate that was once made of bronze or marble The pre-shaping is carried out by rolling the molten glass back and forth across a marvering table and adjusting the angle of the blowpipe to create the desired shape. (http://www.glassonline.com and https://www.muranonet.com).

BULGARI: Beads of various colors and sizes.

BURATINI: A bead of a different color that inadvertently appears in a group of beads of a specific color that are being strung. The word *buratini* means "puppets." (Ninni, 1873).

CALCHERA: A reverberating furnace constructed in a way that the dome of the oven reflected the heat of the flames evenly onto a paved surface. This furnace was used to prepare a frit mixture (see Fritta) which would vitrify at 700-800 degrees Celsius. (Moretti).

CANNA DI LEVAR: An iron pipe used to extract the molten glass from a crucible.

CANNA ROSETTA: Solid or hollow glass cane which is formed with multiple layers of glass of various colors. The multiple layers are created by repeated extractions of molten glass, with each gather pressed into a star-shaped mold to create its pattern. After the rosetta cane is cooled, it is cut into segments that are grounded down on a grinding wheel in order for the star-pattern and multiple layers to appear. The rosetta bead (also known as "chevron") first appeared in Murano in the late 15th century. (Moretti).

CANNA DA SPEO: Large diameter hollow glass cane in which segments were cut and slid onto thin skewers/mandrels (*spiei, spiedi*) and then shaped and rounded to create beads. (Moretti).

CANNELLE: Hollow glass cane, approximately one-meter long, intended for producing conterie beads.

CAPANNONE: The spacious area in a glass factory where the ovens were situated.

CARBONER / FRANGI CARBONE: The conterie production worker who was responsible for operating a machine that crushed and pulverized large chunks of charcoal into a fine powder which was later used as an element in the *siribite* mixture.

CASON CANNA: Venetian dialect referring to the area where the glass cane was pulled.

CAVAORBI: A machine used to separate the good beads from those that had insufficient holes or no hole at all. Beads with no hole were called *orbi*, meaning "blind". (Moretti).

CAVAROBA: The operation and/or name of the worker in the conterie factory who removed the *siribite* compound found in the holes of the beads after they had been rounded by the *tubante* in the *arrondomento* stage.

CARRETTINE: An electric vibratory machine that held dozens of sieves used for separating the beads according to size.

CERNIDORE / CERNITRICE: The female conterie production workers who separated the glass *cannelle* according to diameter.

COGOLI or CIOTTOLI: See Tarso.

COLANA: Five strands of *conterie* beads assembled together with a red thread (the *coleto*) to make one *colana*. (Ninni, 1873).

COMPOSIZIONE / COMPOSIZIONATORE: The composition of glass is the recipe or formula of the glass; the composizionatore is the worker of the factory who follows this recipe and mixes the ingredients.

CONCIATORE: The glass *composizionatore* who makes glass from its constituent materials, adds colorants, and supervises the maintenance and use of the glass melt. (Engle, 2006).

CONJON: A mandrel holder that united the iron staff of the tube/drum to the back wall of the oven that was used by the *tubanti*.

CONZAURA: A long, iron pipe with an end that is dipped into the crucible to gather a small amount of molten glass; the glass is then shaped into a cylinder and then, while still hot, is attached to the end of the *pastone* (prepared by the *scagner*) for pulling the cane. (Moretti).

CONZAURER: The worker who is responsible for gathering the molten glass onto the end of the pipe (*conzaura*) and then attaching this glass onto the extremity of the *pastone* for pulling the cane by hand. (Moretti).

CONTERIE: The term used since the 1800s to describe glass beads made by cutting thin, hollow glass cane. In ancient times, conterie were called *margarite*. Originally the word conterie was used to describe lampwork beads made from smaller solid glass cane created by the workers called the *suppialume*, whereas the larger beads were made from hollow glass cane (a process called a *speo*) by the *paternostreri* workers. (Gasparetto, 1958).

CONTERIE FINE: Conterie beads that are made from a finer quality of ingredients, such as gold and silver.

COPERTA: The Italian word for a "blanket" or "cover"; the *coperta* is the last layer of glass that covers an existing layer.

CORNIOLE: Conterie beads that have two layers—the inner core or first layer (*sottana*) was made of opaque white glass (*lattimo*), and the exterior layer (*coperta*) was made of transparent glass, commonly in ruby-red tonalities.

CORRIDOR: A long corridor measuring anywhere from sixty to one hundred fifty meters in which two men (*tiradori*) pulled the glass cane by walking (or running)in opposite directions.

COTTA: The cooking process inside the drum (*tubo*) during the rounding stage (*arrotondamento*) of the cylinders to produce conterie beads. (Astone Gasparetto, *Il Vetro di Murano,* Neri Pozza, Venezia, 1958.)

CRISTALLERI: Workers who cut, engraved, faceted, and polished crystal.

CRISTALLO STANDARD: Clear glass produced with lead or lead oxides.

CRIVELLI: Sieves used for separating the conterie beads according to diameter.

CROGIOLO: Crucibles, containers, or vases of various shapes (round, oval, cylindrical) made of heat-resistant materials in which raw materials, such as sand, soda, and minerals, are placed and brought to the temperature of fusion to make glass. Hundreds of years ago, the crucibles could hold approximately ten kilos of molten glass; today the crucibles can hold approximately one thousand kilos. (Moretti).

FERRAZZA/FERRACCIO: A square iron dish, approximately ten to twelve inches, on which glass was placed for reheating. The *ferrazza* was placed in a reverberating oven and was progressively moved away from the flow of the heat so that the glass or beads would cool slowly, avoiding thermal shock. *Ferrazze* made of copper were also used in the production of the conterie to round the edges of the cylinders. The cylinders were placed on the *ferrazza* and inserted into the oven. Then, using an iron comb, the cylinders were gently moved around in order for the edges to be rounded. This process was practiced before the invention of the *tubo*. The *ferrazza* containers were also used in the production of the conterie as a receptacle of the hot beads after the *arrotondamento* process, in which the beads were left to slowly cool. (Gasparetto, 1958 and Moretti, 2001).

FERRO DA CANNA: A long, iron rod of approximately one and a half meters long, used to gather the molten glass from the crucible.

FERRO DA TAGIO: A cutting blade used to mechanically cut glass cane.

FIORATO: The name of a lampwork bead with superficial decorations of colorful flowers and gilded with *avventurina*.

FORNO FUSORIO: In the past, these ovens used to consist of a large counter on which the crucibles were placed, and above it was a hearth where firewood would burn. The hot gasses from the hearth passed through a hole in the center of the counter in the chamber where the crucibles were situated. Around the walls of this chamber, usually circular or polygonal, were openings for loading the glass mixture (*miscela*) and for extracting samples of the glass. Through another hole, the exhaust gasses passed in a different chamber, situated above where the glass objects were annealed. The counter and walls were made of refractory materials resistant to temperatures needed for fusing glass. Nowadays, the ovens in the glass factories hold the crucibles in one chamber and are fueled by methane gas which is delivered into the chamber by air. The annealing oven is now a separate entity from the melting oven. (Moretti, 2001).

FREGADOR: The worker in the conterie production who was responsible for clogging the holes of the cylinders with the sirbiti mixture, which was calcium and charcoal dust, in preparation for the next stage of production—the rounding (*arrotondamento*) of the beads in the drum/tubo in the oven.

FRITTA: The result of the first reaction of raw materials used in conterie production until the beginning of the 18th century. Later potassium nitrate was introduced to accelerate the final fusion of glass. (Moretti, 2001). Frit is the calcined or partly fused materials of which glass is made. (Merriam-Webster Dictionary).

GARZON, GARZONETTO: A young boy, apprentice, who helped the workers in various tasks of the glass factory.

GASTALDO: The Chamberlain of Art, representing the owners of the glass factory who elected him annually (from the 13th–18th century). (Http://www.barovier.com).

GIARDINETTO: The joining of many *marini*, each with a different color, making a "garden" of colorful strands of conterie beads. The word *giardinetto* means "little garden."

GOVERNADOR / GOVERNATRICE: The worker in the conterie production who separated the beads according to shape and diameter. In the past, the *governador* separated the beads by hand using appropriate sieves. Later this operation was done mechanically.

IMPACCATURA: Packaging.

IMPIRARESSA / E: Stay-at-home mothers and women who were commissioned by the conterie factories to string the beads into hanks using threads of silk, cotton, and linen. The *impiraressa* (*impiraresse*, plural) reported to a *mistra*—the woman in the neighborhood who administered the requests of the factory. Most of the *impiraresse* were located in the poorest areas of Venice, such as the districts of Cannaregio and Castello.

LATTIMO: A milky-white opaque glass.

LEVADA / LEVAR: Traditional terminology used in the Murano glass factories to indicate a gather, or extraction of molten glass, from the crucible using a long, iron staff. This operation can be repeated several times once the molten glass has slightly cooled.

LIBRO D'ORO: The Book of Gold where families from pure Murano lineage were registered.

LUME: A torch or lantern fueled by animal fat and the air of a bellows in order to heat glass canes to make beads. The artisans who made these glass beads were once called *suppialume*. The glass cane was heated and wound around an iron skewer (*spieo*) to maintain the hole. The *spieo* was treated with a mixture of glue, soil from Vicenza, and slaked lime (calcium hydroxide) in order to easily release the bead from the iron skewer. Today's torches are fueled by propane gas and oxygen. (Moretti).

LUSTRADORI: Workers of the conterie factory who cleaned and polished the beads.

MACA: A type of cane used for fabricating conterie beads where the external sides are multi-faceted. The facets are obtained by impressing the *paston* into a faceted metal or brass mold before pulling the cane.

MAESTRO / MAISTRO: The worker of the conterie factory with the most talent and ability to work with the glass in an artistic way. He is responsible for directing the whole team (*piazza*), the executions of the glass, and the jobs pertaining to the glass production. In the past, he was called the *scagner*, named after the bench (the *scagno*) where he sat and worked with the glass.

MAGGIOR CONSIGLIO: Chief Advisor to the Doge (Duke) of Venice, dating back to the 13th century.

MARGARITE: The Latin, historic name for glass beads called *conterie*.

MARIN: A *marin* consists of forty threads of beads. (Ninni, 1873).

MARMORIZZAR / MARMORIZZADA: The operation of shaping the molten glass by rolling the gather back and forth onto a metal table, once made of marble (*marmo*). (Moretti).

MASSICCIO: Solid glass cane in various diameters and colors used by the *perleri* to make beads and/or lampwork objects.

MAZZO: Totaling twenty strands of *conterie* beads; each mazzo consists of four hanks, each hank (or one *colane*) consists of five strands.

MAZZO INTIERO: Two hundred forty (240) strands of conterie beads.

MISCELA: A powdery mixture of various minerals and chemicals that are blended and weighed according to a recipe and put into a crucible to produce glass. Together with the minerals and sand, a certain percentage of glass fragments (*rottami*) are added. (Moretti)

MISTRA: The woman who was the intermediary between the glass factories and the *impiraresse*. The *mistra* was responsible for receiving the beads and orders from the factory, distributing the stringing assignments to the *impiraresse*, and then returning the finished jobs to the representative/superior of the factory.

MURRINA / MURRINE: The technique used in Murano in the 1870s consisted of bundling together glass canes (while cold) to create a specific design or image using various segments of pre-fabricated cane (of various patterns and colors) to form a polychromatic mosaic. The glass canes are slowly heated in the oven so that the segments fuse together. The bundle of glass cane, in its cylindrical form, is then pulled and stretched carefully as to not distort the pattern. After the glass cane is pulled, it is cooled and then sliced into thin segments. The segments are then polished and rimmed in gold or silver to be used in jewelry. The murrine can also be inlaid into wooden or glass tablets or used in vases and other glass objects.

MUTA or MUA: A team of workers in a glass factory who work in tandem creating glass objects or pulling the molten glass to make conterie beads. The team can be comprised of several workers: the *scagner* or *maestro*, two *serventi*, two *conzaureri/consaori*, two *tiradori* or *tiracanne da ferro*.

ORBA: A bead without a hole (also called an eye). The Italian word *orba* means "blind."

OSELLE: A commemorative medal coined on the island of Murano, made of gold or silver, and engraved with the island's emblem (the rooster) and also Venetian rulers and dignitaries.

PAIN: A wooden crate/box used to transport glass cane, glass cylinders, glass chips, glass beads, and other glass objects.

PALATO: A crucible of various capacity where the *miscela* is fused.

PALMETA: Derived from the word *palma*, a *palmeta* is a gather of needles that are spread like a hand-held fan in the palm of the *impiraressa*. Held tightly, the *palmeta* of needles was swiftly dipped into the sessola to thread the conterie beads. (Ninni).

PASTON: A gather of glass that is shaped into a cylindrical form and then pulled/stretched to create a long cane either with or without a hole/perforation. The glass canes were used for the fabrication of conterie beads, lampwork beads, and small glass objects.

PATERNOSTRI: Derived from the "Our Father" prayer associated with rosary beads, these workers would take sections of perforated glass cylinders, slide them onto a *speo* (skewer/mandrel), and then round off the edges of the cylinders under a flame, making them smooth and creating a small bead. This technique became known as the Art of the Paternostreri.

PERLE A LUME or ALLA LUCERNA: Glass beads that are fabricated using the flame of a torch or lantern fueled by oil or animal fat. By the 1800s, this process was replaced with a gas burner or torch. In the 1600s and 1700s, beads made a *lume* were called conterie beads.

PERLE CO L'ANEMA: Beads that have a different color core than their exterior layer. The word "anema" in the Venetian dialect means "soul."

PERLE FALSE: In Italian, these words mean "false beads." These beads were created to imitate gemstones. In the Venetian dialect, these were known as the *zoje false*.

PERLERI / PERLAI: An artist who fabricates lampwork beads.

PESTRINO: A steam-operated grinding machine.

PIAZZA: A team of workers in the glass factory that is usually composed of four people: the glass master, the *servente*, the *serventin*, and the *garzonetto/garzone*.

PIRIA: A metal container with a triangular-shaped spout.

PORTA-MASSA: Workers of the factory who carried and transferred glass (using wooden crates) from one department to the next.

ROSETTA: Commonly known in the United States as the chevron bead, this bead is made of multiple layers of perforated glass cane, with each layer pressed into a mold of a star pattern, and then pulled to the desired length. The glass cane is cut into cylinders, and the edges are milled to expose the underlying multiple layers. The rosetta bead first appeared in the late 15th century probably on the suggestion of Maria Barovier, a descendant of prominent Murano glass masters, dating back to 1324. (Marascutto e Stainer, *Perle Veneziane*, Nuove Edizioni Dolomiti, Verona, 1991).

ROTTAMI: Glass fragments and recycled glass that is added to the powdery mixture of a recipe to facilitate the fusion of the glass.

RUBINO: A ruby colored glass with a tonality that is achieved by adding gold to the recipe, making it very costly to produce.

RULLO: Rollers made of rubber to help advance the glass cane towards the cutting blades.

SACCOCCIA: A bag that was used in the 1800s to hold the beads and wheat bran, then agitated in order to clean and polish the beads.

SBRIZZADORE: The young girl who was responsible for passing a *sbrizzada* (handful) of glass cane to the tagliatrice.

SCAGNER: Derived from the Venetian word *scagno* (meaning "bench"), the scagner is the glass master who sits on a long bench alongside his tools. There, he rotates the blowpipe (or staff) and manipulates the glass to create an object or glass cane.

SCALDINO: A small heater made of terracotta, the *scaldino* could hold a few pieces of charcoal. The *scaldino* would be placed underneath the chair of the *impiraressa* to generate heat while she worked during the cooler months. The Italian verb *scaldare* means to heat, to warm.

SCARPELLO: Steel blades that are used in the mechanical production of cutting glass cane.

SCARPEO: The lower steel blade that is used in the mechanical production of cutting glass cane. These blades had teeth-like indentations to accommodate a specific diameter of glass cane.

SCHIZZADURA: The worker in the conterie production who was responsible for eliminating the *schizzi* (broken pieces) of the glass cylinders (due to the cutting process) from the whole cylinders. This operation was done using sieves.

SEDETE: Resembling silk, this was a special flax thread used by the *impiraresse* to string conterie beads.

SERVENTE / SERVENTIN: Assistants to the glass master. The *serventin* was more skilled than the *servente*.

SESSOLA: A wooden receptacle used by the *impiraresse* to hold the conterie beads. The *sessola*, filled with beads, would rest on the lap of the *impiraressa*. She would dip the fine needles into the *sessola*, ultimately stringing hundreds of conterie beads onto the threads. A *sessola* is also a wooden or plastic dustpan, commonly used by Venetians to remove excess water, or rainfall, from the boats.

SIRIBITE: A fine, dry mixture of calcium and charcoal used to clog the holes of the glass cylinders (intended to create conterie beads), so that the cylinders would not shrink or close during the rounding stage by the *tubante*.

SMALTI: Enamel or opaque glass.

SOTTANA: The first layer of glass (or core) after which a second layer (*coperta*) is added.

SPEO / SPIEDO: A thin iron rod used in the glass factories to gather small amounts of molten glass from the crucible. The word also indicates metal or iron skewers on which small pieces of perforated glass cylinders were placed, then rounded by the heat of a flame to develop conterie beads or *paternostri* for rosaries.

STELLARIA: A term that was at one time synonymous with *avventurina*.

SUPPIALUME: Workers who made beads a *lume* using a torch that was fueled by animal fat and the forced air of a bellows. The word *suppia* in the Venetian dialect means "to blow." The Art of the *Suppialume* existed until the 16th century. (Cesare Moretti, 2001).

TAGLIATORI / TAGLIATRICE: Workers of the factory (usually female) who cut the glass cane mechanically. These workers were also known as *tagliador di canna*.

TARSO: A specimen of very hard white marble (quartz) of pure silica that was pulverized to make crystal frit in the 1600s. The Muranese found an abundance of these pebbles in the Ticino River in Pavia. (Paul Engle, *L'Arte Vetraria* by Antonio Neri, Vol 1, Heiden & Engle, 2006.).

TIRADORE / TIRACANNA DA FERRO: The factory worker who pulls/stretches the molten glass to make a long glass cane.

TOSCA BEAD: A conterie bead in which its inner core is painted and the outside layer is transparent glass.

TRAMOGGIA: Sieves made of sheepskin with the perforations according to the size of the beads.

TUBANTE: The factory worker in the conterie production who was responsible for the rounding of the glass cylinders (to make conterie beads) using the *tubo* (an iron drum), which was rotated in an oven.

TUBO: Introduced into an oven, this large drum was made of iron or copper and was used to round the sharp and jagged edges of the conterie beads. The *tubo* replaced the previous operation of the *ferrazza*. Luigi Pusinich invented and patented this drum in 1821, which was adopted by most glass bead factories.

VETRO NEUTRO: Neutral glass, a derivative of borosilicate glass.

VETTE: Glass that has been pulled to a very thin diameter (resembling a string), to be used by lampworkers to decorate and gild beads.

VITRITE: Semi-finished black glass used to insulate the brass base (today made of aluminum) of light bulbs, producing a stronger base.

ZOCCO: A small wooden bench or tree trunk that was used to absorb the blows of a chisel while cutting glass cane.

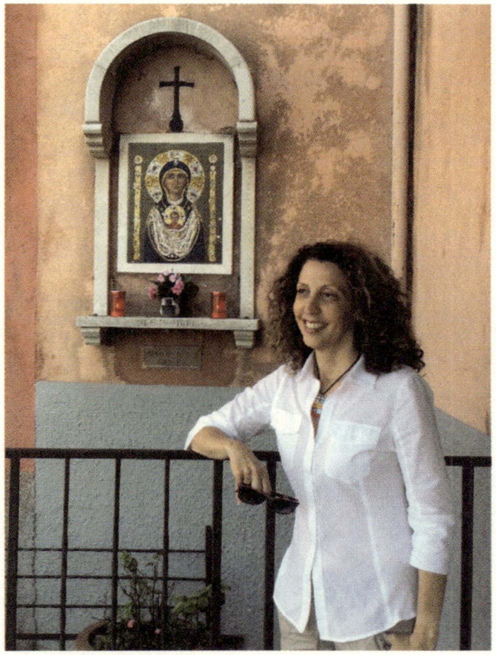

About the author:

Shortly after graduating from Saint Mary's College in Orchard Lake, MI in 1984, Nicole Anderson embarked for Europe and has lived and worked in Venice, Italy ever since. Her interest in beads began when she worked in a glass store near the famous Saint Mark's Square. Nicole now spends half the year in Venice amassing beads (in addition to searching for antique, vintage, and rare ones), and the remaining months in the United States doing trunk shows from coast to coast.

You can follow her on Instagram and Facebook under **The Glory of Beads.**